Liebman Adler

Sabbath Hours

Thoughts

Liebman Adler

Sabbath Hours
Thoughts

ISBN/EAN: 9783743441972

Manufactured in Europe, USA, Canada, Australia, Japa

Cover: Foto ©Lupo / pixelio.de

Manufactured and distributed by brebook publishing software (www.brebook.com)

Liebman Adler

Sabbath Hours

SABBATH HOURS

THOUGHTS

BY

LIEBMAN ADLER

ISRAEL'S MISSION IS PEACE

Philadelphia:

THE JEWISH PUBLICATION SOCIETY OF AMERICA

1893

PRESS OF
EDWARD STERN & CO.
PHILADELPHIA.

TO THE

FAITHFUL KEEPERS

OF THE

PERPETUAL LIGHT

OF

JEWISH FEELING AND PRACTICE,

The Jewish Women,

THIS WORK IS DEDICATED.

PREFACE.

The following fifty-four sermons, one for each Sabbath of the year, with two additional for leap years, were culled from two volumes of German sermons on texts from the Pentateuch, published by the late Rabbi Lieb-man Adler, of Chicago.

The author, in his preface, speaks of how, in days gone by, "when, on Friday, all the preparations for the beloved Sabbath had been completed, and the Sabbath garments had been donned, the Jewish mother began to read, attentively and devoutly, the Pentateuchal and Prophetical portions assigned to that Sabbath, continuing until it was time for the evening service at the syna-gogue, and finishing whatever she failed to read then, on the afternoon of the Sabbath."

It is hoped that this collection of modern sermons on every-day problems may take the place, with the daugh-ters of Zion, of the old-time book of Biblical readings, and therefore it is dedicated first and foremost to the use of the women in Israel. Through all the vicissitudes of this century, the sanctity of the Jewish home has been well maintained, and with it the influence of woman over Jewish religious life. By right of inheritance, she occupies vantage-ground, from whose height she can shape the future. She it is that can keep alive the ancient fervor, and promote an intelligent view of

Judaism and its practices. To equip her with needed knowledge is the purpose of this collection of Biblical discussions, which are conducted from the point of view of modern thought, and with rare lucidity, illustrate the universality and present timeliness of our ancient sacred literature.

Through these same characteristics, our book may come to have another use. There are many towns and settlements in the United States wholly cut off from Jewish teaching, and such communities may welcome these sermons as a source of devotion and as a guide to the study of the Sacred Scriptures, the fount of Jewish inspiration. Indeed, the book will yield its virtue only to him who, with each sermon, will read, in the Holy Book itself, the chapter from which the text marked under the title is selected. Such earnestness alone can restore to us our former distinction, the knowledge of the Law, · which must continue to be our wisdom and our understanding before the eyes of the nations.

THE EDITOR.

BIOGRAPHICAL SKETCH.*

Liebman Adler was born on the twenty-fourth day of Tebeth, 5572 (January 9, 1812), at Lengsfeld, Grand Duchy of Saxe-Weimar, Germany. He received his first instruction in the school of the Jewish congregation and from the rabbi of the town, and continued his Hebrew studies with R. Kunreuther, at Gelnhausen, and afterward in the Jewish seminary at Frankfurt, under R. Solomon Trier and R. Aaron Fuld.

He then passed through a two years' course in the Teachers' Institute at Weimar, and accepted a position in the Jewish congregational school of his native town. A secular school having been established, mainly through his efforts, he became its principal in 1849. But five years later, Adler left Germany, in the hope that America might afford a better career for his children. Soon he was made the teacher and preacher of the Jewish congregation at Detroit, Mich., where his memory is still affectionately and reverently cherished. In 1861, a call came to him from the *Kehillath Anshê Ma'arabh* of Chicago, with which his name was connected until the day of his death, January 29, 1892.

In Chicago his work was varied and laborious. The fulfilment of his duties required strength, perseverance

---

* Adapted and translated, with the permission of the author, from "Liebman Adler, Eine Gedenkrede, gehalten am 14 Februar, 1892, im Tempel der K. A. M. in Chicago, von B. Felsenthal."—[ED.]

vii

and courage, and Liebman Adler was strong, tenacious and honest. Hence, his harvest in Chicago, as in Detroit, was appreciation, reverence and love. After the lapse of years, his congregation made his work less onerous, and during almost the whole of the last decade of his life, he was relieved of all his official duties.

Two phases of his public activity deserve special mention ; he was a true patriot, and in the best sense of the word, a successful, religious teacher. " Five Addresses to the K. A. M." are on patriotic themes, are anti-slavery in sentiment, and express strong feeling with clear, swift utterance. His deeds affirmed the sincerity of his convictions. It was he that induced his oldest son to risk life, if need be, in the service of the Union Army.

In his religious work, he stood upon a .conservative platform, clinging to inherited customs and ceremonies, which to him seemed fraught with inspiration. But his orthodoxy was not the uncompromising rigidity of prejudice. He was a clear, unbiased thinker, and a student of Jewish history, who saw in Judaism a living, progressive force.

The best exposition of his attitude we have in his sermons, of which we happily possess three volumes. They are pervaded by a tranquil spirit, peculiarly characteristic of his mind and life. In simple, cordial language, he has laid down in them the highest wisdom of noble living. They are wholly free from every blemish of polemics, are in no sense dogmatic, or clouded by mysticism. In a word, they are genuinely popular. In the Jewish homiletic literature of our day, they should, along with David Einhorn's and Michael Sachs' sermons, be accounted our treasures.

His published works form one tangible legacy that our revered rabbi has left us. Another and a greater is the memory of his beautiful character. Unassuming and childlike, he loathed all pomp and artificiality, and was content with his own lot in life. As becomes a son of Aaron, he loved and promoted peace, and his lips always and everywhere kept knowledge. The true philosophy which he expounded to others, rendered his own life joyous, prevented every taint of pessimism, and taught him to meet death without dread.

Besides the proof of his patriotism and the statement of his creed, he has left us, in his will, a record of his lovable traits as a man. According to a fine old Jewish fashion, he gives his children directions for their spiritual guidance: "My children! Keep together in fraternal union. Let no sacrifice be too great to ensure your mutual helpfulness and the continuance of your brotherly feelings. Every act of love that you show unto one another will do my soul good. The example of eleven children of one father, standing together in love and faithfulness, will be a more beautiful adornment of his grave than the most elaborate floral decoration, which I would rather not have, though I do not wish to control your desires in that matter.

"The little property that I leave behind, will become yours only after the death of your mother. I know you; I can trust you, you will not show yourselves unfilial in its possession and use. The inheritance, however, which you possess even now is a good name and a training as good as I could give you. It seems that not one of you is destined to grow rich. Let that not disturb you. Only remain honest, true, industrious and economical. Do not speculate. Even when speculation is successful, no blessing rests upon it. Put your whole energy into the conduct of your chosen calling. Serve God, and have him always before your eyes. With men, be amiable, courteous and modest, and all will go well with you even without riches. My last word to you is: Honor your mother! Brighten her sad widowhood. Do not disturb her in the enjoyment of her small estate, and supply the deficiencies in her income.

"Farewell, wife and children! One thing more, my children: I know well that if you would, you cannot practise Judaism according to my conception, and as I practised it. But remain Jews, and live as Jews in the best manner of your times, not only for yourselves, as individuals, but also for the welfare of the community."

These words ring out, and re-echo beyond the walls of his own home. "His image," says one of his chosen friends, "stands before us in clearest outlines, and we look up to it with fervent love and deep reverence. . . . As often as we look upon it, may we renew within us the resolve to walk in his footsteps, and thus grow into the light of a noble life."

TABLE OF CONTENTS.

PREFACE.

BIOGRAPHICAL SKETCH.

SERMONS:

xi

THE STORY OF THE CREATION.

In the Jerusalem Targum "in the beginning" is rendered by "in wisdom." Truly, in the very first word of Holy Writ there is wisdom, since it begins with "the beginning," and leaves untouched all that goes before.

Among the ruins of Nineveh, a library of inscribed stone-flags was discovered. When deciphered, they were found, among other things, to contain a tale of the creation and the story of a flood, which, in many particulars, coincide with the Biblical tales. These ancient accounts from Nineveh may be older than those of the Bible, but the latter excel the former, even as the laconic speech of an experienced sage eclipses the confused bombast of a thoughtless chatterer.

Whereas the Bible is content to begin with the "beginning," the Nineveh document supplies the unknown preceding the beginning with fables and tales of the gods, wildly fantastic and unæsthetic.

The ancients have propounded the question: "Why does it say, 'in the beginning God created,' why not, 'God created in the beginning?' God, the subject, ought to take precedence." The query was considered worthy of various replies, and, with the same idea in mind, the Greek translators have taken the liberty of changing the text. But even when thus transposed, there is wisdom in the words.

The Bible wishes to give man a story of the creation of the earth which he inhabits; it wishes to speak of the "beginning" and not, as does the Nineveh document, tell a tale of the God-head, a theogony. For this reason, "in the beginning" should be more accentuated than "God."

The ancients furthermore ask why the Bible commences with ב in בראשית, instead of with א, as do the ten commandments. The question is scarcely a brilliant one, but the reply is very clever. The letter ב is closed on all sides but one. This signifies that we must not too deeply investigate, we must not permit our thoughts to betray us to the heights of heaven or into the depths of hell; they should not lose themselves in speculation, either about prehistoric ages, or about a future world. Therefore, the Torah begins with neither philosophy nor hypothesis concerning the nature of the God-head, but with heaven and earth.

Portions of the Bible do not meet with universal approval. But we are apt to forget that its wisdom does not consist merely in what it says, but equally, if not more, in what it leaves untouched. Strictly speaking, it contains no theology, no metaphysics, no mysticism, no heaven, no hell, no angels, no devils, nothing of another world. The Bible, according to its contents, may be divided into natural history, history, laws and ethics.

"In the beginning God created the heaven and the earth." This verse brings the Bible into harmony with the most advanced science. When was the beginning? That is not explained; perhaps millions, perhaps an

utterly inconceivable number of years ago. Whence
was the earth evolved? From fire? From water?
Or from both? The Bible itself is silent on that point.
It leaves to science full sway to investigate and decide
the question.

The ancients inquire: "Why does Scripture say
את השמים and ואת הארץ. These words את are apparently superfluous; it would be just as correct to say:
בראשית ברא אלהים שמים וארץ." And they think that these
words signify that heaven and all that is included in the
idea of heaven, and the earth with all its potentialities
were created on the first day, i. e., indefinite ages ago,
but that on earth these forces proved their existence
gradually, each one acting in its own time.

We may consider the story of the creation of the
universe told completely in the first verse. The further
narrative deals exclusively with the earth which we
inhabit; not with its creation, but with its development,
its evolution. It is no cosmogony, but purely geogony.
On the first day, or in the first stage of development, light
found its way through the dense vapor shrouding the
earth. And there was light! But there was not yet
discernible a body whence light emanated.

In the second stage of development, the fluid element
was divided into actual water and the vapor that fills
the atmosphere.

In the third stage, the last, mighty upheavals of the
earth took place. The crust of the earth was sprung
open, mountains arose from the depths, while other
parts fell into abysses, were filled with water, and
formed the seas. And upon the newly-made dry land
appeared the earliest vegetation.

In the fourth stage, the atmosphere had become so clear that the sun, the moon and the stars were visible. Finally, in the fifth and sixth stages appeared life, rising from its lowest forms to its highest development in man.

To-day, as on each Sabbath, we have solemnly taken the Torah from its case, and have thanked God aloud for blessing us with it; the congregation, Bible in hand, devoutly follows the reading of the portion, and at its close, once more gives thanks to God for bestowing upon us the treasure of the Torah.

And what is this that we have read? It is what in science is known as geogony, the doctrine of the formation of the earth, a branch of natural science. Science —this is the distinction—deals with the creation only, regardless of the Creator; whereas the Torah mentions the Creator: " God said, God created, God made," etc.

What could be more potent in urging the Israelite to investigate and acquaint himself with Nature, than the fact that the Torah, his Holy of holies, opens with a chapter of natural science? It does not begin like our catechisms with, " What is religion?" but it tells God's people how the earth developed under God's omnipotence. Man's earthly weal, his fairest, chastest joys, and his pure, sincere piety are the results of this study. The psalmist, in the 104th Psalm, loses himself in contemplation of Nature, and then his surcharged heart breaks forth into the words: " O Lord, how manifold are thy works! in wisdom has thou made them all: the earth is full of thy riches."

If, thousands upon thousands of years ago, in the

infancy of mankind, long before there was any idea of natural science ; before the telescope had brought within mortal vision spheres millions of miles away ; before the microscope had disclosed a new microscopic world ; before the magnet had pointed the path over the seas; before air and water had been analyzed in the crucible; and thousands of other means had brought light and order into the dark bowels of Nature, and revealed a world full of marvels—if, at that early period, Nature was held in such esteem that the holy book, the Bible, was opened with a contemplation upon it; if, at that time, sages and poets, gazing about them and up at the starry firmament, drew thence the inspiration which impelled them to immortal verses and songs of wisdom ; how far advanced must we be, we children of the nineteenth century, in which science, with its innumerable dis-coveries and inventions, has opened so many windows admitting light into the awful depths of Nature ! Alas, we are indeed *children* of the nineteenth century ! The ordinary individual—I mean one of the masses of to-day—is a child in matters of natural science. Yes, we have retrograded. We have, it is true, cast off an im-mense number of superstitions, of absurd explanations and prejudices held by the ancients concerning the phenomena of Nature. But this is not due to intelli-gence ; there is a different reason for it. The ancients inquired into the causes of things, and if a rational answer was not at hand, the query was silenced with a fable. We do not *inquire;* we are, therefore, safe from all misunderstanding, but neither do we arrive at an understanding of these causes. We imagine that we have advanced ; we *have* advanced, but it is not pro-

gress; we are prodded by comparatively few thinkers.
Ask the masses about any ordinary phenomena of
Nature and their causes—about thunder-storms, earth-
quakes, cyclones, shooting stars, volcanoes, eclipses of
the sun or moon. For every one of these, the ancients
had an explanatory reply; but were you to repeat that
reply to one of the masses of to-day, his education would
lead him to deride the credulity of the ancients; yet
no better answer is forthcoming; none is needed, since
none is asked for. In social intercourse there is nothing
more unbearable than an inquisitive person; but in the
intercourse with Nature, the Nature in and about man,
everyone ought to be inquisitive, particularly the
Israelite; and sound and reliable answers can be drawn
from the wells that have been dug and made accessible
to all—from a rich, popular literature.

Ah, how wofully has religious thought gone astray!
Religion and natural science, which, in the first chapter
of the most ancient record of religion, went hand-in-hand,
and appeared to possess *one* heart and *one* soul, now
regard each other inimically, and, like Jacob and Esau,
quarrel about the rights of the first-born. Jacob must
bow down seven times before Esau embraces him; and
when Esau says, "Now let us go forth together like
brothers," Jacob trembles at the thought of such close
companionship, and answers, "We may not go together,
for my flocks might suffer; go thou first, and I will
follow." And when Esau says, "Then shall some of my
people remain with thee to guide and protect thee,"
Jacob replies, "Wherefore? I need it not."

Judaism ought not to countenance this unbrotherly
relation 'twixt religion and science. The Bible is science

—natural science, history, law and ethics. The Talmud, despite the objections and warnings interposed by some of the rabbis, discusses all the branches of science known in these times, as do the best rabbinical writings of the brilliant Spanish school. Only the German and Slavonic rabbinical schools, during times of unutterable oppression, became alienated from science, as also African and Asiatic Judaism has become estranged.

I am addressing an educated, enlightened congregation, one certainly not accustomed to unctuous sermons from its present preacher. Yet, were I to bring a flower into the pulpit instead of a Bible-text, and attempt to prove the omnipotence of God by showing the structure of the stem, the leaves, the calyx, the corolla, the stamens and pistils, the cells and veins; were I to show that the goodness and wisdom of the Creator are manifest in the drop of honey at the bottom of the cup, attracting the insect, which in its intrusion is covered with pollen, carries the pollen to other flowers, and so fecundates them, etc., you would not be greatly edified. You would say, "Such matters are out of place in the temple of God!"

This is the true reform at which we must aim: we must consecrate both history and natural science, by regarding them as integral parts of religion;—בראשית* considered as natural science, must be held equally sacred with Noah,* considered as history.

THE FIRST VERSE OF THE BIBLE.

"In the beginning God created the heaven and the earth."—GEN. I: 1.

Heathens can accept not even the first words of Holy Writ, for, according to their ideas, "in the beginning" the gods were created. The Torahs of the heathens do not begin with cosmogony, the history of the creation of the world, but with theogony, the account of the creation of the gods, and of how one god begat another. After that, how many generations may have come and gone, ere the spirit of research awoke in man, leading him to investigate the origin of each individual creation, and then of the sum of things, the universe, that is to say, ere he reached the idea contained in the words "he created!"

For these words also are beyond the conception of the heathen; he would say "they created." We have revised our prayer-book, substituting "salvation" for "Savior." But a far greater, a far more important and more influential change at the time was that from "they created" to "he created." Nor, indeed, could the heathen say "they created." "Created" signifies the formation of something from nothing, and the power to do this the heathen does not accord to his gods, who may only give form to pre-existing matter. These first words of our Torah, "In the beginning God created," which express a complete revolution in the world of

8

thought, have been given to humanity by Judaism, nor have they yet taken root anywhere but in the soil of Judaism and her daughter-religions. How long, then, may it have been before the human intellect was sufficiently strong and disciplined to sum up manifold creation in two concepts, and to give expression to these in two words: heaven and earth!

Then, for thousands of years, this first verse of the Torah expressing, as it does, a spiritual conquest, was conned by mankind. But in the course of those years, its imperfections have been remedied, and its misconceptions righted. Divine truth can never be clearly enough understood, and much less clothed in words, because, for the divine, we have but a human method of expression. This is shown in the very first verse of Holy Writ, in our text. "Elohim," which is the concentration of the blind, heartless forces of Nature, supposed to have been divided among all the gods, was later transformed into "Adonai," a single Creator, Preserver of the world and Controller of human destinies, an eternal, omnipotent, just and merciful God, a God that is Providence, an all-providing Father, a holy, superior, intelligent Being, free from all faults and passions, asking no service for himself, demanding only that we seek the light of truth, and abide in virtue. Thus, in the course of time, the incomplete designation of a supreme power, " Elohim," gave way to the more comprehensive "Adonai." So, too, have misunderstandings been dispelled. Isaiah's prophecy has been fulfilled with regard to the word " heavens:" " The heavens are vanished like smoke." Heaven, as the ancients understood it, no longer exists for us, not *one*, much less *seven* heavens. At the time, it

was an enormous triumph of the mind to bring all creation under two heads; as time went on, the mind included
all creation in a *single* conception, and expressed it in a
single word: universe, or the even more forcible cosmos.

When we raise our eyes to the glorious azure, which
the ancients called heaven, we, with our modern conception thereof, are none the less disposed to reverential
wonderment, our souls are none the less attuned to joyous adoration, when we think of the Creator of these
glories, of this ether, which at night is illumined by
innumerable lustrous worlds, and in which our earth
floats like a feather. Yea, this azure awakens in us, as
did the heaven of the ancients in them, worship and
adoration of the Ruler of the universe, even though the
azure no longer represents to us a solid edifice, the better
half of creation, the habitation of superior beings.

The word of God is everlasting, but its interpretation
varies. The word "Shomayim" signifies to us what is
beyond human conception, the supernatural, which the
mind sees as in a vision, the inexpressible which the heart
dimly feels. The animal part of man belongs to the earth.
But his higher thoughts and aspirations, his world of
ideas, and all that is beyond animal pleasures: thought,
hope, the consolation of immortality, the belief in one
God, the constant striving better to understand his
being and his will, to live and act accordingly—these
constitute our heaven. To earn what we require is
earthly; but to earn it honestly and fairly under the
most trying circumstances, so to limit our wants that we
may not jeopardize honesty and rectitude, *that* is heavenly. To live in wedlock is earthly; but for man and
woman to live together in love and faith, in peace and

harmony, even though it necessitate daily and hourly sacrifices, *that* is heavenly. To be father and mother is earthly; but to use every endeavor, shunning no sacrifice, not merely to rear children, but to bring them up in the fear of God and on the path of virtue, not only to regard them as the sunshine of the home, a natural delight to the eyes of the parents, but to be ever conscious of the sacred duty to make good, useful men and women of them, *that* is heavenly. To live for one's self and one's family is earthly; but to deny one's self pleasures in order that others may enjoy, to exert one's self that other exhausted ones may rest, to care for others and save them care, and even to risk one's life for that of others, *that* is heavenly. To drift with the tide is earthly, but to stand against the current in the defence of truth and conviction, to stand alone for the right, firm as a rock, even though the tide of public opinion toss and swell around one, and principles totter and sway, *that* is heavenly. Earnest attention to temporal needs is earthly; but to think of the eternal, and to sacrifice momentary good for the sake of eternity, *that* is heavenly.

This heavenly spirit was created as was the earthly. It was the creation of the first day. And in the account of the five days following the first one of creation, we are told of the development of this creation in matters of the earth as well as of heaven.

Thy heaven, oh man, thou carriest within thy mind and within thy heart! Some have only a bit of it, others, all the seven heavens of the ancients: with some, it is clouded o'er, sombre and threatening; with others, radiant in its brilliancy. Rabbi Akiba died a martyr,

after indescribable torture, yet seven heavens were in
his heart. Hadrian's life closed with the blackest skies
within his heart, though as Akiba's emperor, he was
apparently enjoying the greatest earthly prosperity.

God created the heaven and the earth; but just as the
earth became known to man by degrees, a large portion
of it being discovered after thousands of years, and
much still remaining to be discovered, so it is with
heaven, the heaven in the mind, in the heart, and in
social life. It must be sought and found. Progress
means ever to discover new heavens within us, heavens
of knowledge and of culture of heart and mind, patience
and fraternity, peaceful and harmonious existence in
social life, as well as in the intercourse of countries and
nations. This is the sevenfold light, these are the new
heavens which the prophet of Messianic times has
promised us; and to approach nearer and ever nearer to
them is the task of our mundane existence.

THE SO-CALLED FALL OF MAN.

The Bible suffers from two opposing parties—on the one hand, from the simple piety of those that pay it unquestioning homage; on the other, from its enemies. Both accept the words of Holy Writ in their literal sense, even in those portions that are narrative and not legislative.

The one class takes it very ill, if we say, "The word has a meaning, but word and meaning are as different as body and soul;" that they consider the most pronounced heresy. The others say, "What absurdity! and that is supposed to-be Holy Writ!"

We believe that when the Bible commands and forbids, there is no room for subtle interpretations; there the words embody the full meaning to be conveyed, and whoever attempts to wrest the sense to suit himself, acts dishonestly by the book. But when the Bible clothes its teachings in tales and parables, we agree with Rashi that the words themselves cry out, "Explain me!" With regard to the verse, זה ספר תולדת האדם "This is the book of the generations of Adam," our sages say : "So far as the story of the creation and all that is connected with it is concerned, the honor of Holy Writ demands that we take a hidden meaning for granted; but further on, where questions of practical life are involved, the honor of the Scriptures demands an exact and literal interpretation of its contents."

13

Thus do we approach the task that we have set ourselves for to-day's discourse, the explanation of those
portions of the Bible that treat of the "fall." (Gen. II:
15–17; III: 1–7.)

Let us say at once what meaning they convey to us.
The first human beings lived their appointed time in
happy innocence. Then they began to think, and their
innocence was destroyed. Doubt, discord between head
and heart, took the place of a calm spirit and serene
content.

There is a way of thinking that but reflects the
thoughts of others. A child thinks as its parents think;
a pupil thinks as the teacher has taught him to think;
an individual thinks as those about him think.

There is a kind of thought that subordinates itself to
the wishes of the heart, "the wish is father to the
thought!"

There is a kind of thought that will make no conces-
sions to the feelings, but would rule as an autocrat; it
says to the heart: Repress thy desires, they do not please
me. Speculation makes unquestioning enjoyment of life
an impossibility.

Speculative thought banishes innocence. The child
is innocent so long as it follows the instincts of its heart,
and thinks the thoughts of others. But no sooner does
it begin to think independently, than its actions become
good or evil, it can no longer be called innocent. So
what is told of Adam is the natural course of man's life.
Every human being, for a time, lives in innocence, in
pleasant unconsciousness of right and wrong; if left at
liberty, he acts according to the dictates of his heart,
and enjoys his existence.

As the young child need not trouble itself about its sustenance, since it is given to it, so with its thoughts: it thinks whatever is given it to think. A child of a quarrelsome disposition may manifest it at an early age, it is true, and live at variance with those about it; may be easily fretted and angered and excited, but within its heart every child is at peace with itself. No sooner has independent thought asserted itself than heart and reason, inclination and duty, gratification and remorse battle for supremacy. Before thought awakens, we live at peace with ourselves; but awakening thought drives us out of the paradise of childhood, to which we may never return.

This Bible-story does not betray a disturbance in the plan of creation, as if God had had some other intentions concerning man, and these had been frustrated by the sinfulness of Adam. It raises the veil, and discovers to us the underlying idea of the plan of the Almighty.

It is true, it is a great deal pleasanter to abide in ignorance, at peace with ourselves. We live much more calmly, more content with ourselves and the world, when we do not think, or if we think, think as others do. It is much more conducive to peace to know little. Learning and knowledge, inquiry and introspection bring much disquiet into one's own heart and into the world. The Preacher says, "He that increaseth knowledge increaseth pain," and the German prince of poets:

> "Who thinks not of the morrow,
> To him life brings its gifts,
> And yet he's free from sorrow."

The innocence of *not thinking*, of artlessness is, upon closer consideration, not quite so charming as it would appear. The child is guileless, sweet and good, because it is too weak to do any harm, and because its parents and guardians watch over it that it may not abuse what strength it has. But when the natural innocence of not thinking has grown great and strong, and can no longer be watched, then woe to such simplicity and to its surroundings! Innocence, sentiment, but not reasoning, is the attribute of a savage. The savage is a grown child. The savage, like the child, follows his instincts; he is not troubled and unsettled by thought. And like the child, the savage is self-satisfied, he may wade in blood, but he feels none the less innocent. Not only those that we call such are savages. Whoever allows himself to be guided only by his feelings and instincts, and has not partaken of the tree of knowledge, is a species of savage. Were all men but children, mature only in years, we would have no villages, no towns,—only wigwams.

No; innocence is becoming only as long as man lacks the power to do harm. As the years go by, bringing strength to man in their flight, thought, the serpent, the symbol of the ancients for eternity and wisdom, rears its head, and man enjoys the fruits of the tree of knowledge. He is no longer a child, existing in innocence, not knowing what is good and what evil; he is a divine being, rising above nature; he knows good from evil, and can regulate his life accordingly.

At what period does this change take place? In our religion, thirteen is the age assumed for the male sex, and twelve for the more rapidly maturing female sex, as the boundary between irresponsible innocence, which eschews thought, and the responsibility imposed by the consciousness that independent thought may be exercised. Of course, this is only an approximate boundary line, for many a one may grow hoary, nor cast off the innocence of ignorance.

Our story draws a picture of the human race at the very dawn of the history of mankind—not its fall, which the Church teaches as a fundamental truth, but on the contrary, its elevation. On the one hand, it discloses the paradise of innocence: life without moral restraints, truth without investigation, thoughts without thinking, gratification without remorse; no warning, no prohibitory laws, not even a sense of shame to restrain enjoyment. " Of every tree of the garden thou mayest freely eat." But then there is the picture of the tree that man is warned not to touch. This is the tree of thought. If thou partakest of its fruits, thou wilt be like unto a divine being; thou wilt think independently of parents, of teachers and of the times; thou wilt know good from evil. But I warn thee, dearly must thou pay for it. Thought gnaws like a worm at all thy pleasures; the innocent child within thee will die, and thou wilt become as a different being!

But of all trees, this very one attracts man with irresistible power. He partakes of the fruit, and pays the penalty. The careless, thoughtless, joyous Adam is dead; in his place, we see a serious man, upon whose brow earnest thought is mirrored.

It was not intended that man's fate should be characterized by the unbroken regularity of the development

3

of the flower of the field, or of the course of the stars in the heavens. Thought and feeling were to battle within him, and thought with thought. The keen edge of reason was to clip the wings of feeling, and the warm heart was to give of its warmth to cold, cruel, uncompromising Reason, and coax it gently into harmony with life. That which we have lost, the harmony of childhood in the years of innocence, we are to find again in the reconciliation of thought and feeling. This recovered harmony, which is our own merit, even though it be imperfect, is worth far more than the perfect one which was given to us, and which we lost with childhood.

We cannot deny that the tenor of the tale in question is suggestive rather of loss than of gain to humanity; and here, as elsewhere, the wisdom of the people is proved in their proverb: "Not all is gold that glitters." Thought is a double-edged sword, which ofttimes wounds the thinker, and brings misery and unhappiness not only to him, but to the world at large. It can transform rich, luxuriant fields, the scene of joyous existence, into a bleak, barren desert. However, the means to prevent such misfortune is also mentioned. Man is told, "In the sweat of thy brow shalt thou eat bread." When the years of innocence have flown, and thought begins to hold sway, give the boy work, and work also thou as long as thou hast strength, even to old age. Labor is a panacea for all ills; it keeps sound hearts healthy, and heals suffering ones; it keeps thought within bounds, preventing it from straying off into unprofitable regions. Every thinker ought also to be an artisan of some kind, and every laborer a thinker.

Woman, too weak physically, too sensitive in nature

and disposition, to battle for daily bread in the cruel
world, takes upon herself the responsibilities of mother-
hood, and the greater part of the cares, troubles and
burdens of the home and the bringing up of the children, which latter, alas! often entails anxiety and sorrow.
She devotes herself to her children, and sacrifices herself
for them all her life; and this complete devotion of
heart and soul and thought to her maternal duties pro-
tects her equally from temptations of the heart and from
undisciplined thoughts. Intelligent mothers are the
greatest blessing of the human race.

As our first mother induced the first man to eat of
the fruit of the tree of knowledge; as once choruses of
women animated David to immortal deeds, and drove
a king, whom they did not praise, to despair; as the
homage of woman was the one bright spot and the
moral support of the knights in the darkness of the
Middle Ages, so even to-day much of what men do that
is worth doing can be traced to the importance which
they attach to the approval of noble women. Whenever
we meet a man who is distinguished in mind and deeds
above his fellow-men, we may safely conclude that the
spirit of an intelligent mother lives in him, a mother
that guided her son to the tree of knowledge.

Now, that thought may not completely control man,
to the exclusion of heart and feeling, the narrative goes
on to say: "And I will put enmity between thee and
the serpent, and between thy seed and its seed; thou
shalt bruise its head and it shall bruise thy heel." And
what is the world's history but a continuous warfare
between wisdom and stupidity, passion and self-control,
sound judgment and prejudice, civilization and savage

instincts? How often is the head of wisdom trodden upon, and how often do critical thought and finical deliberation drag upon the heel of noble impulses!

No, it is not a fall of which we‧ read. A being as perfect as is our God would not create an order of things so frail and destructible that the first man could disorganize the entire system.

The story is rather a mirror of the noble impulses of man; of his striving after knowledge and enlightenment; of his efforts to comprehend the causes of things; of his attempts to demolish every barrier opposing his progress towards knowledge; of his desire for possessions that floods cannot wash away and flames cannot consume, and for this we must not blame Adam and Eve, our first parents, but rather praise our God.

THE SENSE OF SHAME.

It is a matter of course that the owner of a house, which he himself has built, of which he has laid the foundations, and in which he has always lived, knows more about it than any stranger who has merely passed through its rooms; it is equally self-evident that even an ignorant shepherd-lad is a better guide in his native village than a philosopher from afar; that a manufacturer is more familiar with his own productions than all or any of his customers, no matter how expert they may be.

The Bible is the holy edifice of the children of Israel; the forefathers laid its foundations, the sons completed it, and for many centuries, through good and evil days, they have dwelt in it in faith. In this edifice, then, they ought to feel at home. But one day there came the Greeks, the Romans, the Egyptians; then the Germanic tribes, the Goths and Vandals; and later on the Arabs, tent-dwellers and camel-drivers. The former came from their lecture-halls, their minds full of fantastic theories, which, in their schools of philosophy, passed for wisdom, and the latter came directly from the superstitions of idolatry. But they all chose our Book as the text-book of their faith, and moreover pretended to know an interpretation thereof truer than our

21

own. This explains the difference between our religion and theirs. The new devotees of the Bible, coming from foreign regions of thought, built their new religion upon the old substructure, without a thorough knowledge of the foundations, of the quality of the materials, and of the plan.

The new worshippers read the Bible in its translations: the Romans, in Latin; the Greeks, in the Greek tongue; the Arab chief could not read at all, nor could any of the Germanic, the so-called barbarian accessions of the Church.

The book, read in a foreign tongue, was also interpreted in a foreign spirit. The word of the Bible was taken in its verbal meaning, and adhered to literally.

Unsatisfactory as the translation of Hebrew into foreign languages must necessarily be, yet is it a far easier task than the translation of the *spirit* of the Bible into the spirit of Rome and Byzantium. The *text* of the Bible was but inadequately reproduced, and its *spirit* suffered still more. This is exemplified in the portion of the Torah read to-day—the tale of the fall, as the Church calls it, which it utilizes as the corner-stone of its new edifice. Paradise, the tree of life, the tree of knowledge, the serpent which speaks and beguiles the woman, the woman who tempts her husband to sin, the hiding from God, the curse and the punishment, the expulsion from paradise—every word was interpreted literally by the Church, and whatever spirit was infused into it, was introduced from foreign sources.

The rabbis tell us that there are forty-nine different methods of interpreting a single word or verse in the Bible, and that no one of these is binding as a dogma of faith. In Israel, too, have been attempted manifold explanations of the chapter in question, some of which differ from one another as materially as sense differs from nonsense. But no one takes exception, no one is branded as a heretic, no matter which of them be accepted. Years ago, we took occasion to speak in this same temple, about this chapter, combating its interpretation as the fall of man. To-day, we will confine ourselves to the consideration of a means of grace, which is incidentally mentioned in the narrative as having grown out of the indulgence in the forbidden fruit.

Among the chief characteristics that distinguish the human being from the brute, we generally include his erect carriage, his capacity for thought and speech, freedom of will, and conscience. Many include the power to laugh and weep, and we may, with still more justice, add the sense of shame. Man is the only being in the animal world that feels shame; we need not, as the rabbis think, learn it from cats. It is singular that, of all the commentators of the Bible in past and recent times, none has given heed to this circumstance, which is so prominently brought forward in the tale under discussion. After the first beings—so goes the story—had eaten of the tree of knowledge; that is, had begun to think, the sense of shame appeared as the first consequence. Two human beings dwelt upon the earth, and they felt shame in each other's presence, and sewed fig-leaves together to cover their nakedness. But despite this, they still were ashamed in the presence of God, and when he called them they were afraid, and hid themselves. We are further told that God gave man labor as a safeguard against unbridled thought and action, and toward the end it says: "God made garments of skins, and clothed them."

In a Torah manuscript, written by Rabbi Meir, the reading, "a garment of light," was found in a marginal note. And truly, where, in the first days of creation could the furs or skins of beasts have been found? However, it matters not whether we grossly say "skins," or more spiritually, "garment of light," the point under consideration is the reference to the sense of shame, which is awakened by thought.

Few are conscious of the heavenly gift they possess in the sense of shame, of the angel of mercy that follows and guards them through life. The consciousness of the wickedness of sin in itself, its evil results, fear of heavenly and earthly punishment—all taken together are not so much protection to man against degeneration and excesses, as is the sense of shame.

When the barriers that protect virtue and morality fall, the sense of shame is the last to give way. Woe be to the man that feels no shame, to him who, like the bold ones Isaiah laments about, "Like Sodom, tell openly their sin, and conceal it not." Among the three laudable characteristics of Israel, our sages mention the feeling of shame. The sense of shame is the patent of nobility of the descendants of Abraham. They further say, "They who are ashamed are not inclined to sin."

Shame felt in the presence of others is the lowest degree; but this lowest step is the most important, for all the others depend upon it. Who does not begin at the bottom, cannot reach the top. Therefore, be it not said, "He who does not feel shame in the presence of God, should not feel shame in the presence of man; who

sins in secret should have the courage openly to admit
it, and who does this not will be accounted a hypocrite." The lowest degree of shame should be cultivated
until the higher one is attained. It is well to throw
round one's self the safeguards of shame, even in one's
own family circle. Parents should be ashamed to talk
and act recklessly before their children. Husband and
wife should feel shame in the presence of each other,
even as Adam and Eve were ashamed.

It is well to have the utmost consideration for the
feeling of shame and delicacy in children. Better cor-
poral punishment than insults and scoldings that
degrade them in their own eyes, and dull their sense
of shame. Every laborer, and be he of the lowest class,
has feelings of delicacy which his employer is bound to
respect. Even a beggar has some sense of shame left,
his last treasure; and far more does this apply to the
needy who will not beg. Respect their sense of shame
as well.

The next higher step is to feel ashamed of one's
self within one's own heart, to be forced to say to one's
self: Though no one knows how wicked thy thoughts and
actions are, thou knowest it; thou liest, thou flatterest,
thou art false, thou art uncharitable, thou art dishonest,
thy hidden paths of sin are beneath human dignity.
Be ashamed, oh man, to face thyself. As the sense of
shame leads men to cover their faults with fig-leaves
before their fellow-men, so it leads them to justify their
faults in their own eyes.

There is thus a still higher degree of shame, shame
in the presence of God. Before the eye of God, what
avails the fig-leaf? Man stands there in a "garment of

light;" all his faults show through it, every blemish in his character is apparent. Before the all-seeing eye of God, the Holy One, all assumption of goodness vanishes, the mask falls and every equivocation, every excuse which suffices to still our conscience, stands revealed in its true light. Indeed we who like to call ourselves his children, ought to be sincerely ashamed in our Father's presence, doubly ashamed to sin and then cover our sin with the fig-leaves of sophistry, falsehood and hypocrisy.

Well for him who need not hide in fear, when he hears in his conscience the call of God: "Man, where art thou? thy God seeks thee!" And yet, it is well with him who still has the grace to hide and be ashamed of his sin in the presence of God.

As every gift of God is exposed to abuse, so the sense of shame. Such abuse is termed false shame, false pride. We are ashamed to learn; we hide our lack of knowledge under a fig-leaf, and so cover up our ignorance. We are ashamed to correct a mistake, to admit to ourselves, and certainly to others, that we have been guilty of a wrong, and we prefer to continue in ignorance, in the old faults and mistakes. We are ashamed to subordinate ourselves, to obey, and we adorn ourselves with the fig-leaf of proud independence, often quite unjustifiably. We are ashamed to toil with our hands, with which it was intended that we should labor, and make the earth habitable for man. We are not ashamed to be seen with hands idly folded during the hours of toil. We are not ashamed, though we be young and strong, to seek aid, humbly and cringingly to beg for assistance, and thus forfeit our dignity; but we would be intensely mortified to be seen with a burden upon our shoulders, with an axe or a shovel in our hand, honestly toiling for our daily bread. Decked in borrowed finery, unpaid jewels and ornaments, we do not shrink, in the presence of our rich friends, from boasting of our counterfeit wealth. But we would be inexpressibly ashamed of being found living according to our means, with shabby, but untorn, cleanly and honestly gotten clothing and furniture, and associating with people in similar circumstances. This false shame has done, and continues to do, a great deal of harm.

We have *detectors* to discover the base coin among the true. Our virtues are the genuine gold coins in the media of exchange between men on earth, as well as our viaticum on the journey to the world beyond. But among the virtues, as in everything else, not all is gold that glitters; in the practice of virtue, too, we need a detector to distinguish the false from the true, genuine virtue from its counterfeit. This is true concerning all the virtues, but particularly of the sense of shame.

In conclusion, we turn once more to our introductory words. We remarked that our interpretation of the Bible and its misinterpretation on the part of others mark the line of division between our faith and the newer religions. The understanding of the Bible depends upon our knowledge of it in the original. Every translation is but the translator's exposition of his own conception. We Israelites would have to be ashamed of our pretension to the truer understanding, were the ability to read the divine Book in the original to become as rare among us as it was among the pioneers of the newer religions and the later worshippers of the Book. Not only are we on the point of losing this

ability to read it in the original, but the masses of our
fellow-believers seem more and more inclined to ignore
their ancient religious documents, even in their translation. Alcibiades one day asked a schoolmaster to lend
him his Homer. "I have none." "What! you, a
teacher, and no Homer in your house?" and in his
indignant anger, the boy so far forgot himself as to
strike the old man. Again, thou art an Israelite, and
hast no Bible in thy library? Thou belongest to a
faith that prides itself upon being the nations' teacher
in matters of religion, and dost not know thy own text-
book? It is true, under the present circumstances, not
every one can hope to be able to read and understand
the Bible in the original; in fact, the great majority
must be debarred therefrom. All the more ought everyone to feel bound to support any institution whose object
it is to counteract this evil, so that at least the leaders
and chosen ones of every Jewish congregation will preserve in Israel the inherited, true, pure spirit of the
Bible.

Sense of shame, thou divine messenger, thou guardian spirit of virtue, do not forsake us! Be our good
angel in all our ways, in our journeys, in storm and in
sunshine, until we safely land upon the shores of eternity.

CAIN AND ABEL.

GEN. IV.

"God is with me, I do not fear."

There is a distinction between "God is" and "God is with me;" we may believe in the existence of God, and yet feel forsaken of God. Happy he that can devoutly exclaim, from the bottom of his heart: "God is with me." Woe to him who, like Saul, in dull despair exclaims: "God has forsaken me; he answereth me not even in my dreams!"

How can man know whether God is with him or not? We are led to this question by the subject of to-day's Scriptural portion.

Cain and Abel each brought God an offering. "And the Lord had respect unto Abel and to his offering, but unto Cain and to his offering he had not respect, and Cain was very wroth and his countenance fell."

Who told Cain, how did he know that God had not respect unto his offering? One of the explanations given by the early rabbis is that fires from heaven devoured Abel's offering, and left Cain's untouched. A more recent commentator indicates the answer in an illustrated edition of the Bible. The smoke from Abel's sacrificial altar is seen to rise straight to heaven, but the smoke from Cain's offering is blown sideways by the wind. Such explanations are smoke themselves, and

only dim the clear vision of the reader of Holy Writ.
To know whether God is content with us, we need neither
watch the smoke of the offering, nor wait for fires from
heaven; we need only look into our own hearts; if
there we find that we are content with God, we have
the happy consciousness that God is content with us;
he who can say אֲנִי לוֹ, I am the Lord's, can also say
יְיָ לִי, the Lord is with me!

The tale of the first two brothers is taken from life;
not from the remote, obsolete life of antediluvian times,
but from the fresh stream of life, surging about us to-day.
No malicious, envious, god-forsaken man is satisfied with
himself, or his fellow-men, or his fate, or the course of
things in general; and whoever is at strife with himself,
soured and embittered in spirit, is of the opinion that
God has forsaken him, and that there is no justice in
the world. The gnawing worm of discontent and the
angels of contentment do not ask what a man's station
may be; to them it is immaterial whether he is rich or
poor, learned or ignorant, king or subject; they take
cognizance only of hearts, not of ranks. There are
those that are sated, yet dissatisfied, and others that are
content though starving. A good, honest man, a dutiful laborer or business man will, when his work is done,
sit at the table with his wife and children, in the one
modest room he calls home. Content if the hunger of
all be appeased, he rises, thinking: "God has helped
me to-day, he will help again to-morrow; God is with
me, I do not fear." It does not occur to him to think
that God has forsaken him, that God is displeased with
him, that he suffers unjustly. Instead of making the
old-time offering, he prays to the Lord; nor does he

think: "How can I pray to a God that pays no attention to my prayer?"

The Church puts the words of the Psalmist into the mouth of its founder, "My God, my God, wherefore hast thou forsaken me?" *Our* martyrs did not so exclaim in their hours of torture, when the flames were rising about them at the stake. Even in the throes of death, and in death itself, they did not believe themselves forsaken of God. They did not expire saying, "My God, my God, why hast thou forsaken me?" but with "Sh'ma Israel" upon their lips.

In the tale of Rabbi Akiba's martyrdom, we are told that he rejoiced in his painful death, as an opportunity to seal with his life-blood the averment that he had made twice every day: "Thou shalt love the Eternal, thy God, with all thy heart, with thy life, and with all thy goods."

Cain was a farmer; his farm was as large as the whole earth. So far as his condition, his outer life, was concerned, he might well live content, and· say: "God is with me!" But of what use was all this? His brother was as calm and happy and contented as is every good man that is satisfied with himself, with his fate and with his God. Everything seemed to go well with his brother; he was equally composed in success and failure, always even-tempered and happy. With this condition Cain compared his own wretched state of mind; in the light of the contrast, his calling and work seemed trivial. That which, in his brother's hand, became refreshing wine, in his own seemed to sour into vinegar, or to turn to bitter gall. Then he thought, "God does not love me, he hates me; my offering

does not please him. My brother is his favorite; his
offering has found favor in the eyes of God." And
embittered as he was, he took the first opportunity,
offered by a dispute in the field, to deal the fatal blow,
and he became a murderer.

"The wicked looketh out for his righteous, and
seeketh to slay him," says the Psalmist. That is one of
life's truths, first proved in Cain, and it has continued
to be proved through all generations. He that is dissatisfied with himself is no longer content with God, or
the world, or his own brother. He is not with God, and
therefore God is not with him. In his eyes everyone is
happier than he, more favored by God than himself.

Let us ask: "How is nobility of heart manifested,
and what brings genuine, lasting happiness to the
heart?" To take, to accept without giving in return, if
on account of poverty, is bitter; if from motives of avarice—show me the covetous man whose face is not fallen,
like Cain's, in whose features we cannot read: "Here
dwells neither contentment nor happiness!" Neither to
give nor take, but to live only for one's self, is the manner of low natures; or, as we read in the Ethics of the
Fathers, is the fashion of the lords of Sodom and Gomorrah. It is sweet to give, to sacrifice. If husband
and wife, if parents and children, live and sacrifice for
one another, they will feel divine bliss in so doing; this
happiness is augmented where there exists strength and
opportunity to extend help and kindness beyond the
home, out into the endless world of suffering humanity.
Even the most selfish of men cannot so completely isolate himself, but that he will sometimes be called upon
to make a sacrifice in honor of God or in the interest of

humanity; but he will bring his sacrifice tardily, and
in a surly, grudging spirit. So it was with Cain: "in
process of time," after he had stored harvest upon harvest,
he determined to sacrifice some of his superfluity in gratitude to God, the Giver; but of Abel we are told that
he brought "of the *firstlings* of his flock and the fat
thereof."

When people give with trembling hands and "in process of time," we may know that they are selfish, avaricious, hard-hearted. The noble ones, the Abels, do not
delay their gifts and sacrifices until they have enough
and more than enough themselves, but they give and
sacrifice of their earnings soon, because giving, sacrificing for others, is their greatest happiness. They do
not fear that giving may impoverish them, that they
themselves may want, for "God is with me, I do not
fear." They do not, after the manner of Cain, "in process of time," come to the house of God, and, by their
presence, sacrifice an hour to God; but they appear
before God, and can spare an hour for worship, even one
of their remunerative hours. They do not say, like
Cain: "Am' I my brother's keeper? My brother does
not concern me; I have myself to look after." It gives
them pleasure to be kind to their brother, and to protect
him from evil. Thus are we content within ourselves;
we know that we are with God, and that therefore God
is with us.

They that isolate themselves in feeling, that have no
heart for others, no wish, no hope, no goal but their
own interest, will soon find their spring of joy drained,
their hearts grow cold and ever colder; they become
bitter and more bitter, more unhappy and discontented;

4

they forsake God, and feel god-forsaken, and their very
expression invites the query: "Why art thou wroth,
and why is thy countenance fallen?"

Blessed be they that are content within; blessed they
that are with God, and with whom is God; blessed they
that may in truth exclaim: "God is with me, I do not
fear."

THE BOOK.

"This is the book of the generations of Adam. In the day that God created man, in the likeness of God made he him; male and female created he them; and blessed them, and called their name Adam, in the day when they were created."—GEN. V : 1, 2.

Our text, in two brief, prosaic verses, disposes of the creation of the first human beings, which was described more circumstantially and graphically in a former chapter. The cause of the repetition, and of the altered form and contents, is that the first is an account of the creation of the natural man, whereas the second one treats, as it were, of a second, revised creation, the child of nature being transformed into a civilized being. Civilized man begins with the book. "This is the book of the generations of man" (of the formation of man). With records begins the development of the civilized being: תולדת (generations) is his evolution. Savages remain savages, because they cannot write, and have traditions but no books. If the peoples that now rank as the most enlightened were to forget how to read and write, and were to lose all their books, a few generations hence would see them barbarians. A lifetime of seventy years is much too short for mental or physical progress to be of any consequence. Yet even the little an age can achieve, would pass away with it, and the following age would have to begin over again. Ante-

35

diluvian man must, indeed, have been much longer lived than we of the present day, else even the limited civilization of prehistoric times could never have been attained. The personal experiences of long lives made up for the written records of several generations. But even the nine hundred and sixty-nine years of Methuselah's life, what are they, unrecorded in detail, as compared with the lifetime of one of us, who, through books, can live from four to five thousand years! By means of books, we are contemporaneous with the mental and technical acquirements of hundreds of generations. We live with the earliest inventors, Jubal and Tubal Cain, as with Edison. Books are humanity's savings-bank. The profound thinker deposits his golden thoughts therein; the superficial thinker, his coppers, but each one something. The accumulated capital may be drawn upon not only by the depositor, and in proportion to his deposits, but by all mankind and to any extent. The charter of this bank is entitled: "This is the book of the generations of man," the book that forms civilized man.

Many may say: "I do not believe in books. I read no books, much less have I written any, yet I am neither a fool nor a savage!"

It is true that there are practical men and women who never read, and withal are more useful than many that absorb libraries and exhaust inkstands. Nevertheless, whatever there may be stirring of fertile thought in his brain, or of delicate feeling in his heart, and whatever technical skill he may proudly boast, indirectly the practical man has drawn it all from the accumulated knowledge in the bank-book of humanity; for this bank not only pays back deposits with interest, it does not even wait for people to draw upon it—it does not even ask, " Who was the depositor ?" Its profits benefit all, even those that do not read and write. The bank is not in danger of a run upon it ; on the contrary, it is ever calling and reminding people, " Do not let my treasures lie idle, come and take of them !"

It is equally true that readers and writers of books are not always the best men ; the former often carry away with them the absurdities and the unhealthfulness gathered in some books, and the latter often deposit tin instead of gold—matter to kill time and souls, instead of educational store. But do we not find blight and madwort among the wheat ? So it must also be in the field of human thought.

The first story of the creation has, for its subject, the natural man, and the style of description is chosen accordingly. The man of nature speaks in metaphors. Just as writing begins with picture-writing, with thoughts depicted in colors, so the expression of thought by means of language begins with word-painting. With culture comes the use of prose, and accordingly the second account of the creation, which speaks of the " cultured man," accomplishes in two verses what it took the first an entire chapter to do.

So much for the difference in form between the two accounts of the creation ; now for the difference in matter.

According to the first account, man was created first. But when it was found that it was not well for man to be alone, woman was given to him as a companion. The man was called Adam and his wife Eve—for " she was the mother of all living." According to this account, woman's place in creation would be but as the complement of man ; she is valuable only as the mother of future generations ; for her own sake, her existence would not be justified. This, indeed, do we find the position of woman to be in uncivilized lands and ages ; she is but her husband's beast of burden. The social and domestic position of woman keeps pace with culture.

In the second account of the creation, we are told, " Male and female created he them ; and blessed them, and called their name Adam." Here woman is created not merely as a helpmate to man, as a supplement, as it were ; she is valued not only as Eve, the mother of men, but she exists independently and for her own sake.

" This is the book of the generations of man "—this is the history of man as the book has developed him.

There always have been men and women who exaggerate virtue and piety into a very caricature, and so cause them to be decried. We find the same tendency illustrated in the relation of the sexes to each other. The calm, sensible prose of our text would read that man and woman were created equals, and so every just, enlightened code of laws endeavors to give to woman equal rights with man. Whereas the poetical conception of the story of the creation of the " natural man " degrades woman to the level of a mere convenience to man, the romantic literature of civilized countries goes to the other extreme, and deifies and beatifies the " eternally feminine " (das Ewig-Weibliche). It depicts the world as one of flowers and sunshine, of homage and adoration, and oftentimes are girls and young women embittered for life, unhappy and discontented with their lot, because they fancy themselves wronged, because, in real life, in the world of reality, they find that, in the long run, men and women alike are valued according to their services. Their eyes are opened to the fact that the demands of the home upon the housewife, of the family upon the mother, and finally the husband's assertion of *his* rights, prove to be very different from the hazy pictures of romantic literature.

Yet the charming conceits of romantic literature possess at least the merit of having given great pleasure to the world. Who can count the hours of enjoyment that such reading has bestowed, or the number of hearts that it has softened? Who would deny that it has been invaluable in awakening, fostering and cultivating the æsthetic sense in the majority of its readers? If we had to continue the Bible, who knows but that the influence of romantic literature might impel us to add a third account of the creation of woman to the two already existing? In the first, she is man's inferior; in the second, his equal; in the third, she would be a higher æsthetic being, which neither knits nor weaves nor spins, but charmingly arrayed, like the lilies of the field, would beautify our lives, and "weave heavenly roses into our earthly life." And then, because it were not good for woman to be alone—for who would weave and spin and take care of things?—we would have God create man to serve her.

But exaggeration ceases to be pleasing, indeed, it becomes offensive, when it introduces woman into the arena of political strife, and transports her from the peace and purity of domestic life to the noise and mire of publicity. She has a right to enter upon this life, certainly, just as the dove has a right to mingle with eagles, but the exercise of the privilege would prove fatal to the poor dove. Instinct teaches the animal to keep out of danger. Is there not enough of abuse, slander, fraud and even bloody strife in connection with elections and politics in general among the politically-privileged sex, without casting the other and purer half of humanity into this whirlpool? Men, in their political contests, may calumniate and cast the mire of slander upon one another. A blot on a man's character is easily obliterated, and even his real shortcomings are leniently judged. But the faintest tinge upon a woman's character robs her forever of her reputation and tarnishes her name and being. Woman, more delicate and sensitive, and when good, possessing a nobility of soul which even the best among men cannot approach, would not retain her equanimity as man does in the pitiless strife of politics. She would leave the field of battle hurt, deeply pained and wounded, whereas men of opposing factions cordially shake hands after the battle, as if no unkind word had been spoken. But the cultured, patriotic woman is not debarred from exerting political influence; her spirit may guide husbands and sons in the noblest direction, and kindle them to the noblest deeds. Cornelia did not go into the Forum, but she was the mother of the Gracchi.

"This is the book of the generations of man." The evolution in the history of civilization, the growth of culture, of thought, of enlightenment, of intellectuality in each successive generation, is due to books.

We have noted their influence upon the position of woman. The tendency of culture is to place the weak

on an equal footing with the strong. And thus Israel,
like woman, has been the gainer by the advance of culture. It is weak in numbers, and has been further
weakened by prejudice. Look about you in the different countries of the earth. Wherever you find woman
oppressed, her claims disregarded, there Israel likewise
does not lie upon a bed of roses; and where woman suc-
ceeds in asserting her rights, Israel also is permitted to
grow in dignity. In no land upon earth is woman held
in higher esteem than in our blessed United States.
Here, too, the Israelite may enjoy every privilege. This
is the best evidence that the country takes first rank, in
point of culture, among the nations of the earth. May
it ever remain upon this pinnacle, and be guarded from
the pitfalls of exaggeration!

PRAISE AND BLAME.

"These are the generations of Noah : Noah was a just man and perfect in his generations, and Noah walked with God.—GEN. VI : 9.

In the introductory words of to-day's portion of the Law, in which the Bible speaks of Noah in the third person, he is designated as "a just man and perfect," and again as a man that "walked with God;" but further on, where Noah is mentioned in the second person, addressed by God, it says merely, "for thee have I seen righteous before me in this generation."

Thence our sages draw the lesson that, in a person's presence, praise of him should be moderate, and full praise accorded only in his absence. Generally, this is accepted in its negative sense, as a warning against flattery, as an objection to exaggerated praise. To be sure, if we glance about us in practical life we find that praise, in the presence of the person commended, is apt to be exaggerated, even false, while behind his back, there is rarely any praise at all, neither faint nor unstinted praise.

These thoughts lead us to the regions of flattery and duplicity, tempting the preacher to moralize, and offering him a grateful subject, bound to win for him his listeners' sympathies. They fully approve of his railing against and chiding the insincerity of the world. "The minister is quite right; every word he has uttered is

42

perfectly true!" For each one thinks that the moralist's strictures apply only to the wicked world, and not to himself.

Our principle should be, not that we *may* praise, but that we *ought* to praise others; moderately, yes, and with discretion, but praise them we should. As God spake to Noah, "For thee have I seen righteous before me," so be you ready frankly to show the good man your appreciation. Many people have not sufficient generosity to speak a kind word or give a sign of appreciation, unless it be from selfish motives. "Love thy neighbor as thyself." Surely, no one objects to this fundamental principle of our religion. Well, no matter how modest you may be, you are pleased by an expression of praise which, you feel, you merit. It borders on saintliness to be able to act rightly and nobly, quietly and without ostentation, seen only by God, knowing one's self to be misunderstood, and yet continuing calmly and unconcernedly in the path of the good and the noble.

Do unto others as you would have them do unto you. If you mean to try to live up to the law, "Love thy neighbor as thyself," you must remember that it can be carried out, not only in cases in which your neighbor is in need of material assistance, or requires your personal aid, but also by rejoicing his heart whenever it can be done. Love of mankind gives bread to the hungry and alms to the poor, and makes us obliging to our neighbors. In times of trouble we extend a helping hand to every one that needs it. But when neither hunger, nor trouble, nor aught else, calls for acts of human kindness—what then? Speak a pleasant word

to all! That is the gift that pleases the millionaire as
well as the beggar, and it is always appropriate. It is a
gift precious enough for those dearest to you, and not
too valuable to bestow upon the most·distant acquaintance. If you wish to give pleasure to the faithful part-
ner of your life, if you would sincerely delight her, and
elevate her spirits, you need not go to a dry-goods store,
and purchase the costliest and most elegant material for
her, nor pave the ways of a happy marriage with dia-
monds: tell her something kind; praise her management in her sphere at home. When a man supposes
that he can give a woman no greater pleasure than by
presenting her with woven materials, shining gold and
glittering stones, does he imagine that he is thus showing
the proper appreciation of the dignity of womanhood?
Does he imagine that to be the way to make every
woman happy, from the maiden to the matron? Show
her your appreciation of the dutiful mother in her, of
the housewife, and do not stint your praise of anything
that may be praiseworthy in her, and if she possess but
a spark of true womanly pride, this will make her happier than wagonloads of precious gifts could do.

If you have a laborer with whom you are satisfied,
tell him so! Praise him! He will be better pleased
than with the conventional gift which is supposed to
repay his ardent services.

How delighted pupils are when they are praised by
their teacher, and they may carry the praise home in the
form of a certificate, particularly if they know that the
praise is deserved.

But even our dear, beloved gold, hardly earned, still
more hardly parted with, finds its way more readily out

of our purses, than does a good, kind word out of our
mouths. The penurious man will sooner, though even
that with a heavy heart, make up his mind to the purchase of a diamond, than will the hard man to the
utterance of appreciative praise. Limited knowledge
of human nature is shown by the fact that there is more
complaint of flattery, that is, of too much and undeserved
praise, than of praise withheld, though merited.

To flatter a man in his presence, and then to criticise
him adversely as soon as his back is turned upon us, is
an undoubted sin, of which no one is entirely innocent,
but which everyone regards as contemptible; but when
the kind word that really belongs to another is withheld,
the wrong is not even suspected. Is it because people
are, in truth, so poor in virtue that we hear so few
of them praised? Why, that would be a slur upon the
Creator who made them!

God said to Noah, "Thou art a man whom I have
found good and righteous, 'in this generation,' under the
existing circumstances under which thou hast grown up
among men."

So let us judge. Let us give every one his due; let us
judge of everyone in the light of the circumstances
under which he has lived and been brought up. Let us
give to everyone credit for the good in him, whether it
be great or small, to those near and dear to us, as well
as to those with whom we come but casually in contact.

Our sages say, in an allegory, that God lays the hand
of his mercy upon the scale of merit, when the tongue
of the balance wavers between guilt and deserts. Even
though there may be some doubt as to the unquali-
fied merit of the action in question, praise it! We are

not so conscientious when we come to blame. Many a
hard judgment is passed upon the strength of a mere
supposition, of rumors floating about in the air, coming,
no one knows whence—why be so guarded in praise?
If we take into consideration the circumstances under
which a man lives and acts, much may be praised that
is not exactly resplendent in virtue, and much be
thought clean that has many a stain.

Of course, praise must be, according to circumstances,
merited, then it is not flattery. It must not be over-
done, else it may spoil the one to whom it is accorded.
Moderate praise harms no one; on the contrary, it
spurs him on to be completely worthy and deserving of
it.

Many a one that finds it hard work to utter a kind
word justifies himself by saying, " I cannot flatter! I
am no flatterer and no hypocrite!" Instead of which
he ought to say, " I cannot praise; my heart is not good
enough."

Many a one who can most readily, without the slightest hesitancy or qualm of conscience blame another in
his presence, but cannot bring himself to utter a word
of praise or acknowledgment, considers himself therefore one of the most sturdy, honest and sincere of men.
In reality, he ranks among the heartless, coarse-grained
misanthropes of earth.

Many are not actually malevolent; they blame without condemning; but neither are they kindly disposed.
They utter not a kind word, unless it be forced from
them. But, despite their taciturnity, they are not
philosophers, as they fondly fancy; they are too poor
in love and sympathy for their fellow-beings to give

away even a word. They would not have given Noah
- the satisfaction of saying to him, "Thee I have found
righteous in this generation."

Praise a man moderately in his presence. You are
not asked for valuable gold coins—exaggerated praise;
nor are there very many that deserve such praise. But
be always well supplied with small coins, the small change
of praise, ana scatter it to the right and left on your pathway in life as kindly gifts and just tributes ; for there
are few in whom there is not something to praise.

To cast blame upon a strong man, in his very presence, though it may be justified, requires heroic courage ;
but to find something to praise in a weak one, and
to accord him praise therefor, bespeak a noble nature
and a gentle heart. Blessed be they that can do both,
in whom nobility of spirit, strength of mind and goodness of heart are united !

GEN. VI : 9.

When the moment of separation between life and death has come, and our labors here are ended; when there is nothing more to be added to or taken from our life-work, in what word should we most like to have all our striving and getting summed up, and echoed beyond the grave? Artist? Scholar? Ruler? Millionaire? Or should we like to be remembered as a beautiful, gracious lady? No matter how much importance people, even up to the last day in life, attach to such names, when the last hour comes, on the verge of eternity, there is no longer any delight in the things that seemed of ruling importance during life. The word that we should most like to have re-echo in the world after the grave has closed over us, is that which clung to Noah's memory : "Noah was a righteous man." *Zaddik* is the word; to have lived as a Zaddik would assuredly be our last and greatest desire. We find this word cut into most Israelitish tombstones, in praise of the man resting beneath. Often the praise that the patient stone bears is unmerited, yet the frequency with which it occurs testifies to the high esteem in which the epithet is held.

The handsomest and tallest monument, with the most grandiloquent inscription, has no value, if the one little word "Zaddik" cannot be truthfully placed upon it.

The most touching and the most polished funeral oration is devoid of meaning, if the little word "Zaddik" must of necessity be left out of it. Man may secure posthumous fame through manifold works; he may gain celebrity after his death among those left on earth, but in departing, only that which walks *before* us is of value to us, והלך לפניך צדקך "Before thee shall go thy righteousness"—all that pertains to a Zaddik.

Zaddik is a Hebrew word. What is its translation? It is one of the untranslatable Hebrew words. Even in being defined, it loses its force, just as wine loses its aroma in a chemical analysis. To render it in another language deprives it of its flavor, it is then like wine poured from one vessel into another. The attributes just, honorable, honest, benevolent, god-fearing, may be applied to a man or not—the subject ever remains; but in Zaddik all these attributes are embodied. The one word is the subject and the predicate. We cannot imagine a Zaddik otherwise than possessing all these attributes. The Bible declares Noah to have attained his majority; it tells us that in his generation he was the only one that had reached the nobility of a Zaddik.

At the time of the deluge, there had been no revelation on Mount Sinai, and no Moses called to speak to the people in the name of God. How could there then have been a Zaddik? And how could men be punished for evil or even be called evil, there being no divine laws to obey and none to infringe? The Bible-text teaches us the great lesson that we carry a divine revelation in our hearts. Also to that portion of humanity that was not present at Mount Sinai, God revealed himself and spoke. This revelation continues through all times, and the voice

5

of God, heard in our conscience, does not die away. It is "the loud voice that does not cease." Our sages mention seven Noachian precepts, but it is not imperative to derive them from the Bible, as our sages do. The four into which the seven resolve themselves are, humanity, chastity, justice and the worship of God. These emanate from man's moral instincts, and are the gentle voices of the heart, in which God's will manifests itself. Noah had the same law-giver as his contemporaries, the same teacher and mentor—the moral law within his heart; it was sufficient to make him a Zaddik, to teach him how to earn God's favor, whereas his contemporaries had incurred the deluge.

This story recommends to us tolerance, exercised by God himself, and so often overlooked by religious zeal. Even those who were not at Mount Sinai, and whose ancestors were not there, who never experienced a supernatural revelation, and, therefore, do not believe in any, even they may find favor in the eyes of God, if they lead a virtuous life. Noah's contemporaries met their destruction, because they despised the moral law, and permitted their feelings and actions alike to run riot. "For the land was filled with violence." This, the Bible tells us, was the cause of the destructive flood. So far as their belief was concerned, whether true or false, the sun would have continued to shine for them as it had done before and has done since for millions of idolaters.

In matters of belief, tolerance is a virtue; men of the most varied beliefs may live near one another, and each one live and die a Zaddik. But when the question is purely moral, affecting all men alike; when it is one of nobility, of humanity, of rectitude; when, in short, it falls under the divine revelations made in our hearts, then to practise forbearance, to be indifferent towards the views and actions of men, is sinful, punishable tolerance, of the sort that has ever produced deluges; that is to say, times of social distress, great or slight, according to the prevalence of this laxity of judgment.

In the story, after Noah has been distinguished by the honorable name Zaddik, we read further on, as if in explanation of it: "Noah walked with God!" We spoke of a moral law, which every one carries in his heart, and which renders it possible for every one to be a Zaddik. But where, in history, look where we may, can we find an example of a people or a country or any large community living for any length of time in peace and order and security, based purely upon this moral law? A belief in God or gods, whether childish or rational, has always been the foundation of stable, civil order, and the anchor of the social fabric. Individuals have, at all times, discarded the belief in God, and yet continued to live virtuously, but communities—never. The worst periods of moral depravity, even in heathen communities, have always been those in which irreligion was considered the proper thing, and the masses turned their backs upon their temples of divine worship, and gave up their belief, without substituting a better one.

The praise accorded to Noah, "and Noah walked with God," shows what was lacking in his contemporaries, and what occasioned the moral ruin of the people. They walked neither with God, nor with gods.

Truly, the moral law and the tendency to good are in the human heart; so are the conditions for growth contained in the seed, the earth and the atmosphere, but

the sun must give heat and light, must awaken and
quicken the germ. Thus the heart has its moral law,
and the understanding knows right from wrong, but the
divine spark, which impels the heart to good actions, is
wanting. This animating element is the belief in God.
The chemist knows the component parts of the blood;
he can show us its separate ingredients, but he cannot
make blood of the parts. How to impart life is the
secret of creation. The secret of quickening the moral
law in man is not withheld from us: it is the faith in
heaven, in a higher, superhuman, inconceivable Being.

As remarked before, individuals, guided by the moral
law, may remain in the right path, even though they be
infidels, but never an entire community. Political and
social problems may unite the masses, and move them to
act in harmony, but not permanently, only while the
question is pending. If the moral law is to be the law
of the land, if it is to achieve permanent and thus effective results, it must be informed with a ray of the sun
of faith, dispensing light and warmth from a world
above and beyond ours.

Noah's contemporaries walked not with God, wherefore the Zaddikim gradually disappeared from their
midst, and morality died out among them. Depravity
followed in the train of godlessness. But Noah walked
with God; his belief in God kept the moral law in his
heart fresh and pure, and he was the only Zaddik of his
time; and he is praised as a most excellent Zaddik.
For it is not so difficult to live a Zaddik among Zaddikim. It is infinitely harder to remain true to one's
self among evil, immoral people, to stand firm in the
current of public opinion, and not be carried away by it.

Let us not be deceived because nowadays we find everywhere people who are estranged from religion; infidels, who are nevertheless good and virtuous. Let not such examples mislead us into believing that communities may prosper spiritually, and the world remain moral, without some kind of religion. In a country of fifty millions, hundreds of thousands may live moral lives without religion, so long as millions and millions of their contemporaries worship God, and teach the worship of God, and instil thoughts of heaven in church, in school, and at the domestic hearth—so long as hundreds of thousands of churches and schools and synagogues exist to foster these teachings, and so awaken, support and sanctify the moral law in the heart.

Imagine all the churches and schools closed, the moral guidance discontinued, and each one left to follow the promptings of his heart. Oh, ye philosophers! ye would not win those fleeing from the ashes of their faith, not even your own offspring; the masses deserting God would drag you down into their own whirlpool of unfettered sensualism, materialism and gross selfishness.

It would be the foulest calumny to accuse modern Jews of retrogression in morality, because of the more lax exercise of the rites of their inherited religion. Even the most conservative must admit, upon unbiased judgment, that in many ways things are better than they were in the days of unquestioned orthodoxy. Yet we cannot be sufficiently earnest in our warning against too greatly damping the fire of religion, till the heart is dead to the thought of God. Whoever values morality for himself and the generation in which he lives, as well as for the generations that follow, must practise religion

not only in spirit, but also in a manner that will, by
mutual, external interests, bind together a large circle
of believers. Through abandoning the belief in God,
antediluvian humanity, with one exception, gradually
sank into moral depravity. This one alone remained
a Zaddik, for he was the only one that recognized a
God above him. "Noah walked with God."

Let the precious title of Zaddik not wait for the tomb-
stone, but may the Israelite be honored in life, before
God and man, as a Zaddik!

BE CONTENT TO LIVE IN THE LAND OF THY BIRTH.

"And you, be ye fruitful, and multiply ; bring forth abuudantly in the earth, and multiply therein."—GEN. IX : 7.

In the repetition of the thought contained in the first part of our text in the concluding words, " and multiply therein " our sages recognize a special covenant of God ; or, translated into the language of our day, a law of Nature regulating the affection of man for his native heath. " And multiply therein "—thrive, develop and strengthen in the place where your cradle stood.

It is certain that some such natural law of inevitable force must regulate man's feeling on the subject. The most inhospitable regions of the earth are inhabited by people who, nevertheless, enjoy life ; they strain every muscle to earn a meagre subsistence, while lands, richly blessed, remain untilled. In the rugged mountains of Vermont, in the forests of Maine, among the bogs and marshes of North Carolina, there are light crops and hard work, little pleasure and much privation. Yet people have lived there from generation to generation, clinging to and loving the spot in which they were born, while vast areas of land in the Union, as fertile as the garden of God, as the land of Egypt, still await the pioneer's plow. The Shetland Isles, even Iceland, Spitz· bergen and Nova Zembla are inhabited, whereas Spain, Hungary, the principalities of the Danube, etc., still have room for all their dwellers. As a rule, moreover, people are proud of the wretched bit of land which they happen to inhabit. The Russian, in his smoky cabin, buried in snow half the time, looks proudly down upon the Italian, who must go to the mountains for the snow and ice wherewith to cool a beverage. The lazzarone, who lives on the street, subsists on alms, and can claim nothing as his own but the blue of the sky overhead, yet exclaims, "See Naples and die!"

A Greenlander replied to a missionary, " Who made the sun? I don't know; I have never thought about it; but if it was made by anyone, it assuredly must have been a Greenlander!"

The epochs in history, when entire peoples threw off these fetters, and left their barren homes in multitudes in search of more pleasant abiding-places, have ever been fraught with misery, as was the time of the deluge. What is the burning of Magdeburg, of London, of Moscow, or of Chicago, as compared with the calamities brought on by these hordes? Hundreds of miles of villages and towns were one sheet of flames. Slaying and massacre preceded them, and death, ruin and desolation followed in their wake.

God spake after the great deluge, " There shall be no more a flood to destroy the earth!" Likewise, Providence has, since many centuries, kept the nations within bounds, and not permitted them to deluge the earth. The old covenant, "and multiply therein," is once again in full operation. The entire surface of the earth is inhabited, and despite the partial distribution of favors, each one believes himself in possession of the most favored spot, and there takes root for all times.

So enormous a displacement of the fluid element, as in Noah's time, is a curse; but complete cessation of movement would be equally unfortunate. So the rush of entire peoples, the surging of a sea of humanity over the whole earth, brought with it inexpressible misery and suffering. On the other hand, if nations were to separate themselves from one another by insuperable barriers; were to hate and despise one another, and live each one only within the circle of its own ideas, it would prove anything but a blessing. Regarding this, much has changed for the better. Nations confine themselves within their boundaries, and yet there is easy movement from one to the other. In ancient times, next to death, exile was the most severe punishment, for only one's native heath contained that which was most desirable. "Stranger" was an ugly name; neither the life nor the property of him that bore it was safe; respect, friendship, good-will were out of the question. These conditions naturally strengthened the love of home. The more unkind fate was in foreign lands, the more beautiful did home appear. The ancients used to say, "Wherever I am happy, there is my country!" But no one was happy anywhere except at home.

Nowadays, any good book or newspaper article is translated into various languages, and travels from land to land. The products of the soil or of trade and works of art are taken everywhere; hundreds and thousands of people are employed in scattering them abroad. We of to-day also love our homes; but oftentimes we are better off in a strange than in our native land; since we are secure abroad, and are treated kindly, we no longer consider leaving home a misfortune, or life away from it, exile.

For this, God be praised. Each people lives happily and securely in its own domain, and still each individual may safely remove his home to a distance of thousands of miles. Just as the sea is confined in its basin by rocks and sand-banks, so the peoples are detained within limits by the natural law, "multiply therein."

But as brooks, rivers and torrents beautify the earth, as fogs, clouds and moderate rains refresh and invigorate it, so do men travelling from land to land in families and parties receive and bestow the advantages of new knowledge, of new skill, new views, new conceptions, and animate, refresh and enhance the social life of humanity.

The portion from the Prophets (I Kings XXI), which we read to-day, illustrates the natural law about the affection of man for his native heath. Naboth will not, at any price, part with his inherited vineyard. The soil which his parents tilled and cultivated is dearer to him than any other estate offered to him, even though it be better and more beautiful than his own. When we take into consideration the submissiveness of Orientals to the behests of their ruler, and the perils of provoking his wrath, Naboth's outspoken preference for his plot of ground is explicable only by the compelling power of a natural law.

In this, too, there has been a great change. How many do we find to-day living in the houses of their parents, or cultivating the lands of their grandparents? Who would not be ready to sell his house and grounds for a good round sum? Not once but ten times in the course of his life? If the community wants a piece of ground, hundreds are eager to sell, for a goodly remuneration, little caring that their ancestors once lived upon it.

We ought to regard, as one of Nature's hints, the fact that man is always strongest and happiest and most content in his native home, wherever that home may be: "Here I will cast anchor, and if storms do not drive me away, I will live, work and die here; here would I see my children reared and settled." Staff in hand, loins girded, ever prepared for change, living for the day and mistrusting the morrow—that is not the way to find happiness in life. Choose a country, and love it; choose an occupation, and be faithful to it, working earnestly, perseveringly and trustfully, thus preparing better times. Whatever is yours by inheritance or honest gain should please you, and seem better and more beautiful than royal estates. Unlike those that are ever seeking happiness in change, to whom the belongings of others always seem better and more desirable than their own, who are never satisfied with what they themselves possess; unlike those that are willing to sell anything and everything for gold, and rate the value of every possession according to the gold standard —unlike such, have ye a fatherland that ye love, a city, a town, a bit of ground, a home to which ye are attached, a house in which ye feel at home, in which to live, not to be bartered away from time to time, and thus form ye a link in the family chain, and add to its sacred traditions.

"Bring forth abundantly in the earth, and multiply therein!"

THE TOWER OF BABEL.

GEN. XI.

Was there anything sinful in the building of the Tower of Babel? Upon calmly perusing the story, we find therein neither sin nor punishment of sin. "A tower whose top may reach unto heaven" has been construed as an expression of sinful audacity, as if the builders of the tower had had the intention of storming heaven and dethroning God; whereas, it is evident that the expression "reach unto heaven" is merely figurative, and means "very high," just as it conveys the idea of the superlative in the phrase, "the cities are walled and great *unto heaven.*" Altogether, speculation and tradition have been too active about the Tower of Babel. The main question was not the building of a tower—that is mentioned incidentally—it is really the building of a city that is spoken of. Why, the last words are: "and they left off to build the city." But, surely, the tale must have some meaning! Certainly it has a meaning, but one far more natural and rational than has generally been attributed to it. Let us try to elucidate it.

"And the whole earth was of one language and of one speech."

Two opposing forces act upon man. When two people live together, sometimes from their very first meeting, this conflict of feelings becomes noticeable. The one

tendency is toward individualism, toward a life of un-
trammelled, personal liberty, to do what we will, and to
take what we can. This, according to the Bible, was
the tendency of man before the deluge: "the land was
filled with violence." People in whom this tendency
predominates are just as hard to get on with nowadays.
They cause unhappiness in married life, and dissensions
in societies; they mar the peace of the community, and
are anarchists in political life. But man cannot live for
himself alone; he is a being with social needs, and their
satisfaction necessitates limitations to the personal liberty
of the individual. To find the happy medium between
the two extremes is the duty of every individual towards
himself, and of every one who has it in his power to
adjust the laws of the community.

The extreme of self-control and self-effacement is shown
in the story of the Tower of Babel. After building it,
the people wanted to remain together, to form *one* community, to speak *one* tongue, and, in every respect, to
lead the same life. To accomplish this, each one would
have been obliged to sacrifice almost wholly his individual liberty. This personal restriction, which is imposed
by all despotic governments, to a certain extent by all
monarchies, and even by some republics, renders the
citizen a mere stone in the social structure. He does
not exist for his own sake, but only as a part of the
whole. He is like one of the bricks in the tower. The
brick was not baked for the sake of the brick itself, but
to be used in building the tower.

That, indeed, is the view of conquerors of ancient and
modern times. The man, as an individual, has no
value—of what consequence is he? But he is required

as a stone to assist in building up a monarchy or an empire. What cared Nebuchadnezzar or Cyrus for the welfare of the people upon whom he made war? What cared Alexander the Great for the welfare of the Asiatics? What cared the bloody Roman for the comfort or happiness of the peoples far and near whom he conquered? Did Napoleon go to Moscow to advance the welfare of the Russians? Does Russia care to make the Turks happy? In every case, the object was to secure bricks for the structure of power; and so men and peoples are formed into bricks to be utilized in that structure. Anyone who, in matrimonial or business relations, requires the other party to live only for him and his advantage, and so asserts his own individuality that the individuality of his associate is crushed—on a small scale, he, too, is a conqueror and a tyrant. The people with whom he comes into contact are only bricks to him, to be used at his pleasure and to his advantage. It is one of the violent methods of despotism to force the people under a common yoke, to make them forget their own language, and adopt that of their conqueror. Uniformity in religion, uniformity in manners and customs, but above all, uniformity in language!

Experience teaches us that differences of language and the consequent division of people into separate nations and tribes, protected the liberty of mankind. For liberty, when driven away by one people, always found another somewhere on the face of the earth to abide with. Differences of language prevent the formation of universal empires, which are the graves of liberty. Whenever any such have been welded together, by means of blood and iron, they have soon fallen into their component parts, by reason of the different tongues.

Varieties of language are the safeguard, not only of political liberty, but also of religious and scientific freedom.

Thought may be fettered in some one place, but the power of the oppressor can penetrate no further than his language goes.

Woe to us, had the Latin or the Greek tongue become universal in the Roman Empire, as the Romans and the Greeks, respectively, endeavored to make it! Roman Christianity would then, in its sway, have become co-extensive with the Latin language.

Woe to the world, had the Arabic tongue become universal twelve hundred years ago! If so, Mohammedanism would now be the universal religion. The Reformation could not have gained a foothold among Christians in the Protestant countries, had not the Bible been translated into the language of the country, and thus reached the people. Moses Mendelssohn was no reformer, neither in his life nor in his teachings, but by translating the Hebrew Bible into good German, he took the preliminary step to reform.

Thus, too, the story of the Tower of Babel conveys to us the lesson that uniformity of language and custom was not included in the scheme of creation. God scattered the people over the earth, and gave them different languages to make them live in separate nations and tribes. Man is not to be like one of the bricks in the tower; his individuality demands respect.

"And it came to pass, as they journeyed from the East, that they found a plain in the land of Shinar; and they dwelt there."

According to the ancients—the rule would scarcely
apply to the United States—liberty dwells in the mountains, and bondage in the valleys; in the mountains
there is poverty, in the valleys there is wealth. The
sparse vegetation in the mountains, coupled with the
absence of rivers and seacoast, debarring the inhabitants
from all opportunities for profitable trade, naturally
compels them to industry and moderation, the cardinal
virtues of civil life. The clear, pure light and atmosphere
incite to free thought and ideal living. On the plains
the fertility of the soil and the opportunities for carrying
on trade and thus acquiring wealth, spoil the people and
crush their spirit. In a life of luxury, the higher
things of life are disregarded, and the love of liberty is
lost. "And from thence did the Lord scatter them
abroad upon the face of all the earth." The mountains
were to have dwellers to preserve liberty, while the valleys were to be peopled by those whose mission it was to
garner wealth for purposes of enlightenment and civilization. "Go to, let us build us a city and a tower,
whose top may reach unto heaven, and let us make us a
name, lest we be scattered abroad upon the face of the
whole earth."

The cities are the homes of intelligence and refined
culture, of love of art and the æsthetic sense. There we
find the fostering spirits of all these high endeavors,
teachers of science as well as the self-denying rich, who,
having hoarded wealth, apply it to the furtherance of
noble enterprises. In the cities, the schemes originate
which distribute wealth like a fructifying stream over the
entire country. In the cities, people of genius and talent
congregate; everyone who is pre-eminent in his specialty

seeks the city, where his services will be appreciated.
But in the cities, there is also luxury, extravagance,
corruption, pretence. There, every physical and moral
power is strained and over-exerted to meet the insatiable
demands of city life and customs. Political and moral
sins alike find a most congenial home there. The
rabble that collects there is ready for any crime, even
for treason ; traitors to their country have ever found,
and bought their minions in the city.

In the country, life is more simple ; there is more sincerity, more modesty, more cordiality, more industry
and moderation. On the other hand, there is less intellectuality, less taste for art and science, and less opportunity to cultivate or teach these ; there is less enterprise
and a more limited horizon in every direction.

A country in which city life predominates would be a
misfortune, as has been proved by Sidon and Tyre, Car-
thage and Venice. But a country of villages and farms
and no cities, a land of peasants without business and
tradesmen, such as Uri and Schwyz in Switzerland, would
permit of none but a heavy, clownish existence, a life of
stagnation, in which progress in matters of religion, of
civil law, of art and science, of trade, of constitutional
government, and even of agriculture, would not be possible. When combined with the restlessness of city life
the conservatism of country life is a valuable factor in
the regulation of well-ordered progress. Left to itself,
this conservatism would degenerate into complete inertia.
Therefore, the Scriptural narrative says that " The Lord
scattered them abroad upon the face of all the earth;
and they left off to build the city."

" And it came to pass, as they journeyed from the East."

6

There is a migration of people from the East across the ocean to this country, too. Thence, where circumstances have taught them to live industriously and modestly, they come here to assist in a structure so great and magnificent, that figuratively its top reaches unto heaven. The immigrants build up both cities and villages. Under such circumstances, there is no danger .in building. The increase in the population of the cities is counterbalanced by the ever-increasing country population. But we Israelites, as a religious brotherhood, have not maintained this nice adjustment. The majority of our co-religionists in Europe lived in villages and country towns. There were they brought up in the school of industry and moderation, and there, too, they could live in strict obedience to the behests of their religion, without coming into conflict with the outer world.

Now, in the old world as here, the tide of humanity flows toward the cities; country communities are dwindling away. Here, in our republic, all the immigrant Israelites become city dwellers; the counterbalancing, conservative country communities are lacking. The restrictions imposed by our religion are daily disregarded in favor of the demands of city life. So much for the practice. As for the theory, the teachings of our faith— they are not so readily and blindly accepted by the city dweller, who comes into contact with all sorts of ideas, as by the simple countryman. The rapid transformation in the life of the Jewish people here, in their thoughts and actions, is due to the change from the country to the city; the pious, slow, conservative countryman has become an easy-going townsman.

O would that Israelites, while enjoying city advantages and adopting city customs, did but retain the rural simplicity, steadiness, industriousness and virtuous life of their former rural homes! May they, like the flower transplanted to a new soil, not wilt in their divine heritage, but be ennobled, and bear fruits that will find favor in the sight of God and man!

LEARNING AND FORGETTING.

"Now the Lord had said unto Abram, Get thee out of thy country, and from thy kindred, and from thy father's house, unto a land that I will shew thee."—GEN. XII: 1.

Man has a twofold task here below : to learn and to forget. The latter is the more difficult of the two. Although, at first blush, nothing seems easier than to forget, and nothing more difficult than to learn ; a moment's thought will show us that the most important functions in life, particularly of mental life, are acquired without any trouble. We learn to think, speak, subordinate ourselves, to be ashamed, to be merciful, and to practise other virtues—yea, and some of the vices—of our civilization, by merely living in our country, in our birthplace, in our home.

What we learn in the school-room, in the sweat of our brow, is of minor account; the most important things in life we learn easily, without thought or trouble, involuntarily and unconsciously, in our intercourse with men. Now, if we were to pause reverently before this naturally acquired wealth of thought, feeling, speech and action, there would be neither progress nor development; one generation would follow another, and each one be like the last. Many mistakes and failings, unconsciously acquired, must be forgotten, if there is to be improvement, and this forgetting is very difficult of

68

accomplishment ; the force of habit inclines us to learn
with ease, but to forget far less easily.

From time to time, therefore, there must arise original
thinkers, who, above and beyond the inheritance of past
ages, have ideas of their own, revelations in art, trades,
professions, science or religion. They impel the masses
to follow slowly in the paths they have made. Minor
geniuses direct small matters, the fashions of the day ;
they appear and vanish like meteors on the social horizon. For matters of more lasting import, there are a
few bright minds which shine like guiding stars upon
the human pathway. But for the great thoughts that
revolutionize history, and flood the earth with light like
the morning sun, the centuries prepare and wait, until
the man is born, from whose mind shall emanate the
thoughts that are destined to create a new order of
things in countries and among peoples.

Such a man was Abraham. To him came the divine
message which we have chosen for our text : to leave
his country and his birthplace and his family, and go
to a land that God would show him, a new world of
thought, which he was to be the first to unlock.

When the shock of surprise, occasioned by the discovery of America, had abated, there were many ready
to belittle the merit of the discoverer, saying that
it was a simple matter, that the thought that led
to the discovery was so natural that others besides
Columbus might have conceived it. In the same way,
the thought of one God, in opposition to the idea that
the divine, creative forces are distributed among many
gods, seems so natural that it might have been discovered,
and introduced to the world by thousands and millions

besides Abraham. The logical consequences of the belief in one God—the doctrine of universal brotherhood, and the code of morals governing mankind—are so generally accepted by us, that a large proportion of people, educated and uneducated, particularly the latter when they are prosperous, think that if they be but good and honest, they can get on very well without any God whatever. But we must consider that in Abraham's day, and before and after him, the world, including its thinkers and sages, was heathen, and that the morals that hedge us about to-day are monotheistic not heathenish.

Abraham could never have become what he did, if he had not possessed the power to forget and to unlearn what he had been taught in his country, in his birthplace and in his home. Socrates, Plato, Aristotle and other sages of antiquity forgot a great deal; that is, they emancipated themselves from the mistaken thoughts and fancies of their countrymen and associates. But they remained heathens withal; they could not discover and promulgate the true belief in God, because they did not sufficiently emancipate themselves from the influence of their country, their birthplace and their intimate associates.

In Christendom, there are many bright minds and logical thinkers, possessed of keen powers of analysis, and imbued with the desire to seek truth and truth only, to serve truth and truth only. If, nevertheless, they stand spellbound before their inherited faith, and let it define the circle of their reasoning, we need not at once cry out, and brand them as hypocrites. It is evident, they cannot completely emancipate themselves from the influence of their country, their birthplace, and their home; they are not strong enough to forget and unlearn as radically as Abraham did.

It is thus good to be able to forget. But, on the other hand, forgetting is not an unmixed good. One's country, one's birthplace, one's home should, from another point of view, *not* be forgotten. Abraham held them in loving memory and esteem throughout his life. When, after an absence of sixty-five years, he was seeking a wife for Isaac, he bethought himself of his old home; only there, he imagined, and possibly only in his own family, would he find a woman worthy of his son and of his son's future. We must forget with discrimination; some old recollections and influences must be eradicated, whereas others ought to be religiously preserved.

"Out of thy country" was the command that came to Abraham. Man is influenced by the climate of the country in which he lives. Neither the frigid nor the tropic zone has ever produced a great man. In the northern portion of our hemisphere, in the temperate zone, there are calm, deliberate thinkers; the south gives rise to more emotional, more imaginative men; the former are more active and energetic, the latter are far more impressionable, but they are more indolent and passive in disposition. "Get thee out of thy country" —rise above the influence of climate!

The inhabitants of every country possess advantages and failings, national virtues and national faults. "Get thee out of thy country," free thyself from the faults and failings of the race that claims thee!

Nations and the inhabitants of different districts hate

one another, or at any rate, are prejudiced against one
another. " Get thee out of thy country," value every one
in accordance with his worth, and judge him according
to his bearing, not his parentage.

This Abraham did. He crossed the Euphrates,
traversed Syria, dwelt in the land of Canaan, went to
Egypt and returned, pitched his tents, and dug wells in
the land of the Philistines, and everywhere he met with
kindly treatment, respect, friendship and love. Even
Sodom felt kindly towards him, and favored him by
suffering the presence of his kinsman. For whither-
soever he went, it was as a friend of humanity; he
harbored no prejudice, and therefore met with none.
"Away from thy kindred and from thy father's
house." Two villages, though separated by but a
narrow meadow dale, may be entirely distinct, not
only in the manners, but in the dialect and in the moral
attitude of their inhabitants. This is still more apt to
be the case with the dwellers in large cities. Boston
and New Orleans, Paris and Amsterdam, Naples and
Moscow, Madrid and Stockholm are complete contrasts
in the ways, thoughts and feelings of their inhabitants.
But the difference in the moral atmospheres of the cities
of our day cannot compare with that between the cities
of old. An Athenian was an entirely different being,
in character and moral attitude, from a Spartan.
The serious, stern citizen of ancient Rome was the
exact opposite of the luxurious, careless, easy-going
Tarentine; he of Jerusalem was entirely different from
him of Sidon, or even of Galilee, although the distance
between these cities and the province was very insignificant. To Abraham came the message to tear himself

away from the moral peculiarities of his country, and to enter a new realm of truth and morality, in which the whole earth and all its inhabitants might have a part.

The hardest and most serious task it is to leave the "father's house," to emancipate ourselves mentally and spiritually from our home. The task is difficult because nature, gratitude, the memories of our youth and the sacred reverence we bear our parents, all rebel against it, and because every nerve and fibre of our being is interwoven with the traditions of our parental homes.

The task is a serious one, because its accomplishment threatens to shatter, to its very foundations, the structure of our religious and moral lives. The home is the light-house that shines out across the sea of life to warn us, when the storms of passion or the smooth billows of temptation threaten our destruction. In the hour of temptation, the venerable forms of our parents appear to us, even though they be far away, or no longer of this world; they plead with us and warn us, pointing out the paths of repentance and virtue.

We must remember that Abraham had reached his seventy-fifth year ere he felt himself strong enough to tear himself away from the home and the faith of his father, and without danger to the peace of his soul to follow out his own ideas of truth and piety. Nor did he lose sight of a fixed goal: "Unto a land that I will shew thee." He knew that this goal would more than repay him for all he was renouncing.

The message that came to Abraham, to forget and to learn, comes to us all. It is our duty to leave the homes of our fathers, not only literally but figuratively as well, and to correct in ourselves the abuses, the prejudices, the harshness, and the mistakes of faith, thought and action, that we inherit. But let us beware, lest, in eradicating the weeds, we tear up the roots of our moral and religious life, fostered in the sanctuary of the home.

It was not until Abraham was seventy-five years old that he felt able to cross the threshold of his home, and to erect a new one for future generations. We of to-day forget more readily; we leave our homes in callow youth; not only do we leave the parental roof, but mentally and spiritually, and in matters of worldly import, we throw off its subtle safeguards. Abraham tried to realize an ideal that ever hovered before him; he knew whence he had come, and whither he was going. Do we know whither we tend? We are to forget—very well; but what will we learn, what are we to learn? Where is the land that God will show us? Where shall we stop? We cannot remain and ought not to remain where our fathers were. But let us not leave our homes too hastily; let us carefully and wisely select what should be forgotten, and replace it by what is better worth knowing. Everything that recalls father and mother, and does not prevent the children from leading good, true lives, is a blessing to them. Virtue has no better safeguard than the enduring memory of home, and the anchor of faith is safest, when imbedded in our youth. Let us who are the heads of homes blessed with children, see to it that, when they grow to manhood and womanhood, and measure the worth of the spiritual legacy we leave them, they may find little to forget, and much to hold in honor and in loving, blessed remembrance.

THE MASSES FOLLOW A FEW THINKERS.

"So Abram departed, as the Lord had spoken unto him; and Lot went with him."—GEN. XII : 4.

Abraham and Lot acted alike in leaving their country and their home for the land of Canaan, but from different motives. The former recognized a divine mission; his action was the result of his own mature thoughts and feelings: "And Abram departed as the Lord had spoken unto him." The latter went simply because his uncle did. Had his uncle remained at home, it would not have occurred to Lot to go. "And Lot went with him." Lot merely accompanied him.

Such is the practice of the world. There have, at all times, been only few original, independent thinkers—surprisingly few. The vast majority of the millions and millions of people that have existed and now exist, think, speak and act according to prescribed models. In small circles, comparatively small minds suffice to do the thinking for all; in more extensive circles, more profound thinkers are required to think for every member of the larger constituency. It is the same with regard to periods of time. For short periods, there are minor heralds of thought. Each day, each year, each lustrum, has its . pervading thought, which emanates from some one brain, but with the day, with the year, with the lustrum, the thought passes away. Others,

75

more potent thinkers, influence a quarter, a half or the whole of a century with their thoughts. Generations upon generations come and go, and copy them in thought and speech, and fancy themselves to be original. Then there are independent thinkers that have done the thinking, that have been examples to the world, in thought and feeling and action, for thousands of years. Such an one was Abraham.

Abraham followed neither in the path of his ancestors, nor in that of his contemporaries; his mind branched out into new directions. He went, as God had commanded him. He had the strength and the courage for new thought and independent action, regardless of the past and of his own time.

In Abraham we see the independent thinker of pregnant thoughts, whereas Lot, according to our text, is as a mirror, in which imitators may recognize themselves.

We pride ourselves upon being descended from Abraham; but in our intellectual and religious life, we are more like Lot. We are great imitators. We do not speak of imitation in social life, for that is common to frail humanity. Let us speak of that which concerns us Israelites more particularly. In both camps, into which Israel is divided, there are thousands upon thousands who unthinkingly follow others, as Lot went with Abraham. It is proper that it should be so with the orthodox. In believers, it is a necessary virtue to exclude independent thought from the field of religion. Imitation in thought and action is the essence of a true, firm faith. Thought is employed only to explain and justify inherited thoughts and practices.

But if anyone imagines that there are only thinkers in the other camp, he is greatly in error. There are very few reformers; of the *reformed* there are many.

In the Christian Church, those that have renounced the old doctrines call themselves "The Reformed." That is a modest way of expressing the fact; we are reformed, it may be by birth, or education, or instruction, or example, or by the force of circumstances. Had the reformed of the present day lived four hundred years ago, they would, perhaps, one and all, have joined the Catholic ranks, as they now do those of the reform movement. Huss, Wicliffe, Luther, Zwingli, Calvin—these were *Reformers*—original thinkers in the midst of a Catholic world.

Those among us that have discarded the old teachings, and particularly the minutely regulated, orthodox-Jewish ways of life, have drifted on with the spirit of the times into the reform movement. We are reformed. The Israelites of the present day that call themselves reformers would, in Spinoza's day, undoubtedly have done their share in denouncing the independent thinker.

But we must not be too severe upon ourselves, for such is the way of the world. In every field of human activity, there are but few fresh, bubbling springs of thought, whence the innumerable Lots draw their wisdom. Why, then, should it be otherwise in religious matters? In every family circle, in every association, great or small, there are a few that furnish the thoughts, which the others absorb and adopt, believing themselves to be the originators. Hundreds go to Washington, to Congress; there, also, there are but few that supply the

thoughts, and determine the current of debates, and who
shall say whence those few derive their inspiration?

Among thousands of artists there are but few original
masters that strike out into new paths; the majority
practise art according to old laws and old models.

In the domain of science, there are few that write
books containing original thoughts. As a rule, scientific
men learn what is taught them, and teach what they
have learned.

In pedagogy, it is the same. For three thousand
years, the whole world copied the sage that said, "He
that loveth his son chastiseth him," and the authority of
the rod was second only to that of the father. The indispensable instrument hung just above the family table
in every home blessed with children; it hovered ever
above the heads of the children like the sword of Dam-
ocles.

Toward the end of last century, there came another
thinker, who said, "Who loveth his child, shall not
chastise it." At once all the rods disappeared, and now
the chastising of a refractory pupil in a school is tele-
graphed over the entire country, and the account perused
with feelings of indignation.

Four thousand years ago Moses said, "Honor thy
father and thy mother," and the command was taken so
seriously, and was so much exaggerated, that sons and
daughters scarcely ventured to raise their eyes to the
stern faces of their parents. The very chairs in which
father and mother sat were honored. Contradiction was
unknown. Everyone knows how all this is changed.
How did the change come about? Surely, it could not
have been the result of a revelation made to millions

simultaneously! No; there was one thinker that ventured to have and to express a new thought, and in the
course of time this rivulet of thought has swelled into
the mighty current of general opinion, carrying with it
countries and peoples.

Now, however true it be that all this is the natural
course of events, that there are few that think and many
that imitate, it does not, therefore, follow that we are to
rest satisfied to be, in our own persons, illustrations of
the rule.   It is the natural course of events that there
be rich and poor, yet we are in duty bound to endeavor
to keep ourselves above poverty.   Even death has its
good features, yet we must try to avoid it.

Then, too, we should endeavor to advance, in the
great army of imitators and echoers, to the rank of
commanding thinkers.   Do a little more good than your
father and mother did, a little more than those about
you do.   Let your religion be like a blooming garden in
which all is green and thriving.   But let not your religion be like a herbarium of plants collected by your forefathers, shrivelled into theological dogmas, numbered
and scientifically labelled, and then handed down to you
to be carried about as your religion.   Take pains to
think independently in matters concerning your home,
your business and your relations to God and man.   Do
not be a blind imitator.

After all, Lot did not make the worst choice.   There
were thinkers among Abraham's contemporaries, whom
Lot's entire family followed.   Only the one uncle went
his own way, and Lot followed him.   His contemporaries built altars, brought sacrifices, and called upon
their gods.   So far as these outward forms of religion

go, Abraham certainly had no advantage over others in Lot's eyes. But Abraham was better and nobler in thought and deed, superior to all among whom he lived; for Abraham went as the Lord had commanded him. This determined Lot to follow and to imitate him.

In seeking a standard of merit whereby to measure the claims of rival Jewish congregations, we should not take into consideration the beauty of the Temple, the grand organ, the brilliant preacher, the kind of prayer-book, or the amount of religious decorum; what we may judge by is: the efficiency of the school and the amount of education, of honesty, of modesty, of humanity, of domestic virtue, of patriotism and of faith in God.

Since we follow others, let us follow the best, who, like Abraham, go as God commands them.

VICISSITUDES OF FORTUNE.

GEN. XIII : 1, 2.

Abraham, in obedience to God's command, left the home of his fathers, and went to the land of Canaan. Ere long, famine drove him away into Egypt, but after remaining there for some time, he returned to the land of Canaan. Before his departure for Egypt, he had at most been in comfortable circumstances, but it is more probable that he was impoverished by the famine that had compelled him to leave. But upon his return we read that "Abraham was very rich." Before his departure, while still in comparatively lowly circumstances, we are told that "he builded an altar unto the Lord who appeared unto him;" further on, "he builded an altar unto the Lord," and "he called upon the name of the Lord." In times of poverty and trouble and famine, there is much praying and calling upon the name of the Lord. But experience teaches us that increasing wealth causes the fire on the altars of religion to burn ever lower, and the thoughts of a succoring God to become ever rarer and weaker.

Only at long intervals do the prosperous seek their altars to call upon God; and, moreover, they demand a very different altar from that which contented them in their poverty; it must be pompous and magnificent, else they are ashamed to be seen near it.

7

The Bible tells us, concerning Abraham, that "he went on his journeys . . . . unto the place where his tent had been at the beginning, ... unto the place of the altar, which he had made there at the first; and Abram called there on the name of the Lord." He, the wealthy Abraham, the possessor of gold, silver and herds, returned to the same altar at which the poor Abraham had worshipped, and there called upon the name of the Lord.

There are ten proofs recounted of Abraham's goodness and piety, and one of them is that he did not complain, when famine compelled him to leave the promised land, which, at the bidding of God, he had just entered; but even greater merit, because greater temptation is implied by the fact that, when fortune favored him, he remained unchanged, true to himself and to his God. Poverty is a temptation to depart from the path of honesty and from many another virtue; and whoever, through times of poverty, has remained good, honest and god-fearing, kindly, cleanly, orderly and resigned to his fate, has come forth triumphant from a great trial. But wealth has its trials also, its twofold trials, in fact: in its acquirement and in its application. A thousand spirits, good and evil alike, lurk in money. The evil ones are the tempters to dishonest gain and to its use for the gratification of every passion. There is a magnetic force in money, often more powerful than the hand that holds it, and drawing men whither it will. Then, all honor be to the rich man whose hand is more powerful than his wealth, and who applies it to truly good and noble uses.

Abraham stood both of these tests. When trouble

drove him out of the land, he continued to lead a pious, godly life, and no less so when he became wealthy.

Nothing is more common than to hear the wealthy complain of the faults of the poor, and *vice versa* the poor of those of the wealthy—and nothing is more unjust. The wealthy do not know the sensations of the poor; they cannot feel with them and put themselves into their places. Poverty and misery have a demoralizing influence on character; they deaden the sense of honor, and undermine the ways of truth and sincerity in speech and action, and they impair the love of order and cleanliness and even of economy. We would not imply that poverty must perforce lead one to all these lapses from respectability, but it certainly is a strong temptation thereunto.

Abraham resisted the temptation. Even during the famine he remained good and pious. But we cannot expect everyone to be strong like Abraham; and therefore let the wealthy be cautious and considerate in their judgment of the poor.

Be not angry if you find the poor swerving from truthfulness; be not indignant if, now and then, you are out-witted by a poor man, if he wheedles a gift or a service out of you which he does not deserve. Do not leave him to his fate, because he indulges, for once, beyond his means. Be not too severe in your judgment, if he does not come up to your standard of order and cleanliness. Perhaps, were you similarly oppressed in mind and body, you would be no better.

And they that are poor should be less bitter in their opinion, less severe in their criticism of the rich; they need not pride themselves upon not sinning as the wealthy sin; they simply lack the opportunities and the temptations of wealth.

"Ah, if I had the money, I should do all manner of good with it! But, unfortunately, those that have money have no hearts, and those that have hearts have no money!" We may hear this every day from the needy; and on the strength of it, they consider themselves superior, because they imagine that they *would* do so much more good, *if* they but had the means. "Ifs" and "buts" are no proofs of goodness of heart, so long as the confirmation of deeds is lacking. Only he who, like Abraham, has resisted the temptations, both of wealth and of poverty, is entitled to judge of the rich and of the poor. Only he who has been tried and purified in both furnaces of fortune, is capable of unbiased judgment. Are we not told that Abraham interceded for even such sinners as those in Sodom and Gomorrah?

Abraham had not yet acquired wealth, when he adopted his orphan nephew. Poverty is no bar to a kindly, humane heart, nor does it absolve from the duties imposed by humanity. Abraham became great and wealthy, but he never required any subordination on the part of his adopted son; he ever treated him as his equal. When it became necessary for them to separate, he gave his nephew the choice of going or remaining. "And he went on his journey." The wealthy Abraham was not too proud to associate with his old friends and acquaintances. With him, change of fortune did not imply change of friends and associates.

A man in perfect health is able to endure a change of climate that would prostrate a weaker person. In the same way, a truly good and pious man remains morally sound through every change of fortune, whether he rise from poverty to wealth, or sink from wealth to poverty. He goes "unto the place of the altar which he had made there at the first," and calls there on the name of the Lord. Like Abraham, he remains true to his altar, to his friends and to his God.

FEAR NOT THAT YOU MAY SUFFER BY DOING GOOD.

GEN. XV.

"After these things the word of the Lord came unto Abram in a vision, saying, Fear not, Abram: I am thy shield, thy reward shall be exceedingly great."

"After these things"—after what "things?" After Abraham's victory over Kedorla'omer and his allies? "Fear not!" hardly seems to us an appropriate greeting to a returning conqueror. The only other "things" mentioned before are the meeting with Malkizedek, to whom Abraham gave tithe, and with the King of Sodom, to whom he gave the booty which he had taken in the war. But in neither of these occurrences was there any cause for fear. Surely, gifts do not make enemies. Nevertheless, there was much reason for anxiety on Abraham's part. In giving to others of one's own possessions, in making sacrifices for the benefit of others, a man frequently grows anxious about himself; he is affrighted by his own better self and its generous impulses. The soft heart grows timid in the presence of cold reason, which says to it: "How foolish thou art! Giving is all very well, and self-sacrifice is, indeed, noble, but if thou art so lavish, what will become of thee thyself? If thou art so conscientious in thy business relations and so generous in disposing of thy wealth, thou wilt suffer, and others thrive at thy

86

expense. Think of thy wife and child. Thou owest everything to them. Thou needest not provide for any one else. Let others look to the welfare of strangers." Oh, how the very powers of the body, our hands and feet, hesitate and resist, when we bid them execute the noble impulses of the heart! Such was not the case with Abraham. He gave away willingly and freely the entire booty of the expedition, and even paid tithe in addition to the rest. He was not afraid of a generous action.

Again, fear and trembling may follow close upon the doing of a generous action. A man may think, "It may be that I was too good, too considerate." He recalls to mind instances, in which others, with less conscience and less delicacy of feeling, amassed great fortunes, and now occupy high places in society, while, when the same opportunities offered themselves to him, he went away empty-handed, obeying the dictates of a warm heart and a tender conscience. He remembers that he made numberless sacrifices, and gave untiringly, while others looked out only for their own welfare, and thus acquired ever-increasing wealth. In such reflections, fear comes over him, fear for his own welfare: "How can I continue to exist side by side with these shrewder and more calculating men, who can acquire riches so much more easily than I, and who find it so much harder to share them with others?" To them, our text says, "Fear not! In spite of all that thou hast done, in spite of all the sacrifices that thou hast made, fear not for thy future. Thou wilt not grow poor because of thy generosity, nor suffer for the advantage of others. 'Thy reward shall be exceedingly great.'

The benefit derived from such deeds is greater than their price."

Is not a woman better off for being the wife of a conscientious and noble-minded man? Or are those children not fortunate whose father is strictly honorable, though not so richly endowed with worldly goods as other men? Is it not better for both children and father, if, when the hour of parting comes, the former can inherit the blessed memory of such a father, rather than fall heir to the accumulated treasures of a restless and hardhearted seeker after gold?

To this Abraham responded: "'Lord God, what wilt thou give me, seeing I go childless, and the steward of my house' will be my heir?" Thereupon, he was given the faithful promise of a direct posterity, and assured that after a long series of years, his descendants, grown to be a great nation, would occupy the land in which he now wandered as a stranger. The prophecy closes with the promise: "But thou shalt come to thy father in peace; thou shalt be buried in a good old age."

But were his ancestors not buried in Ur of the Chaldees? Did not his father Terah lie in Haran, while he found a grave in the Cave of Machpelah, far away in the land of Canaan? The prophecy, however, was meant as an assurance to his immortal soul that it would rejoin the souls of those that had gone before in peace. This is one phase of immortality, as we picture it to ourselves: the union of the soul with the souls of those once our beloved companions on earth. This idea is, however, not the whole of our belief in immortality. According to the doctrine of immortality, the soul of Abraham, as well as the souls of all other men that have passed away,

live on in full consciousness of the doings of their children and their latest descendants. What bliss it must
bring to the soul of him that has passed from this earth
to see itself perpetuated in descendants in a manner
pleasing to the soul of all souls! And what suffering
must be the portion of the soul of the worthless man,
upon recognizing the sad truth that it has left no good
behind it, that the evil wrought by it in the world continues its influence far into the future! Fancy can
paint no more beautiful heaven for the good, and no
more terrible hell for the wicked than this picture of the
soul gazing from its eternal home upon the good or evil
wrought by it in this world, as it continues to influence
the lives of men for centuries.

" Fear not, Abram, thy reward shall be exceedingly
great."

" Thy reward shall be great." It shall continue long
after the grave has closed over thee. It shall, first, be
the portion of the son promised to thee, that he may
prove worthy of being thy child, and then it shall pass
on to thy descendants. They shall form a great nation,
and spirit of thy spirit, shall give to the world thy conception of God and thy teaching about God to be a
blessing unto it forever. If it be granted to Abraham's
soul to look down upon the sublunary world from the
celestial heights, then must he say to himself, "Truly,
my reward is great."

Abraham was gathered to his fathers in peace. Not
everyone returns thus to his fathers. Many who are
reckoned among the fortunate ones of the earth, and
are envied because of the happiness that is supposed to
be theirs, pass away from this life at variance with God,

with the world and with themselves. It would be well for us, could we always keep vividly before our minds this thought: The day will come, when thou wilt be gathered to thy fathers; therefore, so live that thou mayest rejoin thy fathers in peace, *i. e.*, with a clear conscience. In the seventy years that we have lived beyond our immediate ancestors, the world, and we, as part of it, ought to have gained somewhat in culture and knowledge; or, at least, we should not have retrograded; our lives ought not to seem barren and empty in comparison with theirs.

How beautiful the phrase, to be gathered to one's fathers in peace! With peace in one's own bosom, without the painful reproach of a mistaken life, without inward struggles in regard to one's faith, unshaken in one's belief in a Providence ruling over life and death! How beautiful to leave this earth at peace with one's household, with the sweet consciousness, "I am leaving my house not divided against itself, not in open strife, and not in sullen resentment. It is not probable that over my grave the beautiful bond of family life will be torn asunder, that hate will destroy the edifice erected by my loving care."

"His sons Isaac and Ishmael buried him." Isaac and Ishmael, different as they were, in disposition and in their relations to their home, nevertheless, stood side by side at the grave of the good father, in fraternal harmony, moved by a common grief. Abraham, upon his demise, left his house in peace.

Next to the idea of the unity of God, we hold the belief in the immortality of the soul as the most blessed doctrine. The more active our consciousness of this immortality, the more joyfully and willingly shall we do good, and the less shall we fear to be at a disadvantage compared with other more worldly-minded persons, who scrape together untold wealth, and keep it fast in their clutches. Our weakness and hesitation in doing what we know to be good and proper may be traced to the fact that we have not true faith in this doctrine of immortality, or else that we do not keep it vividly enough before our minds. Our faith is not so strong as Abraham's, the doctrine is not ever-present to us as it was to him. God said to him, "Fear not, thy reward shall be exceedingly great." And what was to be his reward? The Lord gave keenness to his sight, so that he might see that, when the grass had grown afresh on his grave four hundred times, his posterity, a great people, would take possession of the beautiful land, and as the bearer of a divine message, would become a blessing to all the nations of the earth.

Of what value would be a reward promised for so distant a future to him that lies mouldering in the grave, were it not for the belief in immortality? If eternal darkness is to follow, when the light of this life is extinguished, what interest can the living take in the weal and woe of generations that will not exist until hundreds and thousands of years have passed away? Abraham rejoiced in the promised blessing, and saw in it his greatest reward. It was his belief that he would not pass into eternal darkness from the scene of his earthly life; it was his hope that the dark hour of parting past, the true light would rise for him, and that he would then behold clearly all that had been veiled from him while on earth.

Let us not hesitate to make sacrifices which a pious
and noble life demand of the Israelite, nor fear that we
ourselves may suffer while doing good to others. Let it
be our highest aim to return in peace to our fathers, so
that our existence may continue to be a blessed influence unto the latest generations, and that our souls,
from their eternal home, may behold their reward in
the happiness of children and children's children.

CHILDREN OF THE HOUSE AND CHILDREN OF THE SPIRIT.

GEN. XV : 1-6.

In the narrative preceding our text, we find the divine promise of a numerous progeny to Abraham, which the latter listens to in silence. In Chap. XIII : 16, it says: "And I will make thy seed as the dust of the earth: so that if a man can number the dust of the earth, then shall thy seed also be numbered."

Despite this prophecy, Abraham, in our text, complains of his sad fate, that he will die childless. But after a repetition of the divine promise, Abraham "believed in the Lord; and the Lord accounted it to him for righteousness." Why was the promise repeated? In what respect do the two promises differ, causing the first to be accepted so coolly and indifferently, and the second to be announced and received with gravity and seriousness? Furthermore, the text says, in connection with the second promise, that "Abraham believed in the Lord," which would lead us to conclude that he had not believed the first promise. But is it possible that a man of such piety, as was our ancestor's, could have shown incredulity with regard to God's word? There are plenty of sceptics about us, but suppose the most sceptical of sceptics had been blessed with a divine revela-

tion, and were convinced of its authenticity, would he
not believe it?

Let us endeavor to answer these questions, and to
fathom the text. Abraham laments: " Lord God, what
wilt thou give me, seeing I go childless, and the steward
of my house is this Eliezer of Damascus? One born
in my house will be mine heir." This plaint does not
refer to an earthly legacy, but to higher things.

In the course of their lives, parents acquire a wealth
of experience, knowledge and understanding, and would
fain bequeath to their children this treasure bought with
sorrow and suffering. It is their heart's desire that their
pain-bought knowledge of right and truth, that their
better selves may not die with them. But to how many
parents this happiness is denied! At their death, the
children inherit their worldly goods, but the riches of
mind and heart die with them, and their children are
left morally destitute.

When God said to him, " Lift up now thy eyes, and
look from the place where thou art, ... all the
land which thou seest, to thee will I give it, and to thy
seed forever," Abraham was unmoved; to believe or not
to believe was of no consequence to him.

The promise that his offspring should some day be the
masters of this fertile land was no great blessing in his
opinion. For, is it a blessing to parents to have children that have nothing in common with them in principles, in faith, in feelings and in thoughts? What delights
do children confer that do not sympathize with the joys
and sorrows, the hopes, predilections and antipathies,
and above all, with the faith of their parents? That
hearken to other mentors, follow other examples, and

strike out into other paths? Of what value would a revelation be that shows us a great-great-grandchild living in wealth and plenty?

When, therefore, God repeatedly spoke to Abraham of the great reward in store for him, the latter exclaimed: "'Lord God, what wilt thou give me?' I go childless, if I must walk through life alone, without sympathy for my moral ideals. What would it avail me, though my children be numerous as the dust of the earth, if they be not the children of my heart and mind?"

In the text, Eliezer is referred to as the child of the house. Perhaps Ishmael and Keturah's children were already born at the time, and if so, they were the heirs. But even if they were born later, they were the children of the house merely, and they were accorded but an earthly heritage.

Then God said unto Abraham: "This shall not be thine heir; but he that shall come forth out of thine own bowels shall be thine heir"—he that comes forth out of thy own true self, the son of thy mind and thy heart. He will inherit *thee*, thine own better self will he transmit unto thy descendants. And God said, "Look now toward the heaven, and tell the stars, if thou be able to number them, ... so shall thy seed be."

The simile of the stars is not chosen in order to illustrate the blessing of an innumerable progeny; for the stars visible to the naked eye can readily be counted, and there are not nearly so many as is generally supposed. Plato counted them, and, to our disappointment, could count only one thousand and twenty-two; and even at the present time, with the aid of modern astronomical appliances, the number obtained, by simultaneous counting in the best observatories, with the finest telescopes, does not exceed six hundred thousand. The illustration of the stars is chosen, we should say, in order to indicate the *quality* of Abraham's progeny. Nations and religious brotherhoods, numerous as "the dust of the earth," do not confer blessings in proportion to their numbers. Nor are children a blessing, if their ambition grovels in the dust; if their thoughts are of the earth, earthy; if their highest delights are sought in the mire. But children whose virtues shine like the stars in heaven, a people whose lives and teachings are guiding stars to the world and a light to the nations—happy the fathers and mothers who may call themselves the parents of such offspring.

"So shall thy seed be," even as the bright stars above, counted or uncounted. "And he believed in the Lord." This promise touched and satisfied him. "And he accounted it to him for righteousness." The attitude of mind, which assigns to strong and ofttimes blind parental love a subordinate place; which crushes selfishness, so that man no longer delights in his own good fortune, except inasmuch as it produces happiness for his fellowmen and for future generations; which forces from man's bosom the plaint of Abraham, "What care I what God's gifts be, if I am to be to the world as a barren tree; if my spiritual conquests are to be buried with my body?"—this attitude of mind, God will account to thee, oh man, for righteousness!

"Oh, Lord God, what wilt thou give unto me, seeing I go childless?"

Heavenly Father, of what value are thy gifts and thy

blessings, if we waste our lives, and abuse thy gifts, without making them productive of good to our fellow-creatures and to posterity? If our lives here below leave no trace, and are but as dust? Of what value are children, if they are but as dust of the earth, with nothing holy, ideal or sacred at work within them for posterity? What is the good of saving dollar upon dollar, hoarding an earthly treasure for our children? What is the good of watching and working and starving and worrying, in order that our children may find a rich heritage, while to us, in reality, is given no seed, since our better selves are not inherited by our children, and do not live on in them? "One born in my house is mine heir"—what avails all earthly pleasure, if thy heir be but a son of thy house, and not of thy mind, of thy heart, of thy true self!

In the six sons of Keturah and in Ishmael, Abraham recognized the offspring of his house, but not of his mind or his faith; among eight children there was but one that gave him the pleasure of mirroring his own mind. We have no reason, then, to feel secure in our children, and to expect that they will elevate themselves from the dust of earth to the stars of heaven. Even with the very greatest care, parents may succeed in bringing up their sons and daughters but as children of the house; there are innumerable influences at work in the education of a child, besides the good intentions of the parents. If, however, you would hope for a child of your mind, its education and training must not be a secondary matter, attended to at odd moments, in the intervals of pleasure and business; it must be your chief care and first care every day. Then your child

8

will some day inherit more than your money; it will inherit *you*, and all that is good in you. And have a care, too, that your child, if it do inherit you, inherit what is good.

RELIGION AND ETHICS.

The first division of our reading from the Torah to-day deals with two separate incidents in the life of Abraham; but, in the narrative, they are so interwoven, that they seem like parts of one event. The one is the continuation of the revelation of God, begun in the foregoing chapter, concerning the future birth of Isaac. The second event is Abraham's manifestation of hospitality towards the three strangers. With this conception of it, the story reads about as follows: As observed before, God appeared to Abraham. Meanwhile he saw three strangers approaching his tent in the heat of the day. Thereupon, he turned to God, and said, "My Lord, pass not away, I pray thee, from thy servant!" meaning, "while I show hospitality to these strangers." After Abraham had fully discharged the duty of hospitality, he received the divine revelation: "I will certainly return unto thee at this time next year; and lo, Sarah thy wife shall have a son." Finally, we read in verse twenty-two, "And the men turned their faces from there, and went towards Sodom; but Abraham stood yet before the Lord." (It is said that this verse read originally, "God stood yet before Abraham.") The affair with the travellers was concluded, and the revelation continued.

Thus is explained the use of the singular in the passage cited, and thus we eliminate the displeasing element in the narrative—the apparent use of the name of God in addressing creatures that eat and drink, and appear in bodily form.

For what purpose, however, are the two incidents, divine revelation and the exercise of hospitality, so intimately connected in this narrative? If the appearance and entertainment of the three men is utterly irrelevant to the revelation to Abraham, why is reference. made to it in the Holy Scriptures, and for what reason should it have been thought worthy of preservation for future generations? Let us direct our attention this morning to this point.

Among us who have fallen somewhat behind this rapidly progressing century, the word ethics is but seldom used, but, under the term morality, Israel has always highly honored what the word stands for. Ethics is the high sounding word for that which many a one entirely estranged from religion would gladly see in its place. Religion is, however, the unpretentious root of the tree on which ethics may be said to hang, one of the many fruits borne by it. The root of the tree draws nourishment from the dark earth for the strength of the trunk and the juice of the fruit. It holds the tree firmly, so that it may remain fixed, in one spot, for years and years, and proudly rearing its branches high in the air, may not fall to the earth with all its glory. The root remains modestly hidden in the ground, while all praise is rendered to the tree for its shade, its wood, its fruits and its beauty.

Religion is the root, ethics the fruit. He whose

standard is an ethical one, enjoys only the fruit; he
that lives in an atmosphere of religion, owns tree and
fruit alike, religion and ethics. "Walk before me, and
be thou perfect," Deity says to Abraham. If a man
does not foster religious feeling in himself, but becomes estranged from religion, he falls short of being
a perfect man, for religious feeling forms an essential
part of man's nature. So, too, he that believes—and
lives according to his belief—that piety, pleasing in
the sight of God, may exist apart from ethics, he, too,
lacks much of being a "perfect" man. Only he that is
both pious and good is "perfect." The two incidents in
the life of Abraham, as they are interwoven in this tale,
illustrate the point under discussion. We are told of a
divine revelation, and its narration is interrupted by
an account of Abraham's hospitality. Taken together,
the two incidents show Abraham in the light of a "perfect" man.

The narrative begins thus, "God appeared to Abraham." How did Deity reveal himself to a human
being? Surely, not in a physical form, perceptible
to the senses. A divine revelation can be only an
inward revelation. The soul is filled with the consciousness that the Lord is near, and perceives his holy will in
a manner incomprehensible to us. At such times, the
soul is surely in an elevated and deeply religious mood.
Abraham was in so elevated a mood, his soul was com-
muning with its Maker, when he observed the three
travellers in his vicinity. In their persons, ethics made
its demand upon him, in the midst of his devotion,
while his heart was uplifted by the presence of God.
Ethics represented to him, "Here, Abraham, are

human beings to whom you must offer help. Be friendly to them; welcome and refresh the weary travellers." As at the beginning of the chapter, we have, introductory to this passage, the word וירא. This time, however, its meaning is not *seeing* in any form. As frequently, it signifies, "he deliberated." He deliberated : " Shall I turn from God? Let my God wait so that I may greet these strangers, and offer them my services?" He interrupted his devotion, and hastened to fulfil his earthly duty, the duty of hospitality, the ethical obligation of humanity. Prayer, devotion, the commandments and the restrictions imposed by the ceremonial law; in short, everything in the field of religion that pertains to worship of God, that helps to keep the idea of God alive in us, is of great value, and is necessary to a " perfect " man. As soon, however, as man is needed for earthly duties, and ethics puts forth its claim to his powers, God forgives his turning away, nay, he even commands him not to allow his duty to man to be interfered with by service to God. God and his service can wait until man's wants are attended to, for man, when in distress, craves immediate help. There can be no more sacred, no more divine moment in the life of a human being, than was that in Abraham's life, described to us in the Holy Scriptures, in which his soul soared to the heights of revelation. Nevertheless, he hastened from the presence of God, and turned to human beings in need of help.

But you may tell me that this is the very demand made of man by the worshippers of ethics, of nothing but ethics: "Forsake entirely the barren worship of God! Turn away from the dream of divine revelation, and devote all your powers to the active virtues of ethics. Declare your absolute allegiance to a religion of humanity!"

For such also our text has an impressive lesson, a lesson which we cannot take to heart earnestly enough, nor impress sufficiently on our memories. "My Lord, if now I have found favor in thy eyes, pass not away, I pray thee, from thy servant!" With these words, Abraham turned to God after having extended his gracious invitation to the strangers. "Let me not forget thy service, O Lord, while serving these men!" We daily meet with persons holding the firm belief that religion is confined entirely to acts of benevolence, to humanity of thought and deed. "I lead a moral life; my hand is ever open to give and to render assistance. What more can be expected of me?" "My Lord, if now I have found favor in thy eyes, pass not away, I pray thee, from thy servant!" Oh God, forsake me not in my arrogance, in my over-estimation of the little good that I do upon earth, that I may not lose sight of thy power; that I may not forget thee, from whose hand I have received everything, the little that I give away, as well as the goodly store that I keep for my own use! And if I should gain in piety of thought and goodness of heart, let me not therefore grow neglectful of thy praise, let my faith in thee, Heavenly Father, not lose in fervor!

The poor man that finds himself on the road to prosperity; the prosperous man, on the road to great opulence, should call aloud with Abraham, "My God, do not forsake thy servant in the days of prosperity. In sorrow and distress, I sought thee. I knew then that there was a God, whom it was the duty of a 'perfect' man to serve; let me not forget thee now that no trouble clouds the heaven of my life."

"My God, pass not away from thy servant!" should also be the prayer of the man of science, the man of deep culture. Many a philanthropist forgets his God, believing that he is a "perfect" man by virtue of his benevolence alone, that thereby he has attained the very summit of life. Many a man, rich in wealth and wordly goods, passes heedlessly by his God in his care-free existence. Even more common is this neglect in men rich in learning. They become puffed up with knowledge; their pride forbids them to hold a belief in God in common with common men. But too frequently is this the case in our day. With many of our faith, the first fruit of *learning* is *forgetfulness* of God: "To worship God and still possess culture! The combination is impossible!" Oh, my God, pass not by thy servant! Let me not forget thee, while seeking knowledge! Let my heart not lose the bliss of faith, while I am gaining in wisdom; let me be a man, a "perfect" *man* in knowledge, and let me at the same time remain childlike in my belief in a Father of all creatures!

"Oh God, pass not by thy servant!" may we well exclaim when we consider the condition of religious worship in our time and country. Order and decorum, the gratification of an æsthetic sense are all admirably provided for in our houses of worship, and for this progress we ought to be truly thankful. But all that has been done is not sufficient to bring forth devotion, and elevation of the soul to God, to make attendance at public worship a holy joy, ennobling and strengthening the soul. Devotion is the kernel, all the rest is merely the shell. "Oh God, pass not by thy servants," who assemble in thy name!

A REVELATION AT THE THRESHOLD.

"And the Lord appeared unto Abraham in the grove of Mamré ; while he sat at the door of his tent in the heat of the day."—GEN. XVIII: 1.

This verse stands in complete isolation in the chapter. Are we to understand that God manifested himself in the three visitors of whom we are told more further on in the chapter? Such a construction has, indeed, been put upon this verse, especially by Christian scholars, who have interpreted it as a revelation of the Trinity. For this very reason, we should feel ourselves called upon to find a better explanation of the passage.

Our weekly portion of the Torah shows us how God reveals himself to man. Many believe that Deity can manifest himself only in thunder, as at Sinai, or to extraordinarily holy persons, like the prophets, or at particularly favored places, as in the Temple ; or else they hold that God no longer speaks at all. Our text can teach them a different lesson. God revealed himself to Abraham at the door of his tent, upon land belonging to a heathen. There is surely nothing holy, nothing extraordinary in this situation ; on the contrary, it is highly commonplace in its character. Abraham received the divine revelation while sitting at the entrance to his tent and seeking relief from the burning heat of midday.

Abraham was resting comfortably at the door of his tent, when, in the distance, he saw three men travelling towards him. A shrewd worldling in Abraham's place, supremely conscious of his own comfortable position, would have allowed his idle glance, betokening ease, to rest upon them, and follow them until they were out of sight. If they had turned their steps toward his dwelling, and had asked for assistance, he would have tried to rid himself of them as soon as possible. In the language of our day, he would have provided them with half-fare tickets to the next station. Not so Abraham. He feared that the strangers might pass by his abode, and he hastened towards them, and invited them cordially to be his guests, as if he were asking a favor instead of offering one. He offers them only bread, water and rest in the shade, so that they may surely consent to halt. When they have accepted his invitation, he prepares for them a rich repast, and is as active, as eager and as happy in providing for their entertainment, as if they were kings, who would repay his kindness with gold and honors.

This was the manifestation of Deity. In the pure, childlike heart, in the kindly action of Abraham, God revealed himself.

If, seeing a fellow-man trudging through the sand of the desert, in the burning midday sun, you do not arise from your comfortable position, and are not moved to show active sympathy, until the sufferer himself asks for your aid ; if you then scrutinize the petitioner carefully to decide whether he cannot drag himself along for some distance, so as to be out of your sight ; if you inquire into the *worth* rather than the *want* of your suffering fellow-creature; if you refuse your aid or sympathy to a man, thinking: "He has only himself to blame for his present misery"—then, indeed, not God, but a prudent man reveals himself. The fear of being deceived in the object of your benevolence, the excessive anxiety that a fellow-creature be spoilt by generosity, the principle of helping no one that is not completely lame, of leading none not totally blind, of nursing none that is not sick unto death; to sympathize only with those completely overwhelmed by misfortune, to mourn for the dead alone—these are not manifestations of Deity. But if you go forth to meet strangers, if, seeing that they are in distress, you do not ask of them, whence they come or whither they go, nor inquire into their belief, nor accompany your gift with bitter reproaches for the misfortune which they should have avoided, but feel only the impulse to aid them, to remove the thorns from the path of your neighbor, then you may, even to-day, experience the revelation of four thousand years ago in the grove of Mamré.

Such actions can, indeed, be explained only as a revelation of God. How could we otherwise reconcile delight in giving pleasure to others with human nature? How could man live, work and sacrifice of his own possessions for the benefit of others? Toil and moil to make the burdens of life easier for others to bear? Common-sense approves of the reply to David's petition that a portion of the rich repast that Nabal had prepared for his shepherds be given to him and his exhausted followers: "Shall I then take my bread, and my water and my flesh that I have killed for my sheep-shearers, and give it unto men, whom I know not whence they are?"

Of course, we respect an honest, prudent man. He may be faithful and just, upright and industrious, but these qualities alone do not make an Abraham. Reason certainly does not counsel a man bowed beneath the weight of a hundred years, to hasten from his tent at noon, on a day of tropical heat, to watch for strangers, to offer them the freedom of his house, and to entertain them to the best of his ability. Reason could never convince us that, in certain cases, it becomes our duty to work for the good of others, even at the sacrifice of our own lives. Whenever man is active in promoting the good of his fellow-man through self-denial, we may say that we have a divine revelation, that "the Lord appeared unto" us. Consciously or unconsciously to himself, there exists in his heart the feeling, "There is a God, and all the universe is his possession. Every created thing forms a part of the whole. Whatever I do for my fellow-man, I do for myself as well, for my fellow-man and myself are but a part of the whole. And even were I to walk through the valley of the shadow of death, I should not perish and be lost in nothingness, for there is a God, an immortality, an eternity. Another life will be mine."

Truly, a heartfelt, noble act of self-denial, performed for the welfare of others, is a revelation of God. It is not indispensable that such a manifestation be solemn and impressive; that a man should await its coming in *talith* and *tefillin*, with fasting and prayer, sound of trumpet and peal of organ. At the entrance to one's house, in apparently the most commonplace situation of life, God may make his presence manifest. The good deed is accomplished, the idea realized before reason has had time to apply its standard, and shape them according to its pattern.

What a contrast do the two pictures in our Parashah* present to us. On the one side, Abraham, joyfully and eagerly providing for the strangers, and serving them; and on the other, Sodom—the whole town in an uproar, a mob storming a house with brutal energy, demanding the blood of the strangers. We must remember that hatred of strangers, and unkind treatment of them, was not peculiar to Sodom. There we find the feeling manifested with unusual bitterness. It was the normal condition throughout all parts of the world then known, and it remained a common characteristic, in a more or less aggravated form, down to our own time. Even now, throughout great stretches of country, the sight of a stranger is as welcome as that of a wild beast, and his life is equally safe. In the juxtaposition of these two strongly contrasted scenes, the workings of revelation and reason respectively are pointed out to us. Reason dictates—or at least such was its advice in former times: "Be on your guard against the stranger! He will surely do you no good, and he may work you harm." So spoke the whole world.

In the midst of this ocean of hatred and persecution, arose the lonely island of love and kindness: the picture of Abraham and his guests. In the presence of such phenomena, the Psalmist exclaims, "From the Lord is this come to pass, it is marvellous in our eyes," *i. e.*, here something has taken place that is beyond the grasp of our understanding. In our text, it is expressed differ-

---

* Each of the fifty-four weekly portions into which the Pentateuch is divided.—[Tr.]

ently; there we read, "The Lord appeared unto him." Abraham, the father of hospitality and kindness to strangers, was a manifestation of God, in the midst of a world of cold calculation.

A man of mere prudence and sense may be an acceptable citizen of Sodom, but in him God does not reveal himself. That which his reason does not teach him, ever remains a sealed book to him. Everything great, elevated and beneficent in character; everything that adds to the happiness of the world, the product of the self-denial of a few noble-minded individuals, is a divine revelation.

Oh, may such revelations never pass away from our midst! May the spirit of Abraham, manifested in his blessed revelations, continue to exist in the deeds of his children for ever and ever!

HOW CAN TEN RIGHTEOUS MEN SAVE A CITY FROM DESTRUCTION?

GEN. XVIII, XIX.

We read in Job, " Can a mortal be more righteous than God? Or can a man be more pure than his Maker?" (IV : 17.) This exhortation of Eliphaz to Job naturally recurs to us, when we read the conversation between God and Abraham, concerning the fate of Sodom and Gomorrah. Did Abraham really venture to remind God of his duty, when he asked, "Shall the Judge of all the earth not exercise justice?" Did Abraham dare admonish God, when he exclaimed, " Far be it from thee to do after this manner, to slay the righteous with the wicked?" Abraham, furthermore, implored God to spare the wicked for the sake of fifty, forty, thirty or even ten righteous men in the community. Wherein would lie the justice of such an action? Justice does not demand merely that the innocent shall not suffer; it insists, with equal force, that the wicked must not go unpunished. What would we think of an earthly judge who would refuse to pronounce sentence against a number of criminals, because of the many good citizens in the community!

To interpret this passage literally, as if a colloquy had really taken place, instead of entering into the spirit of the chapter, would be grossly unjust to the Holy Scriptures. The significance of the conversation is indicated in the opening words: "Shall I hide from Abraham what I am about to do, seeing that Abraham shall surely become a great and mighty nation, and all the nations of the earth shall be blessed in him? For I know him, that he will command his children and his household after him, that they shall keep the way of the Lord to do righteousness and justice."

"His children and his household after him" are to keep the way of the Lord, so that they may resemble God in צדקה ומשפט, in "righteousness and justice." The contemporaries of Abraham, who had known the place where the Dead Sea now stretched its waste of waters as a fertile valley, the site of populous cities, and their children, remembering the awful catastrophe, would certainly ask themselves the question: "Must not many an innocent man have suffered in the destruction of so large a number of human beings?"

Abraham did not want the way of the Lord to be judged by his contemporaries or his descendants in the light of an act of apparent injustice. The way of the Lord was to be a guide to them in their earthly career. A man's conception of his God always regulates his life. Nor can more be asked of him. If his God is unjust, he will also be unjust. Abraham's conversation makes it appear that in the doomed cities, there were not fifty, nay, not even ten, undeserving of their fate. His answer to would-be critics was, "The Judge of all the earth does no injustice. Be ye likewise on your guard against wrongdoing in your earthly careers."

Subordinate to the main idea, the manifestation of the Ruler of the universe as the God of justice, and the

significance of the Dead Sea as the everlasting memorial
of his justice, various precious thoughts, which cannot
but appeal to the thoughtful reader, are found in this
passage. As long as there are ten, or speaking generally, a proportionate number of righteous men in a community, so long may it enjoy a prosperous existence, or
the hope of amelioration of its condition be cherished.
Whenever a people has succeeded in working its way
from slavery to freedom; from a state of rudeness to
that of civilization; or has risen from ignorance to culture; or has passed from the darkness of superstition to
the realms of light; or has exchanged rabid fanaticism
for respectful toleration, the achievement has not been
the work of the masses; the movement did not, from its
incipiency, count its followers by hundreds or thousands
—no, the pioneer band always consisted of a handful of
noble men and women, who finally succeeded in infusing
a new spirit into the people at large. Without these
torches to illuminate the path of the beautiful, the true,
the good, the indifferent masses, would never have made
any progress; on the contrary, the baser elements in
the community would have succeeded in directing the
multitude into their paths. Had the one Moses and, by
a generous estimate, the seventy other chosen men been
taken from the six hundred thousand that went up from
Egypt into the light of freedom, then, humanly speaking, Israel would have disappeared from the stage of
history. Without Ezra and Nehemiah, the kingdom
of Israel would probably not have arisen a second time.
Had it not been for Rabbi Yohanan ben Zakkaï, Israel's
Law would have died out. Had it been possible for
George III to silence one hundred men like Patrick

9

Henry, Samuel Adams, and their compeers, the formation of the United States might have been indefinitely
postponed. Even now, perhaps, we should be the subjects of Her Majesty, the Queen of England. The
many prosperous communities, which we behold on
every side in our land, whose activity is a source of rich
blessing to the country, did not spring into life with a
large number of members. They all owe their existence to a few faithful and energetic individuals. The
masses merely followed their good example.

The maintenance and direction of states, cities, communities and associations, like their creation and foundation, must be set down to the credit of a few—the men
spoken of in our text as Zaddikim. It would be doing
a great injustice to the majority of the citizens of our
city, as well as of others, to count them among the
R'shoim, but neither can they be counted among the
Zaddikim, the upholders of the community. One section of the community provides faithfully for the welfare of school and household, taking no thought for the
city or country in general, for congregations, or for associations. Others, again, may take an interest in the
affairs of the community, not however to benefit the
community, but rather to serve their own selfish ends.
The sound kernel, the vital element of the community,
is composed of an exceedingly small number. It is
made up of citizens of pre-eminent probity and public
spirit. Were these lacking, the power of the wicked
would rule the indifferent masses, and transform the
most prosperous community into Sodom and Gomorrah.
This is the second lesson, taught to us in the form of
a conversation between Abraham and Deity—a few

worthy men may save a whole community from destruction.

Was Lot a man of this description? The testimony of the Holy Scriptures on his character is not unexceptionable. We read, " When God destroyed the cities of the plain, he remembered Abraham, and sent Lot away out of the midst of the overthrow." Lot, therefore, owed his salvation not to his own merit, but to his kinship with Abraham. It is true, he practised hospitality, but only " in the evening," as the narrative has it. He desired the strangers to rise up early, and go on their way, without attracting any notice. He conducted the travellers to his home by a side-path (סורי גא). Moreover, this incident was the first intimation that his fellow-citizens had of the difference between his mental attitude and theirs. Up to that time, he had given them no opportunity to find out that he held nobler views than they. Lot was one of those men, common at all times and places, who are good when surrounded by good influences, but who, among evil companions, maintain a timid silence, avoiding any appearance that might betray a difference between their point of view and that of the others, and hence give offence. The men that have power to save, the Zaddikim, whom Abraham had in mind, the men that could have rescued Sodom from destruction, had they been present, must have the courage, not only to harbor an independent opinion in secret, but to express their convictions openly, and to act according to them. We read of " fifty righteous men *within the city*"—not the upright man within his four walls, behind closed doors and darkened windows, not the pious man among pious men, the good man in a community of good men, but the man that shows his piety openly "within the city," caring not what may be the opinion of those about him, caring not whether his sentiments make friends or enemies for him among those about him.

Abraham supposed that fifty such pious men were to be found in the five cities, and there was not even one! To his contemporaries and his posterity, standing with deep emotion on the brink of this dead body of saline and sulphurous water, asking, "What caused this dis- aster? Was it the work of a just God?" he could reply, "Yes, the justice of the eternal law, ruling in human affairs, is here manifested." Not the number of evil- doers, of weakling and indifferent citizens—they are found everywhere—caused this catastrophe, but the lack of Zaddikim, the salt of the masses, who keep human life from moral corruption. It was for the want of such men that these cities and their inhabitants perished. Sodom and Gomorrah are not the only victims of such a fate. Since their day, numberless kingdoms and cities have vanished from the earth, meeting with an end of horror. Associations have been dissolved, others drag out a weary existence, all for want of a proportionate, if small, number of men of strength of character, of noble devotion to the common welfare. The material for a continued existence was at hand, the builders were lacking. The cement was wanting to hold the members together in an existence worthy of their divine origin. The pillars that upheld the structure tottered on their foundations.

These Zaddikim do not always go about with crowns upon their heads, or decorated with orders and medals;

nor do they, in all cases, occupy pulpits and university chairs, and bear the title *doctor* or *professor*. They are sometimes plain, unostentatious citizens, who live quiet, unassuming lives, and quite unconsciously to themselves as to others, exercise a good influence upon their fellowmen. They do not always receive their reward upon earth, neither is their lot, in all cases, enviable. Frequently, indeed, they suffer more or less for their courage in differing from the world about them in opinion, in thought, in action. They frequently hear the cry, "This one man came in to sojourn, and he will needs be a judge." You, who stand quite alone with your antiquated or radical notions concerning things human and divine, you, strange man that you are, you wish to act as our judge! Alas! There are not always angels at hand to take the part of the innovators, when attacked, and to save them. History has many a sad tale to relate of martyrs to conviction.

Every man cannot, therefore, be expected to take a bold stand, and so bring down upon himself the wrath of the multitude. Every one does not possess either the courage or the ability to carry on the fight, and indeed a great number of such bold spirits is not needed in the world. But it ought always to be borne in mind that the existence of the masses, characterized as it is by exclusive attention to their own concerns, depends upon the virtue (זכות) of a comparatively small number. Reverence is due to those capable of exertions for which we lack the necessary strength. Furthermore, what we are not strong enough to accomplish in large circles, let us seek to achieve in smaller spheres. Let each one of us make an earnest effort to become the shining example,

the Zaddik in his family, in society, in congregational
life. " In the place where there are no men, strive to be
a man." Let each one say to himself, " It may be that
the little world of my activity needs just such as I am
to influence it to pursue a moral, a pious existence, and
be saved from destruction." Let us remember, that
some must always be the bearers, while the others are
borne along. Let us put our shoulders to the wheel,
ashamed to allow ourselves to be carried by others, and
to live by the merit (זכות) of other and better men.
And may we, fathers and mothers, make it our highest
aim to be counted among the Zaddikim, when the Judge
of all the earth counts the righteous men of our city
and country. May we be found among those who, like
Abraham, command their children and their households
to observe God's ways, to live "to do righteousness and
justice."

"I THOUGHT, SURELY THERE IS NO FEAR OF GOD IN THIS PLACE."

GEN. XX : 11.

Abimelech, King of Gerar, reproached Abraham bitterly for allowing him to come to the very brink of a great sin. Abraham excused himself, saying: "I thought, Surely there is no fear of God in this place, and they will slay me."

Sin, therefore, must have been discussed prior to the existence of the religion of Israel, and the fear of sin held man in check, even in the time of Abraham. Who can say how much earlier in the world's history this feeling acted as a restraining force? Sin was not, at that time, an offence against morality, a violation of a philosophical code of ethics, but an offence against Deity, and the fear of sin was the dread of the punishment that offended Deity would visit upon man. Without the fear of God, the fear of sin did not exist; where the conception of God was wanting, there was likewise no conception of sin.

In the scene of our narrative, the country in which Abraham and Abimelech came into contact with each other, there was no university, no lecture platform, no library; in fact, no book and no pulpit; neither is there any mention of a temple. The only structure spoken of as devoted to the service of God is an altar, made by

setting up a single stone. And yet men knew what is
meant by "sin;" they recoiled in horror from certain
acts, and recognized that toleration of them would bring
distress upon king and realm.

Such was the aspect of affairs in Abimelech's tiny
kingdom, four thousand years ago. The condition of
Gerar was that of the entire ancient world, and the
description applicable to that time holds good of the
world of to-day. To the saying in the Bible: "The fear
of the Lord is the beginning of wisdom," might be added:
"The fear of the Lord is the beginning of the fear of sin."

That which we term science, is of comparatively
recent development; even in its incipiency, it was the
possession of but few men. So small was their number
that they were counted, and but seven were honored with
the title, "Wise Men."

What occupied the mind of man in that distant day?
The intellect craves nourishment as well as the body,
and its food is thought. What, then, engaged the
thoughts of the individual, when the duties connected
with the management of his simple household had been
fulfilled? What was the common thought of the nation?
For a nation must, of necessity, have a common subject
for contemplation. Religion, the gods—these were the
topics for the consideration of the whole people—their
origin, their dwelling-place, their occupations, the objects
of their love and hate, what angers them, what pleases
them—about all this the wise men taught, and the poets
sang. From this source was drawn thought to engage
the mind, and joy and sorrow, pleasure and pain to
nourish the emotions connected with home, the community, the country at large.

The idea of humanity is of even more recent origin than science. "Ethics," "philanthrophy," "virtue" were unknown conceptions in that early day. They were not present to spur man on to good deeds, or to restrain him from wrong-doing. The fear of the gods alone regulated the life of the individual and of the community.

Abraham said, "'I thought, Surely there is no fear of God in this place,' and therefore, neither life nor the marriage bond is held sacred." The *Elohim* of Abimelech was, indeed, not the *Adonai* of Abraham; nevertheless, the fear of the gods, be they called Elohim or Adonai, was the only bound set to human passion, the sole protection against rude force, the one power bridling wild lust.

Out of the belief in gods grew the belief in one God, and along with the belief in one God came the idea of this God as the Father of mercy, the righteous judge, ruling according to eternal laws, as King, *i. e.*, an all-guiding Providence, and as a holy Being, *i. e.*, a God who, without thought of his creatures' service or gratitude, wills and achieves naught but good. However, in Israel, too, there was no "virtue," no system of "ethics," independent of religion. There was but one idea—the fear of the Lord. The commandments in the Bible enjoining generosity, humanity, morality, or holiness upon man are usually followed by the phrase, " אני "I am the Lord." Thus, "Thou shalt love thy neighbor as thyself: I am the Lord."

"Thou shalt fear thy God: I am the Lord."

In the course of centuries the teachings of the God of Israel had become so completely a part of the form and essence of civilization, that good was recognized and practised under the designation, "virtue," "morality," "truth," the bad, shunned as "vice," "superstition," "falsehood," independently of the fear of the Lord. Then, men could live good, rational lives in which the thought of the fear of God played no part whatever. With the development of *science*, the intellectual food provided was more than could be digested by a whole generation, and so entirely could the new treasures of knowledge occupy the mind that not even *one* thought remained to be bestowed upon God.

If such is the case, wherein lies the force of Abraham's assertion, that where the fear of God is lacking, one must be prepared for the worst? We must admit that there are, at present, individuals and also certain limited associations of men upon whose thought and action the fear of the Lord has no influence whatever, and with whom it is, nevertheless, safe, nay, even pleasant to dwell. In virtue and generosity, they bear comparison with any god-fearing man or woman, and hence, they do not illustrate the truth of Abraham's assertion. Let us seek to make the consequences of such godlessness clearer by means of an illustration.

In Holland, many laborers are constantly working at the dams and canals; were their care and exertions to cease even for a few years, half of the land would be swallowed up by the ocean. Many thousands, living in that country, do not lend any aid in defending the land from the threatening waters; nevertheless, they dwell in security, and partly upon the very soil that has been won by hard labor from the unwilling sea. In like manner, the synagogues, churches and religious schools

—all of which nourish the fear of the Lord—are the dikes resisting the advance of godless materialism. Picture to yourselves the state of affairs without these dikes. Think of all these buildings devoted to the service of God as closed. Imagine that there is neither church nor synagogue, and in their stead, put gymnasia or even scientific institutions. Then would appear the truth of Abraham's declaration that where there is not fear of the Lord, nothing is considered sacred, nothing is secure. The foundation would be taken from under the feet of the moral hero denying the existence of God, just as the comfort and security of the Hollanders would be a thing of the past, were the activity of the workmen at the dikes to cease.

An individual or even hundreds or thousands of men, here and there, may set up reason in place of God, or substitute the doctrine of humanity for religion; the whole body of mankind will not be injured in the least. But woe unto us, were the banner of godlessness to be raised among large bodies of men, and the fear of the Lord attacked by them in closely serried ranks! A great nation, standing upon the very height of civilization, once made such an attempt, and its defiant action did not go unpunished. How much innocent blood was there shed, because there was no fear of the Lord in the land!

It cannot be denied that even the hands of religion reek with blood; that the number of its victims can scarcely be estimated; that religions have been a curse as well as a source of blessing to mankind. But this evil thing was not the true fear of the Lord: it was malice, delusion, avarice, ignorance under the mask of religion, not pure fear of God, free from base alloy.

Yet, the evil following in the train of religion, however great it may appear to us, is scarcely to be taken into account in comparison with the misery that would ensue, were every spark of a god-fearing spirit among men to be extinguished. A dwelling-place among snakes, crocodiles, hyenas, tigers and wolves would be a paradise, compared with life among men entirely devoid of religion, of the fear of God.

The fear of the Lord is the beginning of the fear of sin. None can deny that the fear of the Lord is older than science, than "virtue," than life regulated by pure reason. At the same time, the fear of the Lord is the end of the fear of sin, i. e., the fear of the Lord, as a motive for shunning evil, will outlive all others. The fear of God has ever been victorious over all opposing forces, and will ever continue so. When the fury of wanton spirits is spent, when the attempts to solve the mystery of the world without a God have failed, the thinkers, worn out with their struggles, meekly and penitently return to God in their old age, and confess: "We thought that we were building a system, pointing heavenwards, a system as comprehensive and as powerful as believers teach their God to be, and we have been digging downwards, digging pits into which our thought has fallen ever lower."

Our text warns us of still another danger. Abraham thought that the fear of God did not exist in Gerar, but he was mistaken. Abimelech spoke with horror of the imminence of sin. He was affrighted even by the appearance of a god in a dream. Be, therefore, not hasty in your judgment of a fellow-man's relation to God. Not every man that loudly proclaims his belief in God bears a truly god-fearing spirit within him, and many a one that seldom pronounces the name of the Lord reverences him the more deeply, and serves him the more eagerly. Surely, it is not good to blaspheme, but the heart cannot always be judged from the utterances of the lips. Many a one is indifferent in his service of God, because he knows that God's service is cared for. Conscious of his own upright life, he forgets him that gave us the law of good. Were he to see his faith in actual danger, he would place himself before the breach, just as the Hollander leads a peaceful existence while the weather is calm, but rushes to the dikes, when the tide seeks to destroy the land. There is nothing so arrogant as the condemnation of a whole region, an entire community, with the assertion: "I thought, there is no fear of the Lord in this land." He alone, whom we should fear, knows who truly fears and reverences him. He alone may say: "Surely, there is no fear of the Lord in this place." Man, however, has enough to occupy his attention in his *own* soul. It is sufficient for him to keep alive within himself the fear of the Lord.

EDUCATIONAL INFLUENCES.

GEN. XXI : 9-15.

"And Sarah saw the son of Hagar the Egyptian, whom she had borne unto Abraham, mocking. Wherefore she said to Abraham, Cast out this bondwoman and her son: for the son of this bondwoman shall not be heir with my son, with Isaac."

It would surely have been simpler to speak of the child by name. Why not say at once, "Sarah saw Ishmael." An attentive reader of the Bible cannot, however, have failed to notice that in the description of its characters, those of good as well as those of evil fame, the name of the mother is frequently mentioned. Such is the case here. Sarah speaks of Ishmael as the "son of Hagar the Egyptian." By this designation, she indicated the evil nature of the boy, and justified the demand for his removal. She thus intimated that there rested upon him the spirit of his mother, an abandoned creature from her very childhood, the offspring of slaves in Egypt, brought to Canaan like a bale of goods, a creature without a will of her own, subject to the whims of her mistress. How could anything good be expected of her son and his education?

It is a painful thought that many human beings, Ishmael-like, are born under an evil star. Ancestral imperfections of mind and soul, acting as dominant influences in the determination of character, become the

126

heritage of children and grandchildren. It is difficult
to bring such observations into harmony with a belief in
a just and merciful God. But belief is not an easy matter; were it so, there would not be so many unbelievers, nor so many of little faith. The believer approaches
questions concerning Providence, with the modest ad-
mission : " Here the domain of knowledge ends, and
that of belief begins. A Providence does exist, a divine,
ruling Power, whose ways, however, are too exalted for
our comprehension." Nevertheless, we cannot help but
see that for many men, paths for good or for evil are
designated at birth, and not every one possesses the
necessary strength to forsake the allotted road. The
angel could well prophesy to Hagar that the son born
unto her would be a wild man, whose hand would be
against every man's, and against whom would be every
man's hand. There are many mothers, to whom one
might thus prophesy without being an angel. A Hagar
will ever be the mother of an Ishmael.

Mothers, pre-eminently, are responsible for the moral
condition of their children. The great men, who have
been benefactors to the race in the varied situations of
life, and the myriads of earnest, helpful men and women
in cities and villages, whose unostentatious work in their
limited circle is a source of blessing, owe their usefulness to a mother's influence which rests upon them, and
inspires them to action. On the other hand, the greater
share of responsibility for what is low and mean in their
children rests upon the mothers as well. Many factors
enter into the education of a man to lead him away from
the good or the evil course prepared for him in his
home; but in the training bestowed by home, and in

that element of home training determined by the character and disposition of parents, the maternal influence
is of the first importance.

Do we ask when the education of, a human being
commences? Much sooner than is ordinarily held to be
the case—long before the child is born. The choice of
a helpmate is the beginning of this training, for this
choice decides the character of the family to be founded.
The wild Bedouins, who even to-day, render entire
stretches of country unsafe, and remain implacable enemies to civilization, are the descendants of Ishmael, the
son of Hagar the Egyptian.

Sarah said, "Ishmael must leave my house; he may
no longer associate with Isaac." Here we have the second factor in man's education—association. Of what
avail is the discipline of the home, even when exercised
by the best of mothers; of what avail is a school though
conducted by the most capable and conscientious of
teachers, against the mighty stream of life which flows
threateningly around the quiet home? The mother's mild
words, the wise advice of the father, and the earnest discipline by both, can have but little force against the
power of visible example in the world without. "Example is stronger than precept." Example often insinu-
ates itself into the heart, upon whose hardness entreaty
and solemn warning can make no impression. The
character which father and mother have labored hard
to form is frequently altered, ruined or remodelled by
society. However, this change is not always for the
worse; frequently, indeed, it proves a true blessing.

Parents send their children to school, and believe
them in good keeping. It is true, there they receive

from their teachers the knowledge necessary for them throughout life, but in their associations with the pupils, they learn both good habits and evil ways. Frequently, the advantages of the instruction of the former are outweighed by the disadvantage of the evil influence of the latter. In many a one, the seed of moral ruin has been planted in an institution of learning; there, he has learnt how to bring down his good parents with sorrow to the grave. Sermons with illustrations from real life are preached to them on the play-ground, in the servants' hall, in the workshop, in the counting-rooms. How the remembrance of your words, good parents and teachers, pales in the presence of the living example! In training your children, it is, therefore, not the smallest part of your duty to keep far from the innocent the poison of evil example. "Cast out this bondwoman and her son!" Remove from your children's vicinity all that are morally unsound, from the child's nurse to the frivolous dandy that frequents your house, and shrink not from ridding yourself of hoary age, if its baseness is likely to corrupt your pure sons and daughters.

"And the thing was very grievous in Abraham's eyes, because of his son."

Here we have the third factor in education. Father and mother must act in harmony with each other in the training of their children. Better no education at all than that father and mother should work in opposite directions.

Abraham, doubtless, possessed authority enough to make his will prevail in his house. He could not see that any harm would come to Isaac from Ishmael's continued stay in his home. He felt severely the separa-

10

tion from his son, but a divine voice cried to him: "In all that Sarah may say unto thee, hearken unto her voice." Act in harmony with the mother of the house.

The *discipline* of children and the *education* of children are two different things. Discipline is established in cases in which an energetic father guides the reins of authority in conjunction with a passive mother; or again, in which an energetic mother stands by the side of an insignificant father. The children are well disciplined as long as they feel the restraints of home government. As soon as they think themselves free, they are different beings, and follow different impulses. If, however, father and mother are at one in zeal and purpose, then we have true *education*, then the spirit of the parents informs the character of the children. The house in which children are *disciplined* is like a well-regulated clock, which keeps time accurately as long as it is wound, but stops when the motor power of the spring is no longer active. The house in which children are *educated* is not moved by mechanism, but animated by a soul. Though the parents have long been at rest, or though, if alive, they no longer guide their children's footsteps, still their noble work will continue to bear fruit.

Finally, we must consider the moral value of the educational method pursued in Abraham's home. The purpose of sending away Ishmael, the removal of an evil influence, was good, but what can be said of the means employed? It is true, the circumstances of the time did not permit Abraham to send wife and child to the railway station, and to secure for them comfortable places in a palace car, in which they might journey in safety to Egypt, but surely he could have devised a more hu-

mane method of carrying out the harsh measure. It is
highly displeasing to us to see him show the woman and
her child the door, saying to them, "Here are bread
and a skin of water. Take them and find your way
through the desert into distant Egypt as best you can."
In our day, too, there are men that do not treat their
own kinspeople kindly, but they are not praised for their
behavior, and surely not respected; under certain circumstances, indeed, they are severely called to account
for their actions.

In our text, however, the occurrence is described as if
quite natural and proper; in fact, the seal of divine
approval is set upon it.

This point in the narrative leads us up to the fourth
factor in man's education—time and place. Man is the
child of his century, and as the "heir of all the ages,"
he constitutes mankind. Four thousand years and thousands of miles lie between us and the events of our
narrative. Abraham was a child of his century—the
twentieth since creation, according to Biblical calculation, just as we are children of our century, the sixtieth
since creation, according to the same method of reckoning. Abraham was a child of the Orient; we are children of Europe and America. Surely, we have learnt
something in these four thousand years, especially in a
zone more favorable to culture. And we have learnt
and been taught much that is good and noble, which
was unknown to Abraham and the other patriarchs.
The spiritual achievements of the four thousand years
of the education of mankind can nowhere be more
clearly seen than in the legal enactments about the position and estimation of woman in the marriage relation.

The treatment of Hagar and her child, as the child of a slave, four thousand years ago, in the Orient, was normal, in keeping with the culture of a formative period. To-day, in the midst of the culture of Europe and the countries settled by emigration thence, such action would be inhuman, deserving of punishment.

"He whose actions find favor in the sight of the best of his contemporaries, lives for all time," says the poet. We can demand no more of man than that he should rank among the best of his time. As such, Abraham and Sarah will always be deeply reverenced by us. But woe to the world, were there no times, nobler in their influence than the Abrahamic period; no ideas of mo-rality, purer and nobler than those amid which the patriarchs and the other Biblical heroes lived and labored! In spite of their deficiencies, which we need take no pains to deny, the ancients gain in our esteem, when we remember the deficiencies of their teacher—the time in which they lived. We, however, in consid-eration of the fact that teacher Time has, since those days, gained so much in the matter of knowledge of the good and the right, must demand greater things of ourselves.

"LEAD US NOT INTO TEMPTATION."

Gen. XXII.

"God tempted Abraham!" Did the Omniscient, then, not know what would be Abraham's decision? To lead a man into temptation, deliberately to place sin in his path, is considered unworthy of a mere mortal—how can we, then, ascribe such an act to God? Let us devote our attention to this and other peculiar expressions in a chapter of the Bible that has always been held in high honor by us.

The oldest and most highly venerated prayer of the Christian Church, its show prayer, so to speak, is the Pater-noster. It would be highly improper for me to send forth, from this place, a hostile criticism of anything held sacred by another religious community, were it not that, first of all, learned Israelites have, with much labor, traced each part of this prayer to Jewish sources. Again, many Israelites look upon it as not merely harmless, but of surpassing merit, and it is not at all displeasing to them to have their children join in the prayer in the devotional exercises of the public schools, and finally, I shall really—to use a colloquialism—be minding my own business, since one part of the prayer under criticism is to be found in our own liturgy: ואל תביאנו לא לידי נסיון "Lead us not into temptation."

133

God *did* lead Abraham into temptation. It cannot be gainsaid. According to our sages, he tempted him not only *once*, but even *ten* times.

When the Children of Israel were in the desert, God "led them into temptation." The Bible repeats this assertion again and again with great emphasis. David certainly understood the art of praying, as but few others, and he makes the direct appeal, "Try me and prove me."

A prayer for immunity from temptation, then, finds no support in the Holy Scriptures. On the contrary, to come into God's presence with such a petition seems a violation of the spirit of the Bible.

Long after the death of the founder of Christianity— though at not so late a period that a sharp line of demarcation was drawn between Jew and Christian, between Jewish and Christian literature, as was to be the case afterward—Abba Areka formulated the prayer, לא לידי נסיון "Lead us not into temptation!"

The Church did not borrow this phrase from the Synagogue. It is more probable that Abba Areka conceived this supplication under the influence of the ecstatic, the plaintively sentimental atmosphere surrounding the new sect. We find other traces of the familiarity of this great teacher with the apocryphal books, and also that he did not hesitate to copy from them without stating his sources.

The whole prayer of which the phrase under discussion is a part breathes the Christian dogma of the subjection of the will, and of grace as a means of salvation:

"Teach me to know thy law; lead me in thy precepts. Let me not go astray. Suffer me not to fall into temptation or disgrace. Let wicked impulses gain no power over me. Keep far from me all evil associations; and let all my powers learn to serve thee."

Breathes there through this prayer the spirit of our strong, sound and rational belief? our idea of God and of the dignity of his morally free children? No, forgive me, Abba, thou great and pious teacher, no Israelite can repeat thy prayer in sincerity! It is not a growth from holy Israelitish soil. The twigs and leaves extend into the field of our pure faith, but the trunk is rooted, if not in a rank soil, at least in mould in which doctrines concerning God and human nature foreign to us are fostered.

God does lead us into temptation! Of Abraham's temptations only ten are recorded. Fortunate Patriarch! Our temptations mount up into the thousands. No day passes in which they do not assail us. Certainly, temptations assail us, but how is it with our power of resistance? Most certainly, we, too, withstand them. He must be, indeed, a weak creature who, in the whole course of his life, has not found within himself the strength to resist temptation at least ten times.

Wherein would lie the strength and the excellence of virtue, if the temptation to yield to other inclinations did not have to be resisted? Would self-restraint be a virtue, were it not for the temptation to yield to desire? And where would be the merit of piety, were it not for the temptation to forsake it, and follow in the seductive path of worldliness?

Among the earliest passages in the life of the first human pair recorded in the Holy Scriptures is the account of the temptation which preceded the first sin: "And when the woman saw that the tree was good for food, and that it was pleasant to the eyes," etc. Was not that a temptation? Sin always appears to us in an attractive guise, challenging our attention, while virtue, unassuming in appearance, rests quietly in the corner, alluring none, waiting to be wooed. The first temptation is placed beside the first duty. Duty and temptation are of the same age.

He that prays, " Lead us not into temptation !" asks that God change the order of nature, the very plan of creation; that he make man cease to be a man, and change him either into an angel or a brute, neither of whom knows temptation, and is, therefore, also incapable of virtue.

Let us understand very clearly that God does place temptation in our path, from morning until evening, from evening until morning, from youth to old age, from our earliest awakening to consciousness till the last spark of life dies out within us. The child is tempted to gratify its sweet tooth, to play during school-hours, to tell falsehoods. The youth and the maiden are assailed by temptation in a different form. The man and the woman, in the strength of their years, are likewise tried, and even old age is not safe from folly, i. e., from temptation. Prayer is here of no avail. " Help yourself!" is the admonition. Every prayer with such an object in view is an " idle prayer." Resistance to temptation constitutes the moral element in life, and lends grace to man.

Remember, O rich man! your wealth is a temptation to luxury, to arrogance, to idleness. A temptation assails you in the method of gaining riches, and in the method of disposing of them. Wealth will be a test as to whether you are to rule money, or to be its slave.

And to you, poor man, poverty is a trial. Prove that a great soul can exist in an humble hut; that you can preserve a heart pure and noble, even in want.

Beauty is likewise a temptation to its possessor. Many a one, in the consciousness of this great gift of nature, wastes his years in frivolity, and in the care of the beautiful shell, neglects the moral kernel.

Intellectual power is no less a temptation. Frequently the man of average intellect achieves a higher development in morality, in well-being, in usefulness, than his more richly endowed brother, whose very genius proves his ruin.

Whatever be the fortunes of your life, be they pleasant or adverse, say to yourself, "This is a temptation. I must summon up all my strength to resist it."

Whoever has passed a difficult examination before strict judges knows what heart-felt bliss was his, when the hours of anxiety were over. A like blissful feeling is ours, when after a day of severe trial, our conscience assures us that we have come forth victorious from honest battle.

In connection with temptation, one need not think of murder and homicide and other capital crimes. Small are the temptations which glide through our lives like shadows. They constantly surround us, poisoning existence with their stings, in our business activities, in our calling, in our domestic intercourse, in our friendship, in our appetites, in the use of our tongues, etc.

Verily, God does tempt us. Let us remember that at all times. Yes, he tempts us, and therefore we rank above the brutes, and, if we resist, above the angels.

In this point, however, we must not imitate God. We

must not lead a man into temptation; we must not
place a stone in the path of the blind.   When man deals
thus by his fellow-man, he is not tempting him, he is
leading him astray.

If you fawn on the base man, and praise the sinner;
if you flatter the rich and powerful; if, by pomp and
show, you attract attention to yourself, and give occasion
for extravagant imitation, then you are leading your
neighbor into temptation, you are misleading him.

CONFLICT OF DUTIES.

Isaac had grown old, and he felt that the time had come for setting his earthly affairs in order. His most precious possession was the blessing which he had received from his father, and which, in turn, he intended to transmit to his first-born and favorite. Out-witted by Rebecca, he laid the blessing upon the head of Jacob.

The memory of Rebecca is sacred to us. She is one of our pious mothers in Israel, and it would grieve us sorely to be compelled to look upon her in an unfavorable light, but truth and the virtue of truthfulness among men are also holy, even holier than the memory of Rebecca. In what light must this narrative of the Scriptures be regarded, so that full justice may be done to truth, without detracting from the character of our revered Mother Rebecca?

A collision is one of the incidents of life that so often make existence unpleasant; frequently, indeed, involve loss of life. Physical collisions, in which two bodies coming from opposite directions strike against each other, are of daily occurrence. Sometimes there is even danger that our planet may collide with a comet whirling towards us through space. There is another kind of encounter, an invisible and noiseless one, in which neither bones nor muscles suffer injury, but which is,

139

nevertheless, quite as disastrous in its effects. Spirits come into conflict with each other, and in the course of the struggle temper becomes heated. Clashing interests meet on the narrow path of life, and obstinately push on with diametrically opposite ends in view. Ideals of the good, the true, the beautiful are dragged down into the whirlpool of stern realities and the barren prose of life; as when, for example, the young wife, with her ideal of a "knight without reproach," and the young husband, with his dream of fair angels, stand before each other as they really are—reality seeming to mock pitilessly at the images created by fancy.

The moralist's task is an easy one: he preaches moderation and self-restraint. There is, however, still another sort of conflict, in which even moderation and the extreme of self-control are ineffectual; that is, when there is a conflict of duties.

Two conflicting duties, of which the one can be performed only at the expense of the other, may claim our attention at the same time.

Let us make this proposition clearer by some examples.

A married couple may have the choice between peace and amity in their own home, on the one side, and the preservation of friendly relations with parents, who may be hostile towards one of them, on the other. An Israelite may have to decide between living strictly according to the dictates of his conscience, and his and his family's temporal welfare, or their very existence. It may happen that in fulfilling the duty of self-preservation, we are forced to act in violation of the demands of love of country and of our fellow-man. The elder Brutus acted

as judge in the case against his son, who had been guilty
of treason towards Rome. Here, there was a conflict
between the father and the judge in *one* person. The
younger Brutus, one of the murderers of Cæsar, his
friend and benefactor, had to decide between the duty
of gratitude, on the one side, and his duty towards the
community, on the other.

We, too, in our days, may have to choose between
respect for the written law of the land, and regard for
the higher law—the eternal one—of reason and morality.

Our revered Mother Rebecca found herself in a
similar position.

Happy the woman that can look up to her mate as to
her superior, the director of the household, the guide
and teacher of her children ! Unenviable is the lot of
her who has to direct without assistance the affairs of
the household, and the training of the little ones. The
strong women are not the happiest women. So unenviable a lot was Rebecca's ; she had to bear Isaac's share of
life's burdens as well as her own.

Isaac exercised blind authority in the household,
worse for Rebecca than if there had been no one but
herself to appeal to. As it was, his power was but a
useless and disturbing element. She knew well the
wild, untamed nature of her older son, and could picture to herself his wretched future. And to him his
father was willing to entrust the traditional blessing of
the family and the welfare of future generations!

The children of our day also prize highly the blessing
of their parents, but not so much from a belief in its
efficacy, as from a feeling of reverence for their parents,
and for the assurance it gives them that they have per-

formed their duty to their loved ones, and have given them pleasure. In ancient times, however, a blessing from the mouth of the father was God's voice. The blessing·hand of the father was the ,hand of fate, and Isaac was going to err so far as to lay his hand upon Esau's head! Was it not clearly the mother's duty to interfere? Truly, such was her duty, but she was also under a moral obligation towards the infirm and blind old man. Was it proper to distress the unhappy, aged father? Would it be right for her to open his eyes to the true character, the unworthiness of his favorite, his first-born? There was no hope of amelioration, for Jacob and Esau were no longer children. Esau was a married man. Indeed, according to the reckoning of the Bible, the brothers must have been sixty or seventy years old at the time. The truth would have broken Isaac's heart; it is even questionable whether he could have been brought to look upon it as the truth. Men, otherwise extremely sharp-sighted, are frequently afflicted with an incurable blindness to the qualities of their own sons. In this case, then, there was a struggle between conflicting duties. At the expense of truth, Rebecca secured the father's blessing to the proper person.

I am far from believing that we should set up as a rule always to be followed, when the straight path does not lead to the good end, choose the crooked one; if unalloyed truth has no prospect of gaining a victory, choose equivocation and cunning. In such cases, every one must be a law-giver unto himself; in the struggles of conscience, he must be his own adviser.

Make this a rule of life, build your philosophy of life

upon it as a fundamental principle, " I will be true in thought, speech and action. I will allow nothing to cloud the honesty of my words and deeds." But do not lose sight of the fact that we dare not fulfil even our duty without testing the wisdom of our course.

In over-zealous and one-sided practice of duty, in unswerving attention to the behests of stern conscientiousness, we may, perhaps, be treading a path of duty that is paved with sin, with disregard of other duties. Our sages call this attaining a desirable end on the path of sin.

Test the worth of everything—even of the virtue of truthfulness, the very corner-stone of all the virtues. Examine everything in the light of place, time and circumstances. In your criticism of your fellow-man, be not too ready to stigmatize every neglect of duty as absolutely bad. Remember, there is frequently a conflict of duties, in which the one must be subordinated to the importance of the other. Perchance, the neglect of the duty apparent to you may be the price paid for performing another—a more important—obligation, of whose existence you are entirely unaware.

Let every good mother give thanks to her Creator, if her household is so constituted that she stands before her spouse and her children as a pattern of strict truthfulness and uprightness. Should a mother, however, believe that her position requires her to follow the path of duplicity, then may the reasons for her action be of so urgent and holy a nature, as were those of our revered Mother Rebecca, blessed be her memory!

TEMPERAMENT.

"Esau said in his heart, The days of mourning for
my father will be at hand; then will I slay my brother
Jacob." Commenting upon this phrase in the Scriptures, our sages say, "Esau spoke *in* (בלבו) his heart;
thus all evil men speak and do. We read in the Psalms,
'The fool says *in* his heart,' Jeroboam spoke *in* his
heart, Haman spoke *in* his heart. They are all governed by their hearts, while good men control their
feelings; therefore, it is said 'Hannah spoke *to* (literally
on, על-לבה) her heart,' 'David spoke *to* his heart,' and
thus also did Daniel express himself, imitating their
Creator; for the Bible says, 'God spoke *unto* his heart.'"

God, the Creator, alone has power to create; man
can merely modify what has been given him, using it for
good or evil purposes. As it is not in his power to create,
so also he is unable to annihilate anything existing
according to nature's laws. He may work havoc and
ruin, he may be the author of unspeakable evil, but
annihilation is beyond his power.

Man is born with a certain disposition, which frequently proves a most troublesome factor in his education, both at home and at school. A man's nature is
the work of creation, and cannot be destroyed. Education, therefore, must not seek to stifle nature, but rather

144

attempt to develop it into character. Jacob and Esau form a case in point. They were endowed, by nature, with different dispositions—"the children struggled within" Rebekah. Jacob was, by nature, a cool, deliberate thinker. Esau was wild and excitable; guided by impulse in his good deeds as well as in his evil ones. Their widely different qualities were revealed in their choice of a vocation. Jacob's quiet shrewdness inclined him to cattle-raising; his brother's wild courage selected the bow and arrow as a means of obtaining a livelihood. Esau is described to us as coming home from a hunt, excited and very much fatigued. Surely, the paternal larder, his mother's kitchen, might have supplied him with food, had he but asked for it. However, with the impatience, characteristic of such a nature, he insists upon eating the meal prepared for his brother. For this privilege, he resigns his birthright. He eats and drinks, laughing all the while; he had satisfied his heart's desire —the desire of his master, for his heart controlled him completely. But when his father, although ignorant of the compact between the brothers, bestowed the blessing of the first-born upon Jacob, then Esau's heart was heavy, and his lament over the loss of his privileges was commensurate with his animal spirits upon resigning them to his brother. He complained that Jacob had cheated him out of his birthright. And in his heart he said, "The days of mourning for my father will be at hand; then will I slay my brother Jacob." If, however, the blessing under discussion was worth a contest, Esau ought to have considered that it would effectually shield Jacob from any evil that he might plot against him; but by virtue of his temperament, he lay at the

11

mercy of his feelings. Again, we are told that his choice of wives grievously embittered the life of his parents. His unfortunate choice was the act of his wild feelings, entirely uncontrolled by reason. The teachings of morality, the suggestions of prudence, consideration for the feelings of his parents counted as nothing against the wild tumult in his heart. In one of his good moments his heart was moved by the sorrow of his parents, and he added a third wife to the two so displeasing to them. Finally, he is pictured to us nursing in his heart wrath, which has been accumulating through twenty-two years of separation, and, with four hundred men at his back, moving towards his brother, whose blood he is bent upon shedding. Instead, tears of emotion flow in profusion. He kisses and embraces his brother, lying upon the heart that he had purposed to pierce with his steel, and speaking to Jacob in the soft, loving tones proper to brotherly intercourse. Here, again, he acted as his heart prompted him. He was completely under the control of his heart. In one moment, the venomous poison of hatred within him was transformed into the wine of love.

In Jacob's life, on the other hand, we find evidences of thoughtful deliberation rather than of rash impulse. Jacob does not speak *in* his heart; he speaks *to* his heart; he is master of his heart, not its slave. These children, so entirely different in temperament, were the offspring of the same house, of the same father and mother; even more than this, they were twins. What a sad picture of family life is here presented to us! One of these sons is compelled to flee the paternal roof in secret, so destitute of means that he bears with him naught but the staff in his hand, and is forced to spend a night under the open sky. The other remains at home, at variance with his mother, and nursing thoughts of murder in his heart. Can the parents be blamed for their own and their children's unhappiness? Esau's temperament was ever the same from birth; so, too, Jacob's. Esau's mother could make no peaceful shepherd of him, nor could Jacob's father train him to be a bold, reckless hunter. Man cannot annihilate. He can merely mould and modify natural endowments. Disagreeable as may be the consequences which they entail upon us throughout life, they cannot be suppressed or destroyed. Those traits of Esau's nature, which were especially objectionable to his mother, she mistook for malice, and her heart turned against him. She thought that Esau lacked but the will to be like Jacob. Isaac, again, considered the qualities displeasing to him in Jacob as unmanly and deceitful cunning, and his love for his son gradually cooled. " Why is he not like Esau ?" he asked. The divergent opinions about Jacob and Esau, held by their parents, are still current in the world. Pious Judaism loves Jacob, and hates Esau. The best possible construction is put upon Jacob's actions, while Esau is denied all good qualities. Another class of Bible readers, again, shows a decided preference for Esau; they attribute to him knightly qualities, while in Jacob, they see an artful knave, wanting in brotherly feeling. Both the parents and the critics of the brothers take it for granted that all human beings, if such be their will, can pattern themselves or be patterned after the same model of virtue. And when Esau fails to be like Jacob, as it was his mother's desire

he should be, or Jacob, in growing up to be unlike Esau,
does not meet with his father's wish, the boys' will
is declared to be at fault. Had Esau made the greatest
effort to please his mother, or had Jacob done all in his
power to comply with his father's wish, neither could
have been successful; Esau could not have made a
Jacob of himself, nor Jacob an Esau. Their natures
were different, and natural inclination cannot be destroyed. Such is the experience of parents with several
children, and of teachers to whose care a whole school
is entrusted. Children cannot all be modelled after the
same pattern; both parents and teachers must take disposition into account in their work of education. Not
that nature is to be allowed to pursue its course unchecked, any more than it should be forcibly suppressed!
By means of education, disposition ought to be elevated
into character; it should be placed on a foundation of
morality, so that man may not be the slave of his emotions, but that his emotions may be subordinate to him
and his intelligence.

The educator's most difficult task is to find the method
appropriate to the nature of each child in a home or a
school, and to apply it so skilfully that the children may
not notice the differences in their education. The problem is so difficult that we parents ought not to be too
severely censured if we fail to solve it perfectly in the
training of each of our children. Were not Isaac and
Rebecca unsuccessful in their efforts? It is true, we
can see a special reason for their failure. The parents,
themselves, were not at one in the education of their
children. Under these circumstances, Esau's untamed
savagery and Jacob's artfulness are in nowise remarka-

ble. Jacob leaned toward his mother, while Esau was more attached to his father. Miserable discord ensues when the two guides do not confront the children as *one* being, *one* thought, *one* heart and *one* head; when appeal is made to the one from the other; when children use one parent as a shield against the other; when the one smiles, while the other storms; the one permits what the other prohibits; the one assents, and the other refuses; or, even when the opposition of the one side to the activity of the other be but negative.

Let us parents mark well the dreadful words of the son, whom his father had spoilt and his mother did not love because of his disposition: "When the days of mourning for my father come, then will I slay my brother Jacob." Let us so train ourselves and our children that they may not, like Esau, like Jeroboam, like Haman, speak *in* their hearts, the seat of unbridled nature, but *to* their hearts, like Hannah, like Job, like Daniel, like God himself, according to the words of the Scriptures, which read, "And the Lord spoke unto his heart."

DOES MAN NATURALLY IMPROVE WITH AGE?

GEN. XXXI.

What a contrast the picture of Jacob's departure from the home of his childhood, drawn for us at the beginning of the portion, presents to the scene depicted at the end, the description of his home-coming, the subject of our Biblical selection this morning!

In the account of Jacob's departure from the paternal roof, a fugitive, bearing with him naught but the staff in his hand, we read that when night overtook him on his journey, he laid him down under the open sky, and slept the sweet sleep of youth. Twenty years later, grown to be a rich man, he complains "sleep has departed from my eyes." Upon leaving home, he dreamt of angels, of a ladder connecting heaven and earth, of God standing beside him. Twenty years later, upon returning to the home of his youth, he dreams of his flocks, of rams and goats. At the beginning of his journey, he declared himself satisfied with "bread to eat, and raiment to put on," and these things were given him in abundance as the fruit of his labor. Now, however, he is no longer content with these simple blessings. He says, כי אנכי גם-אעשה איתי מתי "I must also provide for the future of my house."

Having become an inmate of his uncle's house, he

150

makes light of serving seven years twice over in order to gain the beloved of his heart. This same man, of warm feeling and poetical imagination, we see, in the Biblical narrative read this morning, grown twenty years older, and in the very prosaic situation of contemplating a stroke of business, accomplishing his end by the device of the ring-streaked rods!

In presenting so sharp a contrast between youth and old age, Jacob's life is not anomalous, it merely illustrates the *natural* development of a man in the course of years; it accentuates the difference between the sentiments of the young and of the old: idealism in youth, the practical side of man's nature developing with increasing years; poetry at life's entrance, prose constantly growing more prosaic at the other end of our earthly existence; in youth, self-sacrifice, generosity, living and expending for the pleasure of the moment, weaving rosy dreams of the morrow, as the years go by, selfishness and calculation, distrust of the future. The belief is erroneous that man *naturally* grows better with years; that the spirit approaches nearer a state of perfection; that man dies better than he was when born. Every man grows more *knowing* with age; his intellect expands; he becomes richer in experience, the necessity of adapting himself to existing circumstances grows ever more urgent; through practice, he becomes more and more an adept at dealing with persons and contingencies according to their natures. Even though he grow no wiser, prudence comes to every man with increasing years, but he does not inevitably grow better with time; by a natural development, indeed, he changes for the worse.

If impulsive youth commits a folly, if a young heart

loves rather too well than wisely, we may always plead
youth in extenuation of the fault; the German saying,
with years alone comes sense, may serve to assure us
that all will yet be well. If, on the contrary, the conduct of a *young* man be cruel, heartless, uncharitable,
unchivalrous, avaricious, envious and spiteful—then,
indeed, it is useless to seek comfort in the thought,
" These faults will disappear in time; this is the way of
youth." No; it is not so! These qualities will only
become more and more marked with increasing years.
An evil-hearted youth will surely develop into a still
more evil-hearted man. Age never corrects faults of
the heart. If man desires to be good and constantly to
grow better—and such both ought to and can be his
aim—he must seek earnestly to preserve in age the treasure of his youth, the good impulses of his heart. The
root of all the good and noble qualities of the heart lies
in our youth. It is the privilege of age to nourish this
root, to make it send forth strong and enduring shoots.
Therefore, there is no religion of reason. Reason can
rely on itself for support; the heart, on the other hand,
craves the help of religion. Religion appeals to the
heart alone. Its office it is to guard and foster the emotions of the heart, so that the innate love of the good
may not wither through neglect. Religion cannot *implant* good in the heart, but it can rouse and stimulate
the good already in existence. It can fan the spark of
nobility into a flame. It may guard against evil influences, and so, with advancing years, the heart may grow
purer and better.

Since, as far as qualities of the heart are concerned,
youth is *naturally* better than age, since the child has a

more tender heart than the old man, the rational training of children, the training that will make good men
and women of them, does not consist in teaching many
maxims of morality, but in exercising strenuous care to
keep baneful influences at a distance. Parents and
teachers must be untiringly vigilant over their own
actions, lest they thoughtlessly reveal weaknesses, which
cannot fail to produce an effect like blighting mildew
upon the heart of the child. The harm thus done can
scarcely be made good by subsequent preaching and
moralizing, by reproof and punishment. If parents
take great pride and pleasure in the precocious cleverness of their children, they may, by stimulating their
activities, by conversation and discussion, aid such early
development. It is, however, questionable whether the
intellect thus reaps permanent good results. He who
arises too early feels worn out when the strength of him
who has enjoyed sufficient rest is at its height. But as
far as the qualities of the heart are concerned, an early
development of cleverness is certainly harmful. Let
the children be childlike as long as they are children
in years. Feed them on worldly wisdom with a spoon;
do not overwhelm them with it by the bucketful. Do
not hasten to make gentlemen of your boys, and ladies
of your girls scarcely out of the cradle. Do not lay
upon them too soon the yoke of etiquette, and still less,
the harness of trade. An hour spent in play is much
more effective in developing mind and body, as well as
in fostering the pure and natural content of childhood,
than all show and finery, than precocious chatter and
worldly wisdom. The fermenting juice must be allowed
to rest, if good wine is to be made of it. Unspoilt chil-

dren are easily satisfied, and need but little for their sum of happiness—like Jacob, in the days of his youth, raiment to put on, enough to eat to satisfy hunger, and the enjoyment of the dream of life · by indulging in sport and gaiety. Children, clad in magnificent garments, and decked with jewels are not only hindered in their childish games by a regard for their fine clothes, but when they arrive at the period of self-consciousness, they do not dream of angels passing to and from heaven; their unchildlike visions are of show and vain display.

At length, whatever we may do, arrives the time in the life of every individual, just as it came in Jacob's life, when a serious question presents itself for solution: "I must provide for my future and the future of my house." Idealism, generosity and lovely dreams of angels cannot found a house, neither will they alone enable a man to preside over it honorably. Sagacity must be quickened and brought into action; but in the struggle, hold fast to your childlike nature. Do not degenerate into a soulless threshing-machine, busied only with gathering the grain. In the midst of labor, preserve a cheerful spirit; let tender feeling exist side by side with sharpness of insight; in careful and minute investigation and research, keep your childlike faith in God and his Providence. A forward, worldly-wise child is not an agreeable phenomenon, but the sight of a man, hoary of head, yet young in heart, is most pleasing; an old head above a heart beating with youthful enthusiasm, a grave, hard-working man, occupied with the sober cares of business, who, when he dreams, unlike Jacob in his prosaic, old age, is not visited by visions of flocks and herds, but still beholds heavenly apparitions stealing about his couch.

HUMILITY.

Filled with dread and anxiety, Jacob journeyed towards his home. It was no idle, spectral fear that made him tremble. Esau was moving towards him with four hundred men. For twenty long years had anger been boiling in Esau's bosom, wrath gnawing at his heart-strings. At last, the hour was at hand, when he might pluck the sweet fruit of revenge. What means did Jacob adopt for his protection? Our sages include them in three words דורון תפלה ומלחמה gifts, prayer and war. First, he sought to allay his brother's wrath with *gifts*, then he turned to God in *prayer*, and finally he prepared himself for the worst by getting ready for *combat*. Esau, however, with knightly courtesy, refused the gift; matters did not come to such a pass that it was necessary to fight; and whether to prayer is to be attributed the favorable outcome of the meeting, God alone can know. In the ordinary course of events, God helps man by giving him strength to help himself. Jacob, surely, held this belief, or he would have been satisfied to pray, and would not have sought other means of rescue as well. What was it, however, that cooled Esau's burning wrath? What changed his bloody intentions so suddenly into kind, fraternal feelings? It was the friendly word, the fraternal tone and the humble

approach of his brother. The warmth of Jacob's greet-
ings, his modest speech had already thawed slightly the
ice-crust about the heart of his wrathful brother. When,
however, the brother upon whom his father had laid the
blessing of the head of the family, came into his presence, bowing himself to the earth seven times, then the
icy crust gave way, all the brotherly feeling, so long
repressed, rushed forth. Gifts, it is true, are a mighty
lever. Gifts can buy worthless rabble without limit,
and even win the sympathy of better men. A gift to
the needy is a true kindness, and to the rich, it is a
pleasant mark of esteem. Combat and bravery subdue
cities and countries, found states and kingdoms, and
strike down those that neither bend nor yield. But
more effective than the richest gift, more agreeable to
the spirit than the finest offering, more powerful than
the strongest arm, more victorious than steel-clad valor,
is the soft tongue, the mild speech, the well-chosen word.
He that humbles himself conquers him before whom he
kneels. The meek one himself becomes the victor.

Esau, the man of the sword, the experienced warrior,
skilled in arms, rushes forward with four hundred con-
federates at his back, who merely await his signal to
draw their blades, and speed their arrows. A helpless
shepherd approaches, followed by trembling women and
children. The shepherd, however, bows himself to the
earth seven times, and the weapons fall to the ground;
a brother lies locked in a brother's tender embrace.
The weak shepherd was the conqueror; the mighty
Esau, the vanquished one. Seven obeisances had sent
four hundred and one swords back into their sheaths.

A heavy burden fell from the heart of Jacob; mountains of oppressive care were removed from the spirits of his beloved ones. The blackness of night was changed into laughing sunlight. On the part of Esau, the viper of anger, the serpent of hatred, the hyena of revenge, which had gnawed incessantly at his heart, and torn his very entrails, were suddenly transformed into dove-like tenderness and the patience of a lamb. He had set out on this expedition with murderous intent, and he retraced his steps, a kind and loving brother. What magical power had wrought this wonderful and rapid change? What is the name of the talisman? Humility! This is the magic spell!

It is eighty years since our own Benjamin Franklin recommended this talisman to youth as a means to success. It is four thousand years since Jacob tested its power.

I well know that this Israelitish method of stooping in order to avoid a blow is entirely out of harmony with Hellenic or Teutonic ideas. Greeks, Romans and Teutons alike look with contempt upon the bowed head of humility. To bow seven times is a sevenfold manifestation of cowardice and servility. According to their conception of honor, Jacob and his followers should have met violence with violence. Had he fallen in the encounter, and had his whole family perished from the earth, they would have erected a monument to his memory, their poets would have celebrated him in immortal songs. However, we are not teaching the morality of the Romans, the Greeks and the Germans, but Biblical, Israelitish ethics, which calls to us, "Hide thyself for but a little moment, until the indignation be passed away!" What would have become of Israel, if, instead of proving itself buoyant like the ship, it had stood up proud and unbending like the mighty, heaven-aspiring cedar! Long ere this it would have been uprooted and dashed out of existence.

His submissiveness in the presence of superior strength has won for the Israelite the reproach of cowardice. If the Israelite be, indeed, an enemy to strife and to fighting with deadly weapons, it is as much from dread of inflicting death as from fear of being killed.

Our text reads, "Jacob was greatly afraid, and he felt distressed." Our sages interpret this verse as meaning: "He was greatly afraid for his own life and the lives of his beloved ones, and he felt distressed that he might be put under the necessity of inflicting death on others."

Submission, it is true, is a virtue to be practised only within narrow bounds. Humility and compliance may be low and mean qualities, unworthy of a human being. The narrow limits within which submission is praiseworthy are well defined in Jacob's story. First of all, Jacob humbled himself before his older brother, and the re-awaking of brotherly love was the reward of his deference. Secondly, Jacob was conscious of the wrong that he had done his brother.

Well may one bow seven times over, and even more, if thereby a wrong can be expiated, the memory of an act of injustice be blotted out!

It was not alone the humility of bowing low that conciliated the wrathful brother, but the soft word, the mild speech, the brotherly tone as well.

I know of no limits that ought to be drawn to the use of gentle words. Be ever mild in the form of your

speech, even though decided in your purpose. Always
be friendly. Do not cultivate glibness of tongue, but
be ever ready with a kind word. I well know, one cannot always be agreeable; one cannot answer amiably at
all times, but this is true only because in this, as in all
other respects, we are imperfect. He that strives after
perfection in all things will in this direction, too, try to
do his utmost.

There is no happiness on earth—indeed, our sages
say there is no God—where there is no kindliness, and
as a result, not good cheer. What good does it do you,
you husband, if you heap up treasures, and lay them at
the feet of your spouse? What avails it that you are a
paragon of virtue; that your spirit can soar far above
our common life; that you are a marvel of deep learning, if, having all this, you lack friendliness of speech?
Is your wife a happy woman? Are you happy? And
of what avail, oh wife! is your beauty, your charm,
your wit; what matters it that you are the very personification of fidelity and self-sacrifice; that your house
welcomes the visitor by the cleanliness, the order and
the good taste there manifest? You do not rest from
morning till night. You are a pattern woman and
mother, but if you are lacking in that one virtue—
kindliness—what matters all this to yourself and to
others? If your speech is sharp and cutting; if you
cannot bow down even seven times, if necessary; that is,
if you cannot accommodate yourself to people as they
are and to existing circumstances? And, you children,
it matters not that you feed and clothe your aged parents
with the best that can be procured; that you provide
abundantly for their comfort, if you are unwilling to

bow before them in childlike reverence, if your lips
know not the speech of kindness.

Gifts, combat and prayer bring forth prosperity, dominion and piety, but friendliness makes happiness.
The key to one's own happiness and that of others is not
of gold or iron. A cheerful spirit and a pleasant word
will open the kingdom of bliss.

TOLERANCE.

"Then said Jacob unto his household, and to all that were with him,
Put away the strange gods that are among you, and cleanse yourselves, and change your garments.

"And let us arise, and go up to Bethel ; and I will make there an altar
unto the God who answered me on the day of my distress, and was
with me on the way which I went.

"And they gave unto Jacob all the strange gods which were in their
hands, and the ear-rings which were in their ears ; and Jacob hid
them under the oak which was near Shechem."—GEN. XXXV : 2-5

What may be considered the distinguishing mark of a
man of true culture? What characterizes the nation
that has progressed farthest on the paths of civilization?
The answer to these questions may, we think, be summed
up in one word—tolerance !

If we allow the various nations of our time to pass in
review before our mental vision, we shall find that those
nations possess true culture whose social relations and
legislative codes breathe a spirit of tolerance ; and the
degree of tolerance characterizing a community may
serve as a standard of its grade of culture. So, too, in
the world's history. Page after page reveals the fact
that, with the dawn of culture, the first traces of toleration may be discovered ; gradually tolerance spreads
farther and farther, borne on its way by the progress of
civilization, and, in turn, aiding the latter in its development.

History has also a story of retrogression in culture to

relate, and the first sign of each retrograde movement is
the spread of intolerance.

Let us next turn our attention to individuals.

We must premise that by a person of culture, we, of
course, do not mean one dressed in the height of fashion,
whose house is furnished as fashion demands, and whose
demeanor accords exactly with the rules in vogue in the
society of the day. Neither does the term convey the
idea of a man crammed with deep learning or polite literature. Whenever you find a man strict towards himself, true to his own convictions, but at the same time
tolerant of others, then be assured that you are dealing
with a person of culture, whether the individual belong
to the upper or the lower stratum of society; whether he
appear in a smock frock or wear threadbare clothing, it
matters not, that person is cultured, even though ignorant of Latin and Greek.

Toleration and intolerance do not, as is commonly
held, manifest themselves only in the field of religion, so
that if religion did not exist, these conceptions would
also be unknown; they assert themselves in social life
generally, in whatever relations human beings may
associate with one another. If you can quietly sit
by, and listen while some one gives expression to an
opinion, offensive to you, and according to your way of
thinking, utterly false; or, if you can hear a question discussed from one point of view, while you would treat of
an entirely different phase, and you do not obtrude a
correction upon your opponent, then you are tolerant.
If you can allow every one to pursue his own path, follow out his own views and inclinations—if you be a
husband, permit your wife to carry out her own ideas in

the management of the household; if you be a master, suffer your workman that does his duty faithfully to work according to his own method, and not lay down arbitrary rules for him to follow—then you are tolerant, and you bear the stamp of true culture.

Intolerance is especially decried in the form which it takes in religious life; there its appearance is like that of a roaring lion, a loathsome, hissing serpent, a hyena from whose pollution not even graves are safe. But it is in the family circle, in the relations of every-day life that this beast is nourished and fostered, without the least suspicion that many of the evils attending our career may be traced to the same intolerance that has won for itself such ill fame in the domain of religion.

It is frequently said that heathendom knew not the curse of intolerance, that the scourge was brought upon mankind by Judaism in the first place, and that Christianity intensified its virulence and enlarged its dominion. This is false, first of all, because toleration and intolerance, as we observed before, are not confined to religion alone, but manifest themselves as phases of character throughout life. The observation is, moreover, intrinsically untrue. Pharaoh believed that the Israelites could serve their God in Egypt, and Moses replied to him, "Would not the Egyptians stone us, if we sacrificed a lamb?" It seems, then, that as early as the days of Egyptian supremacy, men were stoned in honor of God. We may remember, in this connection, how Daniel, Hananiah and their companions were threatened with death; Kambyses, with his own hand, put to death the adored Apis of Egypt, and not content with that deed, he ordered a massacre among the Egyptians, who had been unutterably shocked by the enormity of the outrage committed.

Our Chanukah festival annually reminds us of the religious persecutions of the Israelites under Antiochus. Both before and after the destruction of the Temple, the Jews underwent much suffering, because they would not consent to give divine adoration to the Roman Emperors. Socrates was sentenced to drain the cup of poison, because he was accused of contempt of the gods, of leading astray the youths under his control, i. e., of teaching them to despise the gods.

It is true, nevertheless, that the instances of intolerance in heathen history are few in proportion to the large number of heathen on earth, and the length of time during which paganism held sway. This apparent tolerance may be traced to the fact that the various religious beliefs of the heathen did not clash with one another. Many gods were worshipped, but nothing definite was known concerning their number, and hence a few more or less made no vital difference. New gods were discovered, as we discover new planets. A stranger, finding other gods than those worshipped in his home, was in nowise troubled by this fact; he added the new gods to the old ones, or recognized in the former deities already familiar to him. A Roman coming to Greece found Jupiter in Zeus, in Germany he discovered him in Wodan, in Egypt in Osiris, and in Phœnicia in Baal, and in like manner, he found the counterparts of the other gods and goddesses known to him, with only the names changed. In Athens, a special altar was erected to the unknown gods, so that no insult might be offered to a god of whose existence the Athenians were unaware.

Such was not the case in Israel, and, therefore, our faith was looked upon as the source of intolerance. There is only *one* God, and he is better and more powerful than all your gods put together, and, at the same time, invisible! With this assertion, Israel cast down the gauntlet to the entire heathen world. No matter in what place the Israelite found the temple doors standing open for him, he could discover no god, worthy of his adoration; even the sun was nothing to him in comparison with his God. He allowed no god to be likened to his God, and would not yield an inch of his ground in matters concerning the Deity: " Your gods are nothing at all, our God alone is God! Your divine law is folly, ours alone is the law of wisdom. Your morality is an abomination, ours alone is pure and holy. Call our God neither Jupiter, nor Zeus, nor Wodan, nor Osiris, nor Ormuzd, nor Trinity, neither speak of him as Ideal, Nature, Reason. Our God is *God*, and neither definition nor comparison can encompass his greatness."

It is true, this sounds like intolerance; and this intolerance has, for thousands of years, incited all the nations of the earth to enmity towards us. This intolerance has made bloody work for the hangman and the torturers, the princes and the rabble of all times. But we cannot act otherwise. This intolerance, which refuses to have any comparison made between the belief of Israel and other beliefs, has never done any one an injury.[*] Israel, alone, has suffered thereby.

Turning to our text, we read that Jacob demanded of his followers, all the idols that they had with them, and " he buried them under the oak near Schechem."

---

[*] King John Hyrcanus' treatment of the Idumæans excepted.

For nearly twenty years before this event, Jacob had allowed the practice of idolatry in his family. Before her flight, Rachel had taken possession of her father's household gods. These images had therefore been worshipped by her as long as she had been at home. And Jacob had borne with this idolatry up to that time. He had probably thought, "Better a pious heathen from conviction than an unimpassioned believer in God, holding to the faith under coercion." This is an example of true tolerance.

Later, however, when he journeyed to Bethel to erect the long-promised altar to the service of the Most High, he would endure no discord, no mixture of idolatry and the worship of the one God. Here, again, we have intolerance, but intolerance proper to the circumstances. When standing upon ground holy to us, we dare not, only to please others, mingle the sacred and the profane.

In last week's portion of the Torah, we read how Laban swore to Jacob, "The *gods* of Abraham and the gods of Nachor shall judge between us." Here we have an instance of heathen intolerance which accepts all manner of gods. Jacob, however, would not lend himself to this form of tolerance. Jacob swore not by the gods of Nachor; he swore by the God of his father. That is intolerance, resting upon strong, personal conviction.

Be intolerant! Remain true to your belief in that which your conviction assures you to be divine, true, pure, holy and noble. Stand firm! Be not seduced by promises of earthly gain. Be not affrighted by any harm that may come to you; do not let ridicule move you from your position. If they call to you: "Come, be not so stubborn. Give us a finger, if you must refuse your whole hand! Come to us! We shall be able to agree. Give way somewhat yourself, we too will do the utmost in our power to meet you. See, the difference between us is not great. We are willing to say, 'the gods of Abraham;' surely, you may then say, 'the gods of Nachor.' Be tolerant!"

No! Be intolerant! Between Judaism and philosophical Hellenism, as between Judaism and Christianity weakened to Unitarianism and Universalism, there yawns a deep chasm. We believe only in *one* God, a Divine Providence, ruling the world, in whose sight all men are equal. We cannot add anything to this belief, as, for instance, ascribing divine qualities to a human being, nor can we give up any part of it, as, for instance, endowing our God with human accidents.

In regard to the beliefs and the actions of others, however, be tolerant. Honor their temples and lecture halls, their priests and teachers, their congregations and audiences, even though in principle and practice they clash with your convictions. Throughout life, in narrower as in wider spheres, allow every one to reach his goal in his own way, without offering officious advice as to better methods of attaining his end.

Universal "enlightenment" is not the climax of happiness to which mankind may hope to attain in the course of time. Equalization of mankind, whether on a high or a low plane, is a dangerous principle. This principle guides a gigantic northern power which makes great exertions towards bringing about uniformity of belief. The accursed work of the Inquisition was inspired by this idea, and such is the motive of the advo-

cates of "enlightenment," who aim to lead the world on
to enlightenment and—unbelief, and grow impatient
when they find that they cannot accomplish their end.
No; never will all mankind think alike! The Fiji
Islander and the scholar in a Berlin lecture hall will
never occupy the same point of view. The world is
meant to present a varied, not a uniform aspect. Universal toleration is the hopeful dream of mankind—an
ideal, not incapable of realization.

But do we not exclaim daily with the prophets, " On
that day, the Lord will be One, and his name One?"
We, who are here assembled in this house of worship,
we all believe in one God. For us, God is even now
" One and his name One," and yet how widely we differ
in our conceptions of the divine and in our line of conduct. Acts, whose performance seems a sacred duty to
one, are less than trivial in the eyes of another. Nevertheless, we live together in friendship and amity. The
wide divergence of our paths in the "light of the Lord "
does not disturb our peace. That such a relation may
exist among all men is the hope that we cherish for
the great day of our prayer; not one shepherd and one
flock, but many flocks and many shepherds, and all the
shepherds at peace with one another, serving one Master. We possess a sufficient assurance of progress, when
we see believers of widely varying faiths, as well as
those differing within the confines of a single belief,
dwelling side by side in peace, enjoying like privileges;
when pope, mufti, grand lama, rabbi and philosopher
do not curse and defame one another, but rather dispose
their followers to peace, so that all sects may dwell
together in unity and concord.

Those were evil days, when the word tolerance was unknown in the domain of religion, when tolerance was not a virtue but rather a crime. So, the best time is to come, when the word toleration will again·disappear.

The word *tolerance* is of Latin origin, and signifies "bearing." A man consents to *bear* an injustice meekly rather than become involved in strife and contention. The German speaks of *Duldung*, forbearance, patience. We speak of bearing with misconduct. Parents are patient with their children's misbehavior; teachers, with pupils of limited capacity. Such was, and is, the general conception of tolerance. The individual looks down upon those holding a different opinion with grim forbearance, or smiles pityingly at the childlike simplicity of the people; he bears with it, suffers it. For the present, let us rest content with this conception. It is the medicine that will cure the dreadful disease of intolerance.

Sound morality, however, knows not tolerance, not intolerance. It recognizes only the natural right of man to exercise freedom of thought, and especially to determine his relation to heaven, according to his own judgment and conviction. Man must even be allowed the right to fall into error. There is no need to practise forbearance or *sufferance*, because one man is orthodox in his faith, another is a reformer, and the views of a third differ from both of them; because this man is a Jew, that one a Christian, and the third a heathen. Each one has a right to be what he is. Not toleration, not forbearance, but one right for all!

One's conviction naturally becomes ever more fixed in nursing fanatic zeal towards other beliefs; while in

looking indulgently upon the beliefs of others, it is difficult not to become careless of one's own belief, not to
allow respect for the convictions of others to make one
falter in one's own faith.

We Israelites find it a difficult task to preserve a
pious, Jewish faith, while practising universal toleration.

Let us ever remember Jacob, who bore with idolatry
for twenty years, but removed the idols away from him
upon erecting an altar to the one God, and founding an
independent household. He allowed the heathen to
swear by all the gods. He, however, swore by the God
whom his father feared. Let us say with Joshua, in his
farewell speech, " Choose for yourselves this day, whom
ye will serve; . . . . but as for me and my house,
we will serve the Lord."

As we thank thee, O God, for the sun, which brightens
the day, for its light and heat, so we thank thee for the
sun of reason, which gives promise to mankind of a
beautiful day—a day of peace and concord, when upon
the sacred soil of thy adoration, neither blood nor tear
will flow, no violence and no hate be manifested, neither
cruelty nor bitterness be known.

Bless our country, the shining example of toleration
to all the other nations of the earth! Bless the fathers
and mothers, who encourage pure faith in thee in their
family circles, and who implant it in the tender hearts
of their offspring! Bless the teachers in the pulpits
and in the schools, who teach thy law and urge the
people to continued fidelity to it, and who, at the same
time, proclaim peace—peace to him that is near and to
him that is far, truth and peace! Oh, thou, God of truth
and peace!

BELATED EDUCATION.

GEN. XXXVII.

For thousands of years men dwelt by the shores of mighty rivers, without knowing the fountain-head, whence the water issued in such volumes, ignorant of the mountain, whose springs fed the sources of the streams. Of the origin of many of these streams we are ignorant even to-day. Even more emphatically is this true of the springs of human actions, the influence at work in the lives of mighty nations. Great events pour their streams into the ocean of history. Individuals and millions are raised on high on these waves of the world's history, and again are sunk beneath its billows. But we know not the cause of these phenomena, reason fails to find their origin, which is frequently quite insignificant. Throughout thousands of years, Israel, like the gulf stream in the vast waters of the ocean, has preserved its individuality in the complex history of the world. When Israel poured forth from Egypt, it was a considerable stream. With the sojourn among the Egyptians and the exodus following thereupon, Israel's story ceases to be the record of a series of family events and develops into national history, and, thereafter, plays a part in the history of the world. Where must we seek the fountain-head of this nation? We do not mean the stock from which it sprang. For that we are referred to Abraham. It is the elementary, moving force of this wonderful national story that we seek. We have read of it to-day, and have found it condensed into the words that form the heading of the chapter. "These are the generations of Jacob," this the issue of Jacob, namely, of Jacob's discipline of Joseph, a training, it must be admitted, long delayed. Jacob's eyes were not opened to the true condition of Joseph's spiritual life until the latter's seventeenth year, and then we read " his father rebuked him." But it was too late. Joseph grew up, we are told, with the sons of the maid-servants. His mother was dead. There remained, in his home, his father, his mother's sister, adult brothers, with their wives and two other wives of his father, but all these together could not, in his education and in their care of him, be a true mother to the boy. Had Rachel, his mother, been alive, it would probably not have been necessary for his father to rebuke his son in his seventeenth year. There would have been no enmity between Rachel's son and the sons of her sisters, and all the trouble springing out of this hatred, which finally ended in the removal into Egypt, might have been avoided. His father allowed the motherless child to grow up in its own way among the children of the maid-servants, and failed completely to observe the growing discord between Joseph and his brothers until too late for remedy. "Joseph brought evil reports of them unto his father." Jacob listened without rebuke to the *boy* Joseph's criticism and complaint of his brothers, who were *men* in years. Jacob's own early experiences ought to have impressed upon him the full significance of fraternal strife and the consequences of family dissen-

sions. In his intercourse with Esau and Laban, he
ought to have learnt this lesson well. But he did not
see that the same weed was springing up in rank luxu-
riance in his own house. When he finally noticed it,
it was too late. The rebuke was in vain. "Israel loved
Joseph more than all his children—and he made him a
silken garment." (פסים is thus rendered in the Midrash.)

It is true, we cannot control the inclinations of our
hearts ; we have no power to decide whom we shall love,
and how much affection we shall bestow. It was unfortunate that Jacob loved Joseph more than his other
children, but he was not responsible for this feeling.
Duty and common-sense, however, should have warned
him not to slight his less-beloved children, nor to allow
them to feel that he held them in less regard than he had
for Joseph. He acted like many other fathers, heedless
of the dictates of reason, guided by the heart alone.
Jacob's love for Joseph did not lead him to watch over
his child more carefully, and to discipline him for his
own good ; he left him to the tender mercies of Bilhah
and Zilpah. On the other hand, he made his son a
silken garment. Joseph's brothers, clothed like shepherds, tended their flocks, while his father's favorite
went about in lordly clothing. It is scarcely a matter of
astonishment that dim visions of authority over his
brethren should have loomed up in Joseph's mind. We
cannot accuse him of having harbored clearly defined
thoughts on the subject. The idea of the rulership of
one brother over another was not so very fanciful.
Such had ever been the case in his family. Isaac was
preferred to Ishmael, Jacob was set above Esau in
receiving the paternal blessing. The bitter feelings

aroused by Joseph's narrative of his dream, which could so easily be interpreted as foretelling the future authority of Joseph over his brethren, were therefore not produced by over-sensitiveness. His brothers broke out into the cry, "Shalt thou indeed reign over us? Or shalt thou indeed have dominion over us?" Even the father believed, though he kept the belief locked in his own heart, that the dream might be realized. "His father noted the matter." Finally, however, Jacob recognized the danger in such visions to the general peace of the family and to that of the dreamer, in particular. Thereupon, his father spoke to Joseph, not clothing his *words* in fine silk, for he rebuked him harshly. Here, again, we have a parallel to the course of so many fathers among us, who have not the heart to say a stern word to the *boy*, the mere *child*, but are ready, in their anger and excitement, to upbraid the *youth* in the harshest terms. But the rebuke came too late. Through the belated education of Joseph, the house of Jacob lost its firm balance, and thereupon rushed helpless upon its fate, through the pleasant days when the family had been saved from famine, into the ensuing darkness of slavery. Joseph's individual destiny, however, led him through the depths of slavery and imprisonment to rulership over Egypt.

A father neglected his motherless child, allowing it to follow its own inclination, instead of leading it with tender care ; he attended to the education of his son only when the latter had become a youth. This it was that decided the destiny of a nation for centuries to come. " This is the issue of Jacob, Joseph being seventeen years old," etc.

When Jacob's last hour came, and he had gathered his sons about his death-bed, he spoke harshly to the three eldest of them. Our sages say : "Jacob addressed Reuben in these words, 'My son, thou mayest ask, Why I did not ere this address these words to thee? Because I feared that thou mightest turn the reproach back upon me.'" Our sages would not merit the title bestowed upon them, did they give us this narrative as of an actual occurrence. In this speech, they wish to teach us that fathers must not rebuke their children when they are grown, just though such reprimand may be. It comes too late, and can effect nothing but bitterness of feeling. It is easy to recognize the fault of beginning an education too late in life. Those that commit this error, finally, though it may be too late, come to the conclusion that their efforts were too long delayed. The fault of waiting too long to cease from discipline is less commonly recognized. The influence of the parental will upon the will of the child must make itself felt but lightly at first, and gradually increase in its influence. So, too, the removal of this discipline must be a gradual process, until at its completion, the son and daughter are left completely at liberty. Many parents embitter their own lives as well as the lives of their children by neglecting this principle; having once seized the reins of government, they know not when to lay them down. Everything on earth has its time of growth, of blossom, and finally of ripe fruitage. The same is true of education. A ship leaves the harbor. The steersman places himself beside the helm, surely not with the intention of steering the ship about upon the ocean aimlessly, but in order to guide it into another haven. The helmsman then leaves his post; the cargo, if the ship carry any, is unloaded. If it bear no cargo, but comes to shore with empty hold, the rudder may be turned again and again; it is of no practical use.

Our weekly portion in the Torah furnishes us with an example of the uselessness of belated education, and shows us, at the same time, how apparently trivial incidents in family life may decide the fate of future generations. The consequences of events that occurred in Jacob's tent fills the richest, the most interesting pages of history for thousands of years ·after that time. Through the inverted lens of time, we see, like a drop on the edge of a cliff, this nomad family of the dim past in the midst of family dissensions, deplorably frequent at all times. As the drop helps to feed the spring which swells into the brook, into the stream, and finally into the mighty river, so family events become the source of an historical stream of mighty import.

It is a mistake for man to hold too high an opinion of himself, and think too meanly of others. This is the characteristic commonly called pride. On the other hand, it is unfortunate, if a man holds himself of too little consequence; that is, in his relation to mankind as a whole. It is unfortunate if a father thinks: "My attention to the education of my children or my neglect of them concerns only myself and my family. Of what consequence is my petty existence, are my actions within my own walls, to the world at large?" In this respect, one can scarcely hold too high an opinion of one's self. A man *dies* for himself alone; he *lives* for the world. His achievements and his omissions do not affect the present alone, nor do they pass away with it, but they continue to influence the fate of others, first of his immediate descendants, and then, of more distant posterity. His good work in the education of his children is a benefit to the world, his neglect of discipline an injury.

Finally, the fact must not remain unnoticed that Joseph, in spite of all, after suffering keenly for his own petty faults and for the doting love of his father, grew up to be one of the most noble-minded of men. His early home had been the abode of piety and the fear of the Lord, and in spite of all the faults of his training, this could not but produce good results. The impressions of the parental home are not lost. For a time, they may appear forgotten; they may lose some of their freshness in our intercourse with men; amid youthful frivolities, their memory may grow dim; the conceit of youth may not hold them at their true value; but they will rise to the surface again, as oil floats ever upward, and finally gains the surface of the water. A child that has spent the first seventeen years of its life in a house permeated with an upright and god-fearing spirit may, indeed, if left to its own devices, go astray; may sink from one folly into another, but it will surely find the path of righteousness again. It will not be morally ruined. Whether discipline be early or late, the spirit of home will be the deciding influence. They are, indeed, favored whose youth has been passed in a god-fearing home; they will, at the end, live an honor to God.

THE IMPORTANCE OF LITTLE THINGS.

"No human being, no hour in life, no moral action is without significance."

The world's history, and, as part of it, the fate of the individual, lie before us, dark and impenetrable as the mighty ocean. The sea rolls majestically before our eyes, terrifying us with its mighty waves and billows, its restless tossing and raging. And yet, what our eye can take in is merely a drop in comparison with the vast stretch of waters, and even this drop covers, as with a cloak, the secrets of the awful deep.

We raise our eyes to the firmament; our vision scans immeasurable distances. When the eye is tired out with gazing, not only the eye of the average man, but also the well-protected organ of the most skilful astronomer and the boldest thinker—it drops, and man must acknowledge to himself: "My vision can penetrate only the least part of that which is on high; I can comprehend only the smallest section of what I have seen, and that which my understanding can master—what does it signify in the plan of the Architect of the universe?" The vast design is entirely concealed from us. So with our insight into the mysteriously woven fate of mankind and of the individual.

The number of events chronicled by history, compared with the vast sum of past occurrences, is as the

178

limited horizon of man in comparison with the whole universe. Only an insignificant number of events is observed at all; the majority receives scarcely any notice, and is forgotten, and that which is observed, noted, and made a part of history is not understood in its relation to the whole. As in the world's history, so also in the life-history of every individual. If a man, at the age of seventy, were to take an inventory of his memory, noting all the clear recollections of his past life—how soon would his task be finished! How insignificant would be the sum thus obtained! Of an inconsiderable number of his experiences as compared with the sum total, has he taken cognizance; of this number, only the smallest portion has been impressed upon him; most of these impressions he has forgotten, and of that which finally remains fastened in his memory, he fails to understand the purpose, and what its relation to the whole. It is true, he can tell what he considered pleasant and what unpleasant events, what sad days and what joyful ones, but it may be that the unpleasant experiences were a source of blessing to him, while the pleasant ones were harmful in their consequences.

In the life of Joseph and his family, the Scriptures show how marvellously a man's life, contrary to his own actions and desires, he, indeed, unconscious thereof, may shape itself in a given way. The story further illustrates how the most trivial action, even of an insignificant man in an obscure corner of the earth, may continue to affect the destinies of others in the most distant future, unto the latest generations.

Who can say that he is not a Joseph in his own way? Or that each one of his actions does not play a part in

the lives of others ; that its influence is not felt in ever-
widening circles ? In the life of Joseph, the Scriptures
unveil for us the life of a single man. How many pass
through life without solving the riddle of their own fate,
and of their influence upon the lot of other men ?

No human existence is without significance, no hour
in life is unimportant, no moral action is a matter of
indifference. " There is nothing without its appropriate
place, no man without his opportunity." Originally,
Joseph was an unimportant personage for the world at
large, a mere shepherd lad, running about with his
brothers in the fields of Mesopotamia. Despite his
humble beginnings, however, he, in the end, not only
shaped the destinies of the house of Israel, but also
impressed his personality upon the development of distant, mighty Egypt. Truly, the life of every individual
is of significance in the plan of the universe. Do not
estimate any man as of too little worth to be either useful
or harmful to thee. It is true, not every stone the builders reject becomes the chief corner-stone, but for each
one the Creator has provided a place in the great world-
structure. The smallest may be a stumbling-block
placed in thy path for weal or for woe. Do not force
thyself upon the great ones of the earth, nor be too
anxious about their favor or displeasure, as if they,
alone, could bring blessing or curse upon thee. Had it
not been for Pharaoh's dreams, the chief butler, powerful though he was, would have allowed Joseph, forgotten of all, to perish in prison. As far as our fate is
governed by outward circumstances, it follows its own
rules, to which both great and small must submit.

Neither underestimate thine own value, thinking,

"Nothing of all this concerns me. I am too insignificant; I can lend no aid in the world's work." In this sense, no creature on God's earth is insignificant, or exists for itself alone. To be of use in the world, one need be no philosopher, rich in wisdom, nor hold sacks of gold in his grasp, nor boast an arm of iron. Man, thou art an instrument in the hand of Providence! Look to it that when thy hour of usefulness comes, thy edge be not dulled and rusty.

Neither is any moral action a matter of indifference. Thy action, thy speech, thy omissions, and thy silence are either good or not good, and the actions that seem a matter of indifference—why, this very thinking that an action can be indifferent is one of the things that are *not* good. It is wrong to act thoughtlessly. To relate a dream, or to remark in a conversation that a certain person has done a certain thing, is considered a perfectly harmless proceeding. Thus Joseph must have thought about his own childish prattle. Jacob probably also considered it morally indifferent, whether his son was clad in silk or in linen. And yet how important were these things in deciding the fate of a large family and of an entire kingdom! No word falls upon barren soil; no action is lost in the sands of time. From it may spring a tree of life, or through you, and others like you, it may bring forth thorns and thistles.

Our text furthermore teaches us that we lack the insight to determine which of our experiences are truly good, and which are bad. We can discriminate only between pleasant and unpleasant experiences, for what is agreeable to us and what is good for us are not always united, nor is the disagreeable in every case evil. How often a few days of joy, of pleasure, are followed by many days of sadness! Frequently, after gratification comes deep regret, serene happiness follows close upon bitter affliction, and after pain may come blessing. Joseph's brothers thought that, by selling him, they had rid themselves forever of the troublesome boy. This was *pleasant*, but not *good* for them. How frequently must they have felt bitter remorse for the unkind deed! Their hearts must have been pierced as with knives, when they saw their father sinking under the burden of his grief. Twenty-two years after the deed, we hear them, in their distress, breaking out into lamentations, " Truly, we are guilty concerning our brother, in that we saw the anguish of his soul, when he besought us, and we would not hear; therefore is this distress come upon us."

So fared it with the brothers. To Joseph, on the other hand, the treatment that he received at his brothers' hands was anything but agreeable ; but it was merely unpleasant, it was not evil. His way into the light lay through dark night. In order to rule, he had first to be a slave. The bottom of the pit was for him the first step of the throne. His suffering was the salvation of his family. Whatever is ordained by God, whatever is ordered as our lot, may be unpleasant, bitter, deeply painful, but it is never evil. Nothing *evil* can proceed from the hand of God. Let us, then, not be too extravagant in our delight in a pleasant experience, nor entirely cast down by grief when trouble comes upon us ; we know not the end for which Providence has sent the joy or the trial. Neither be too indignant against him that has wounded thee by word or deed, and has injured thy worldly prosperity. It may be that, though seeking to do thee harm, he has in reality benefited thee. Hold firmly to the belief: God directs everything for the best. No matter what man, in envy, in anger, in hatred, or in folly, plots against man, he can do no harm, if such be not God's will. Here and there a man is allowed to see the problem of his existence solved in his lifetime, and then he may exclaim with Joseph, "Ye thought evil against me, God meant it unto good." In most cases, however, we never receive any light on the subject, but grow old, remembering in bitterness the injuries that our fellow-men have done us. But it is our firm belief that there, where all errors vanish; where the spirit is entirely freed from earthly dross; where truth shines forth in brightness—there the ways of Providence will become clear; there shall we recognize that the happiness and the salvation of mankind are not promoted by the good, the wise and the upright alone, but that all men assist in the work—the good because such is their desire, and the foolish and the malicious, because they must.

"DEATH AND LIFE ARE IN THE POWER OF THE TONGUE."

(PROVERBS, XVIII : 21.)

GEN. XLI.

The turning-points in Joseph's life form an excellent illustration of the wise saying, "Death and life are in the power of the tongue."

Joseph's seventeenth year and his thirtieth may be looked upon as critical points in his career. In his seventeenth year, he was on his way to the misery of slavery and captivity, his thirtieth finds him scaling the summit of earthly honors. In each case, the weak tongue was instrumental in bringing about the crisis.

In ascribing most important results to the use of the tongue, Solomon does not refer to words that are carefully weighed and considered before they are spoken; for in that case, the tongue is merely the irresponsible instrument of the mind. The text refers to the thoughtless use of the tongue, which is like the undirected play of a child. Like a child, it causes much trouble, and again wins all hearts by its artless simplicity.

In another one of his sayings, Solomon explains the meaning of this dictum. He speaks of a prattler, a babbler, who is like a careless marksman playing with arrows; yet, while working havoc and destruction, he declares that he means no harm.

In the life of Joseph, we find an illustration of this

184

proverb. Joseph meditated no evil against his brothers. It was no fault of his that his dreams were so displeasing. It was his misfortune thoughtlessly to babble of them without taking counsel with his heart or his understanding. He manifested like thoughtlessness in repeating his brothers' improper talk. He reported nothing but the truth. Children speak the truth; but they, too, tell it with the *tongue*, without discretion or consideration.

Turning to the change for the better in Joseph's fortunes, we again find his lot decided, not by the discretion but by the *thoughtlessness* of his speech.

One morning Joseph found the two high Egyptian officials, who shared his dungeon, much depressed in spirits. His good nature prompted him to ask the cause of their sadness. His *reason* did not urge him to put the question. Joseph was no physician, neither was he the friend of these men. It was his habit to exchange a friendly word with every one, and in this spirit, he put the sympathetic question, which really meant no more than our "How do you do?" Yet it was precisely this glib word of his tongue that became unto him the word of salvation. In vain did Joseph address the butler in well-chosen words, when the latter returned to fill his high position; in vain his explanation of the injustice under which he was suffering; in vain did he entreat his late fellow-prisoner to intercede with Pharaoh on his behalf. These words were inspired by his reason, yet they were of no avail, while the careless, forgotten "How do you do?" the trick of his tongue, saved his life. Two years after the words were spoken, the thoughtless courtesy of his lips sprouted into a tree of life for himself and his family.

"Death and life are in the power of the tongue, and they that love it will eat its fruit."

Joseph tasted these fruits, the bitter and the sweet alike.

From his story, we may draw the general inference that the heart is not always so unfriendly, nor the judgment so severe as the careless tongue would proclaim.

The kind-hearted and pious Joseph would have been the last man intentionally to wound his brothers and his parents, but his unguarded tongue irritated his brothers, and enkindled their wrath, and so brought misery upon his family and himself.

Do we not all know men like Joseph, kind of heart, but cutting of speech? A bad habit, lazy good nature, and the dangerous gift of wit, all seeking expression in conversation, are responsible for this sharpness of speech. The consciousness that no ill-will is harbored induces a careless use of stinging words.

A clear perception of this trouble may be useful. in teaching us two things. First of all, we ought not to weigh sharp words on too delicate and accurate a scale. We must not mistake the tongue for the entire man. A person may be a Joseph at heart and yet speak with the voice of Esau. Again, after having indulged in unguarded language, we may not comfort ourselves with the thought that our intentions are good. We scarcely comprehend our own hearts fully; how, then, can the world be expected to judge us according to our hearts? The opinion of the world is based upon our words.

From Joseph's life we may furthermore draw the lesson that any word of ours is liable to light upon inflammable material, which, catching fire, may work

havoc and destruction, though we had meant no harm.
In the brain of man, much thought ferments without developing into definite conclusions or practical results.
The masses wait only for a watchword to be given them,
to which they then adhere unquestioningly.

In one hour Joseph's brothers, swayed by the suggestions of successive speakers, changed their minds three
times. Their feelings were roused to enmity against
their brother, but the decision necessary for action was
wanting. "Let us kill him!" "Yes, he shall die!"
"We will cast him into the pit!" "Away with him to
the pit!" "We will sell him!" "Yes, let him be sold!"

Remember, therefore, your words spoken in the family, in the pulpit, in the halls of legislation, in society,
without thought of harm, may be harmful in their *consequences*.

Not death alone, also life lies in the power of the
tongue.

Many a slandered man wraps himself in the cloak
of his innocence, too proud to clear himself, although
before one word of explanation, evil opinion with all its
evil consequences would vanish. Others, again, lack the
courage to speak a good word at the right time, if that
word opposes the current of general opinion. Reuben
gives us an example of such cowardice. He would
gladly have returned Joseph uninjured to his father,
but he had not the courage to speak the word that would
have saved him. Too late he revealed his true feeling
in the matter—when he found the pit empty and Joseph
sold. His tongue had not uttered the right word boldly
at the right moment.

Have the courage to proclaim your opinion openly and

without disguise. Care not how high the waves of opposing opinion may run, if, by your courage, you may aid a good cause, prevent harm, or be helpful to innocence.

The Talmud makes Balaam, Job and Jethro take counsel together as to the fate of Israel. The one spoke in favor of its preservation, the other of its destruction. Job timidly held his peace. For this silence, it is said, he atoned by his well-known sufferings.

There are many such Jobs to-day, who, through timidity or through false modesty, are silent at times at which it would be proper for them to speak.

Finally, Joseph's story should teach us the worth of a tongue accustomed to friendly speech in intercourse with our fellow-men. Language is not meant to serve merely as a vehicle for conveying our ideas, but in our associations, it is to perform the office of oil between the parts of machinery that rub against each other. Language does not offer us only the threshed grains of wheat, but straw and chaff as well; not the fruit of thought alone, but also beautiful, variegated leaves and blossoms. Language is a fully developed plant, not merely its fruit.

Were nothing to be spoken but the words necessary for human intercourse, life on earth would be very quiet. The world would be a vast cloister of Trappists. Easy, pleasant conversation, maintained by the expenditure of but a very small percentage of thought, forms part of the amenities of existence.

The question put by Joseph to his fellow-prisoners belongs to this class of speeches, the offspring of the tongue, not of the brain. The greatest wisdom, the most remarkable fluency of speech, could not have opened the prison doors for the innocent man. An empty, thoughtless phrase, a word of mere courtesy, led him from the dungeon to the throne.

Our sages, in recommending strongly the use of the most pleasing and the choicest expressions, refer to the passage in the Bible, which reads, "Of every clean beast . . . . and of beasts that are not clean." In this verse, in order to avoid the unæsthetic word טמאה, unclean, four words are used in paraphrase of this term. Let us, too, eschew all harsh expressions in our daily conversation.

One of our greatest teachers exultingly mentions, as the ripest evidence of his worldly wisdom, the fact that no one had ever anticipated him in greeting, not even a heathen or a child—not the meanest of mortals with whom he had come in contact in life.

How many of us gathered together in this house have brought clouds into our lives by a thoughtless word or through disregard of a friendly form of greeting! Others, again, may be living comfortably in the sunshine of prosperity through the aid of friendship, which all unconscious they have won by means of a helping hand.

We are apt to think that "life and death" must depend upon great and difficult exertions, earnest labor and deep thought, while in reality, a word frequently forms the delicate hinge upon which our fortunes turn.

We must cultivate not only the feelings of the heart and the powers of the mind. Let us also accustom the tongue to speak words of kindness, of gentleness, of courtesy—for "Death and life are in the power of the tongue."

HOME INFLUENCE.

" Joseph recognized his brothers, but they recognized not him."—GEN. XLII: 8.

Family life is like a light-house. The occupants see the ships leave the harbor, and follow them with their eyes, until the last sail is lost to sight below the horizon. In the darkness of night, the crew of many a vessel, far out on the waste of waters, peers eagerly into the darkness to catch a glimpse of the tower, one ray from whose lantern will inspire the men with renewed hope and strength. The watchers in the tower rest secure in their accustomed places, though wind and wave may beat about the house. They are safe and at rest. They know not of the fearful hearts of the sailors, whose eyes are strained anxiously towards the tower with its lamp of rescue.

So, when a member of the family takes leave of his home, there is sorrow on both sides; the one departing and those left at home are filled with sadness. But as days, weeks and years pass by, although the absent one be not forgotten, and though he be recalled to mind occasionally, yet he is no longer constantly in the thoughts of those still at home. Life at the homestead goes on in its usual way, even though there is one less in the family circle. As for the one that has left home, if the sun of fortune smiles upon him, and his ship of

190

life, laden with rich cargo, sails through calm seas, he, too, may, for a time, not think of the loved ones whom he has left behind, as the mariner does not look anxiously for the tower with its cheerful lamp, when the light of day is about him, and the weather is clear and bright. The son and daughter may, however, fall upon evil days while in a strange land; the dark night of despair may reign in their hearts; merciless fate may hem them in, leaving no way of escape. When such days come, the fearful heart seeks the paternal roof, the home of love and sympathy, of kindness and benignity, the home of happy, youthful days. Imagination overcomes the obstacles of land and sea, which may separate the child from home, and fancy conjures up a picture of the days spent under parental care. Home is the light-house which the child seeks with deep longing, when surrounded by the darkness of night, when driven by the fury of the storm. At home, on the other hand, the days pass quietly and monotonously in blissful ignorance of the misery of the absent ones, whose hearts, weighed down by trouble and distress, beat yearningly at the thought of home.·

How fervently, from the very depths of his soul, Joseph must have called upon his father on that dreadful day in the pit! The dear, sheltered home, now lost to him forever, must have seemed a veritable heaven. On his way to Egypt, in his career as a slave, later when wasting the best years of his life in prison, though innocent of any crime, how frequently, in blessed dreams, in thought, in desire, in reverie and imagination, he must have been transported to the home of his youth! Its memory ever remained fresh within him. Later, when

his fortunes changed for the better, when his first son was
born to him, he named the child Menasseh, which means
to forget, "For," said he, "God hath made me forget all
my toil and all my father's house." This very incident
shows, however, that he had not forgotten his "father's
house," for on that happiest of days, when giving his son
a name, he showed by the name that he remembered the
home of his youth. It was, therefore, natural that Joseph
should recognize his brothers. In spirit he had been at
home so frequently that his family had not become strange
to him. They, however, recognized him not. The explanation usually given for this circumstance is that
Joseph was almost a child when he left home, and when
his brothers saw him again, he had become a man. But
Benjamin was even younger than Joseph; Gad and
Asher were but little older; even Reuben, the oldest of
all, was only thirteen years older than Joseph, and nevertheless Joseph recognized them all. The high position
in which his brothers found him may, it is true, have
made recognition more difficult; but even this circumstance could not have obscured the memory of features
once well known to them. As observed before, the one
leaving home is easily forgotten, his memory fades away
quickly, while the recollection of the loved ones at home
is never effaced from the mind of the absent one. Joseph's memory must, furthermore, have been a bitter
reproach to his brothers, so that, far from cherishing
remembrance of him, they rather sought to keep him
away from their thoughts.

Oh, well beloved home! Happy family life! Thou
paradise of our childhood and youth! Who that has
tasted of thy joys can e'er forget thee! He, whom fate

has too soon driven from the paradise of youth, or who has early been deprived of its guardians, he knows not of how much of the happiness of life he has been robbed, as little as the Esquimau can understand how greatly his dull, gray sky would suffer by comparison with the heaven that smiles upon the land of the citron. Even though years have passed since we left the home of our youth, though it exist no longer, and we ourselves preside over homes as fathers and mothers, with children confided to our care—its memory is always dear to us, the recollection of the happy youth spent within its walls is ever a delight to the soul.

When Joseph was tempted by sin, he said, "How then can I do this great evil, and sin against God?" This was the influence of his recollections of home, a warning voice from the home penetrated by the fear of the Lord. Our sages say that the revered face of his father was thrust between Joseph and sin, and that thus he was kept from doing evil. What better guardian can a young man take with him into a strange land than the memory of the sanctuary of home, the memory of his father and mother? When a child in a distant land has taken the first step toward committing a sin, and his own self-respect no longer holds him in check, then there comes over him the remembrance of his parents. "What would they say, were they to know of my evil ways? How ashamed of me they would be! How they would grieve over my fall!"

Father and mother must, therefore, make the family life one of peace and harmony. Nothing does more to mar the happiness of children, nothing makes the remembrance of home more painful, than discord between

14

father and mother. Make your house a pleasant abode for your children according to the means at your disposal. Not plenty and show, but kindness and love everywhere perceptible make home a happy place; their presence is felt in the very air of the house, in the pleasant relations existing among the various members of the household.

If the recollection of home is to be an active, blessed memory, the father must not only have a house, the house must also have a father and a mother, who are a part of it, not ever on the streets, in company, attending to business, seeking pleasure and distraction of all kinds. "Home" means father and mother living in the midst of their children. The memory of a youth spent amid such associations does not die out in the hearts of the children, and, as with Joseph, an absence of twenty-two years cannot efface the recollection of home. Where there are such memories, brother will not say to brother, "I do not know you!" "Joseph recognized his brothers." Their likenesses, their remembrance had never departed from him. In spite of all the unkindness that had come between them, he felt himself at one with them.

A child's pleasantest recollections of home—pleasant and yet earnest enough to be deeply graven upon its mind—are, after all, those of the piety of the family life, especially of the solemn and joyous festivities, attendant upon Sabbaths and Holy Days. Even though the parents feel but coldly towards these celebrations, they have no right to deny the enjoyment thereof to their children. To compass this end, children may be denied some pleasures during the week, so that indulgence in

them on the Holy Day may make the season addition-
ally pleasant by aid of sensuous delights.

It is useless to speak to the men of these things. They
go on in their own way, heedless of words of advice. The
mothers, however, should consider it a sacred duty to
impress upon their children the true delight of the day
of rest properly celebrated, and of joyful festivals,
and weave the memory of such days into the child's
recollections of home. A son whose home was never
more to him than an eating house, whose father was
simply his provider, whose mother, the lady of the house,
will not be the one to exclaim in the hour of temptation,
"How then can I do this great evil, and sin against
God!" God forms no part of his childish recollections,
and the moral fear of such a father and such a mother
is not a sufficiently active memory to deter him from
sin.

As your children are dear to you, oh, parents! make
your home-life pleasant and attractive. Mingle innocent, sensuous delights with religious earnestness, so that
the remembrance of home may be a blessed memory to
your children throughout life!

EXISTENCE AND LIFE.

"And Jac-b said unto Pharaoh, The days of the years of my pilgrimage are one hundred and thirty years: few and evil have been the days of the years of my life, and I have not attained unto the days of the years of the life of my fathers in the days of their pilgrimage."
—GEN. XLVII: 9

Even in the time of Jacob, one hundred and thirty years were no short span of life; besides, Jacob was still alive, and might hope to attain as great an age as his forefathers, and perchance live longer than they. It is also difficult to see the force of Jacob's remark as a reply to Pharaoh's question.

Were a question like that of Pharaoh to Jacob to be put to one of us, we should find it easy to answer, easier than Jacob, because we should not have to glance over a series of one hundred and thirty birthday-anniversaries, in order to make a reply. Such, however, is the case only when the question is merely about the length of existence. If we are asked about the length of time during which we have enjoyed life; if we subtract from the days of the years of our pilgrimage, the time that we have spent in idle dreaming; that we have frivolously wasted; the time passed by us in trouble and distress, in dread and anxiety; those long periods, the wishes and hopes and labor of which ended in bitter disappointment; if we deduct all these items from the sum of the days of our lives, we should have to cast up the aggregate of the periods of our lives remaining, before giving the actual number of years that we have lived.

In this spirit, Jacob replied to Pharaoh: "You ask about the length of my existence? The years of my pilgrimage in various lands are one hundred and thirty; but how long have I really *lived?* To that question, I cannot give you an answer. The sum of my *life*, in the best sense of that word, is very small. In these one hundred and thirty years, I have *lived* but little. My father and my grandfather saw better days. They lived more than I in the years of their sojourn upon earth."

Even the bright spots in his existence, the short period in which he really *lived*, Jacob calls evil.

Men upon a low plane of culture, lacking, as they frequently are, in self-knowledge, lament bitterly, when days of distress come upon them. They possess a soothing balm, however, for their suffering—they throw off all responsibility, and rail against man and Providence as the cause of their trouble. When good times return, they enjoy them, and that without allowing self-accusation to mar their pleasure.

Upon a higher level of culture and—what is synonymous with it—of self-analysis and self-comprehension, men bear sorrow quietly and with resignation. They neither reproach Providence, nor attribute their misfortune to the malice of wicked men. They recognize that the root of most of the evils that plague us lies in ourselves. The consciousness of our own culpability hangs like a gray mist even over the bright spots of life.

A glance at the career of Jacob may show us the justification for his complaint about the short duration of his life, as well as for his acute consciousness of his own culpability.

Esau and Jacob were born at the same time. In temperament they were the very opposites of each other. "The children struggled together within" Rebekah. You who have brothers and sisters, kind, loving and self-sacrificing; you who dwell together in brotherly and sisterly love, throw no stone of condemnation upon Jacob, because of the unfraternal relations between him and his brother, because the deceit plotted by the one aroused murderous thoughts in the soul of the other. Remember, your brother is not an Esau! In counting up the days of his life, Jacob had to strike out the days spent in the home of his youth. Home becomes a veritable hell, when it is the theatre of deadly enmity between brothers.

Another cloud obscured the brightness of Jacob's early days. His parents were not in harmony in regard to the education of their children. In painting scenes and characters, the Bible does not lay on the colors heavily. In a few light and seemingly accidental strokes, a picture is placed before us. In this narrative, we read simply, "Isaac loved Esau, but Rebekah loved Jacob." This is the theme. It needs no genius, no rich fancy to compose the variations upon it, and every variation of the numberless ones possible will be sad. Every child whose youthful recollections are of parental strife and discord, may, like Jacob, strike out the years of his childhood from his book of life.

Jacob was *placed* in these unfortunate circumstances, he was in nowise responsible for them. The good man, however, always sees cause for self-reproach in the trials and tribulations of life.

No one can be asked to enter into a bond of friendship with a man like Esau, but it is a brother's duty to manifest a brotherly spirit even towards an Esau. No matter how difficult it may be to continue in fraternal relations with your brother, *you* dare not give him up. It is not for *you* to break loose from him. Others may criticise your brother harshly, and treat him as he deserves to be treated; your judgment is not free, your course toward him is marked out to you by the tie of blood between you.

Jacob's life after he left the paternal roof was a mere existence—an existence full of thorns. His work was heavy and momentous. After the toil of the day was over, he did not find rest and inspiration in the circle of his loved ones. No; dislike, mistrust and envy met him on the threshold of home; he encountered everywhere glances of reproach and contempt. This existence finally ended in secret flight.

A life passed among kinsfolk is an enviable lot. As every tree in the forest is sheltered from the elements by those about it, while the solitary tree in the open field is broken by the storm, so we are protected by loving relatives, ever ready with help and sympathy. But how sad the sight of kinsmen at enmity with one another! The wrath of the offended kinsman is more passionate than that of another, his stroke is surer, more fiercely burns the wound inflicted by him.

Whoever has, like Jacob, lived at variance with his relatives, or in his business relations, has daily had to bear with ill-will from those associated with him, may strike out those years of his existence, as a time during which he has not lived.

Again, it was not Jacob's fault that he had so shrewd

and slippery a man as Laban to deal with in his family and business relations. Nevertheless, he could not but reproach himself for finding no better way out of his difficulty than to meet cunning with cunning, and to employ deceit and flight in severing his connection with the brother of his mother and the father of his wives.

Accompanying Jacob upon his homeward journey, we see his constant fear of the meeting with his brother; the misfortune of his only daughter; the critical position in which he was placed by the uncontrollable passion of his sons, Simeon and Levi; the early death of his beloved Rachel; the discord among his children, which he saw breaking out again in his house like an hereditary evil, and finally the twenty-two years of grief for the supposed, horrible death of his favorite. We should far exceed the proper limit of time for our discourse, were we to discuss all these points so minutely as to show how they illustrate the text.

The general meaning of the text is, however, clear to us. It teaches us the difference between *existence*, "the days of the years of my pilgrimage," and *life*, "the days of the years of my life."

Our text contains Jacob's self-accusation. Man is permitted to judge himself according to a severe standard. Jacob scorned to acquit himself of wrong-doing by urging the untoward circumstances under which fate had placed him.

The Bible records the age of the departed Patriarch in these words, "the days of Jacob, *the years of his life*, were one hundred and forty-seven years."

In the sight of the all-wise Father, Jacob had *lived* throughout his whole existence. What seemed as lost to him, the bitter trials and the oppressions of his heart, were the birth-throes of his soul, his training for a higher destiny.

In the economy of nature, there is change of form, but never absolute loss; so, too, in the domain of the moral actions of mankind. That which is our greatest trial, if considered by itself, may, in the complete plan, prove a beneficent dispensation, though we frequently lack the insight to see it in its proper light.

Whenever, oh man! you succumb in honest contest with fate, remember that your failure is that of a mortal, whose weaknesses and imperfections are well known to him, who has made you as you are; in whose spirit the Holy Scriptures testify concerning Jacob, "He *lived* full one hundred and forty-seven years."

IMMORTALITY.

GEN. XLIX.

"There are more things in heaven and earth than are dreamt of in our philosophy."

Shakspere's profound observation that there are "things in heaven and earth," of which man has no knowledge, does not refer to those natural forces which reason has as yet failed to comprehend, though undoubtedly true also of them, but to a spiritual world, whose nature can be grasped neither by physical perception nor by the finest powers of the human intellect, a world whose borderland we may tread but in dreams and vague presentiment.

In our discussion of this proposition in regard to "things in heaven and earth," we shall try not to soar into high and unaccustomed spheres, but shall remain as near earth as possible, dealing with those problems that obstruct the path of every thinking being.

Let our text be the assertion of our sages: "The patriarch Jacob did not die."

Jacob went down into Egypt with seventy followers. During his seventeen years' sojourn in that land, this number must have increased considerably. Nevertheless they continued to form one family. The dying patriarch was as ever its head, holding all its members together. To his three oldest sons, themselves advanced in years, he addresses stern words of reproach. He takes from the oldest son the highly-prized birthright, and no one ventures to remonstrate, much less to gainsay his decision.

Families are not held together by the force of reason. If such were the power of reason, if intelligence could bind together the various members of a family, our hold on family life would be as strong to-day as it was in Jacob's time. We have lost nothing of intellectual power since his time; neither has the faculty of reasoning been taken from us. Nevertheless, it would be impossible for twelve large households, with children and grandchildren, to hold together as one family. It is difficult nowadays for the adults of a single household to look upon themselves as one body. The more extended the power of the intellect, the more limited the range of that subtle "in heaven and earth" which we do not understand. Among these things must be reckoned the recognition of the ties of kindred even in the limited degree in which it exists to-day.

No one can have failed to observe that the most intelligent are not the most obedient nor the most affectionate as children; not the most faithful in conjugal relations; not the most self-sacrificing as fathers and mothers—in short, not the ones most cognizant of the claims of kinship. Goethe's correspondence with his mother was carried on through a valet. Moses expected the sons of Levi, whom he had placed in the exalted position of teachers and guides of the people, to have sufficient strength of soul to disregard their feelings for parents, for children and kinsmen, if necessity demanded the sacrifice. If we wish to see true beauty of family life, tenderness in parents, obedience in children, warmth of affection for kindred, we must not ascend too high in the strata of intelligence.

The old world can boast of an entire class of men of supreme culture, with whom, in the United States, only individuals, not a class, may bear comparison. Nevertheless, as a whole, the people of this country may be considered the most intelligent among the nations of the earth, or rather, we may say, this country has the smallest number of uneducated and narrow-minded citizens in proportion to its population. But, on the other hand, it must be said, a chilling indifference, penetrating the very heart of the people, characterizes its family life. The American can not be denied credit for unexampled nobility and public spirit in generous gifts to charitable and educational institutions, but the lack of warmth in family relations may perhaps be one of the causes of this extraordinary liberality. The fortunes of his heirs after his death trouble an American but little.

It is not agreeable to contemplate the consequence of the stronger family feeling existing among the Jews —less readiness in making great sacrifices for the common good ; Judah Touro has as yet had no successor.

Intellect is, therefore, an obstructing rather than a fostering element in the recognition of the claims of kindred. Union may exist among the members of a family, even though there be no sympathy among them, no harmony in inclinations of mind and heart. There must, therefore, be some common *soul* element in the family, handed down from dead and gone ancestors, sometimes tracing its origin far into the past, which makes the descendants of a common stock feel a bond of kinship uniting them.

Such is the subtle bond thrown about us Israelites. In spite of our patriotism for the land in which we dwell; in spite of our intimate associations with the professors of other faiths; in spite of the differences among us, in culture, in religious opinions and practices, we Israelites, scattered over the whole earth, as we are, possess a common "something" inexplicable by reason, a prevailing family feature, something that reason neither grasps nor courts. "Jacob is not dead." Jacob's soul continues with his family in immortal life. The soul of Jacob is not exceptional. The souls of all of us continue to live in our descendants. Our fathers and mothers live on in us, and our spiritual characteristics are transmitted to our grandchildren and great-grandchildren. This truth is a ray of immortality itself.

The proof of the existence of a life far removed from the earthly life of reason; of a life unfathomed by the understanding, lies in the very stronghold of the intellect, namely, in science. Can mere *reason* explain how it is that man gives up his whole life to the cause of science? Does *common-sense* ever make such a demand upon man?

How many men of noble character and high attainments, while seeking to extend the domain of knowledge, have met their death in the icy regions of the Pole, in the swamps and sands of Africa! But no matter how many may thus perish, the number remains great of those that, undeterred by the fate of the pioneers, follow in their footsteps. How many Crœsuses of learning have languished in attics, and have, finally, perished in the act of enriching science with the result of their labors! Such phenomena may be included among the "things in heaven and earth," beyond the comprehension of reason.

In our own days, have we not had a sad instance of such devotion to science in the fate of the two men* that sought to do that in attempting which hundreds before them had perished—to tame the strong winds of the air for the use of man? Would cold reason urge man to risk his life in such a cause, were there not, at the same time, a vague presentiment in him of the "things in heaven and earth," of which the intellect can tell us nothing; did not an inward voice whisper to him, "If the worst happen, your body may perish in the venture, but no harm can come to your soul?"

What would science be or what would become of it, if left to the control of reason, which it worships as its god; were it not for belief in immortality, which it refuses to accept?

In spite of the initial expense of a musical instrument and the cost of instruction in its use, it is not uncommon to find one in our homes, while in scarcely one of a hundred dwellings is there an apparatus for physical experiment; in one of ten thousand, perchance, a laboratory. Hundreds of private tutors in music, in arithmetic, in penmanship and orthography are employed, against one engaged to teach history and natural science.

The education of children is frequently directed solely with a view to their worldly success. The study of history and natural science does not contribute to this end. The poor instruction in these branches offered in the

---

* Donaldson, who, with a companion, made an ascent in a balloon, and never returned.

public schools—if, indeed, they be included in the curri-culum—is deemed sufficient.

There are, however, some human beings to whom these subjects are of the greatest interest, by whom days and nights are given to the advancement of learning that can bring them no practical gain in a world of reason. Such devotion proves to us that the soul soars in another world even during its life on earth—a world, in which there is no death, though everything above us, in the world of reason and the senses, be hushed, and our friends lament and bury us as dead.

When Jacob called Joseph to his side, and gave him instruction as to the manner of his burial, suddenly the thread of his discourse was broken off, and as though in delirium, he began to speak of Rachel, who had died many years before. In distant Egypt, with the shadow of death already upon him, his spirit hovered over the lonely grave on the road to Bethlehem.

What explanation can be offered for this contact of the soul of the living with the dead, unless we admit the existence of that "something," soaring far above our atmosphere of cold reason, on the heights of fancy and presentiment?

What was the earnest wish that Jacob expressed upon his death-bed? He entreated Joseph to convey his body to the home of his youth, and there bury it beside his forefathers. The task imposed was no light one. Its execution demanded the assistance of quite a little army, for the way was long and difficult. In our days, the bodies of those wrecked off the far English coast were taken up from the bottom of the sea to be laid away to rest in the earth of home, in the western part of this country.

Is this the prompting of reason? Common-sense
says: "Let grass grow over the graves. Let oblivion
spring up in the hearts of those left on earth. As for
the remains still visible to us, let them be removed from
sight as soon as possible." Science offers its aid, and
builds an oven for the speedy destruction of the body.
And it would seem as though the spot in which dust is
returned to dust ought to be a matter of indifference.

Is reason not right in its opinion? The world, however, from Jacob's time to the destruction of the *Schiller*
in our own day, has refused to become reasonable on
this point. It cannot be gainsaid, there is an immortal
something "in heaven and earth," which was before our
time, exists during our lives, and will continue to be
after we have passed away. The deaf man has no conception of sounds, the blind man knows nothing of
colors, so it may be that we live in the midst of glories
for whose perception we have not the proper senses, and
to understand which we lack intellectual strength so
long as our *physical* existence continues, so long as the
soul, hidden within the body, is limited to the perception
of the things of this world.

What we call the future life is not a kingdom of
heaven, a preternatural world entirely separate from
this one. It forms one world with our own. As long
as the soul wears its earthly garb, we can perceive only
so much of it as our senses reveal to us, and intellect
and reason teach us, and as a "something" tells us—
something beyond the reach of intellect or reason.
Like a disembodied spirit from another world, it flits
across our consciousness; like lightning's flash, it illu-
mines our souls; like a ghostly echo, like faint sounds

dying away in the distance, it rouses vague thoughts within us.

A man may presume to doubt the existence of God; he may scoff at those that believe in the immortality of the soul and find comfort in this belief. He cannot argue out of existence that spiritual "something," spoken of by Shakspere, soaring above the senses and beyond reason. Let him call it an incomprehensible something. To us, it is God and immortality.

THE DEATH OF THE FATHER.

"And when Joseph's brothers saw that their father was dead, they said, Peradventure Joseph may now hate us; and then he would certainly requite us all the evil which we have done unto him."—GEN. L : 15.

As a flickering light flares up in sudden strength, illuminating the surroundings with ghastly effect, and then dies out forever, leaving dense darkness behind, so family affection, the consciousness of a close union between brothers and sisters, once more leaps into life in their hearts, when they stand about the newly-made grave of their father. In their common grief, they feel, in the very depths of their hearts, that they once more are united. But when they return to the house of mourning, which the father has left forever, the protecting roof seems to have been removed from the home, so long the abiding-place of peace and happiness, the walls appear to totter on their foundations. The importance of the individual, the "*I*," develops with amazing rapidity, while the idea of unity, the "*we*," fades into the background.

One of the consequences of the death of parents, and surely not the least melancholy of them, is the loosening of the family tie, the relaxation of the bond of union between brothers and sisters.

Not until Jacob's body, after elaborate funeral ceremonies in Egypt and Canaan, had been laid away to rest; not until many months had passed and the sons were once more gathered together in their own home,

210

did Jacob's children actually *see* that their father was dead. From the death of their father until their home-coming, they had *felt* their common loss in their common grief. Now, close upon the exhaustion of the emotions followed the actual perception of what had occurred. They saw that everything had changed. The brothers confronted each other with mistrust and estrangement. Each one presupposed that the change, which he perceived in his own mental attitude—the substitution of the individual for the body, of "*I*," for "*we*"—had taken place in each of the others.

An infirm, blind old man had died and been buried. As a matter of fact, the event caused rather a feeling of relief than of loss to those left behind, and to the deceased himself, death brought welcome release. But the influence of his mere existence among them, even though he was stretched helpless on the couch of pain, as now of his death, was marked and powerful. The home had received a severe shock. Its regular life was destroyed. Everything had to be measured by the new standard, and adjusted to the new order.

The impression that their position in life was insecure prompted the anxious thought of the brothers, "What is our relation to Joseph?" For their father was dead, and they had to be assured anew of their relation to Joseph, before they could trust him. Joseph, after his father's death, might prove a very different person from the Joseph of Jacob's lifetime. But there are noble souls in the world, which stand all tests successfully, and pass through every crisis without losing in magnanimity. They cannot understand how it can be otherwise. Such a soul was Joseph's. He could not conceive of himself

as changing towards his brothers, and he wept when
they came to him with mistrust in their hearts and on
their lips.

It is, indeed, touching to look upon a group of eleven
grown men, helpless and fearful as a flock of sheep after
a thunder clap, throwing themselves at the feet of their
much-dreaded brother, with the entreaty, "Allow us to
live protected by the dying wish of our father!" But
the picture of Joseph appeals to us even more strongly.
We see him overpowered by this speech, weeping and
comforting them, acquitting them of all wrong, nobly
covering up their evil deed with its good consequences,
and finally promising to care for them and theirs as he
had done before his father's death. So beautiful are his
words and so noble his behavior, that children, upon
returning from their father's grave, instead of sitting
upon the ground and reading Job, might well peruse
this chapter of the Bible daily, and take to heart this
example of the magnanimity of a brother after the
death of his father.

The *brothers* of Joseph, not Joseph himself, saw that
their father was dead. No change had been wrought
in Joseph's filial and fraternal feelings by the death of
his father. He, therefore, suspected no change in any
one else. Not so his brothers. They had given but
poor proof of brotherly love. Joseph might have told
of an instance, not exactly noble in its nature, of their
brotherly devotion. Later, too, when Benjamin's safety
was at stake, they had shown but little brotherly love
and solicitude. They had been distressed, and had cried
aloud at the thought of their father's grief, were they to
return without his favorite. These selfish men felt that

the death of their father released them from irksome authority, and they supposed that Joseph shared this feeling with them.

One's own frame of mind is the mirror in which the world is reflected. The man of guilt suspects every fellow-creature of wrong-doing. The innocent sees nothing but innocence about him. The blemishes that we see in others are frequently only the reflections of our own imperfections.

His brothers interpreted Joseph's speech and actions, his silence, his omissions, in the light of their own distrustfulness.

How often is this phenomenon repeated in life! We attribute importance to the gestures of others, read significance into their words, and draw inferences from their actions, and no ulterior meaning was intended. All this is merely the reflection of our own souls. It were well to examine carefully, whether like Joseph's brothers, we have not read amiss, before we put an unfavorable construction upon the thoughts of our fellow-men. There are many such sharp-sighted men and women in the world, who know more about us than we know ourselves. They know what we would think, if we thought; what we would say, if we spoke ; they know the purpose of our actions as well as of our failure to act. They know our reasons for looking to the right and not to the left, for looking to the left and not to the right. They pride themselves not a little upon their insight, and look upon themselves as demi-prophets. What a pity, all these cogitations are entirely without rhyme or reason !

"One must know much in order to know how little

one knows." This is a well-known truth, but we limit ourselves too much in its application. Usually, the aphorism is understood as referring to book-learning. We recognize that a person must be very learned in order to know what an infinitesimal part of knowledge is his own possession. But the phrase is applicable to all men, not to the learned alone. Every one, no matter what his station in life, must possess rich experience and a goodly share of the knowledge of human nature in order to understand how frequently, in spite of all wit and cleverness, he may be on the false scent.

Parents themselves may be in error in regard to their children and their children's futures. How harshly Jacob spoke of Simeon and Levi, and how mistaken he was about Levi. In the blessing of Moses, the tribe of Levi was lauded in the highest terms, and throughout many hundreds of years, the position of its members was the most sacred and the most influential in Israel. Ephraim, who was preferred to his brother, and blessed with Jacob's right hand, turned out to be a destructive element in Israel.

Two persons may dwell side by side in the marriage relation, growing old and gray, without ever sounding each other's hearts to their very depths. Most of our knowledge of the soul-life of our fellow-man, upon which we so pride ourselves, is like the acquaintance of Joseph's brothers with his thoughts and emotions. They *imagined* that they understood their brother, and they thought that they would make use of this knowledge by very delicate and clever means. "They sent word unto Joseph." They invented a speech, and had it reported as spoken by their father upon his death-bed. They then came to Joseph, threw themselves down before him contritely, and offered themselves to him as servants. Then Joseph confronted them in his innocence, and it became clear to them that they had been on the false scent. This is an every-day occurrence, which, perhaps, does not always strike us so forcibly as in the Scriptural narrative about the children of Jacob.

Finally, the narrative teaches the effects of an evil conscience. Joseph could forgive his brothers, and they could thus escape punishment for their evil deed. Conscience, however, is not a merciful, noble-hearted brother, but an inexorable judge. An evil conscience gnaws ceaselessly at man's heart-strings; an evil conscience is his companion at bed and board.

Forty years had passed since their brother had been sold. Joseph's kindness and tenderness, his forgiveness of their deed, had not been able to lay this perturbed spirit of conscience, and these forty years had been powerless to still the upbraiding voice, penetrating to the very marrow of their bones.

O that after the father's eyes are closed upon this world, it could never be noticed in the relations of the family circle that the head of the house, he who during his life kept all together, is dead! May helpless orphans, upon returning from the burial of their father, never want for a brother like Joseph, who will take upon himself the leadership of the family, and keep its members united, so that it may not be *seen* that the father has passed away!

GRATITUDE.

Ex. VIII.

In regard to the first three plagues recorded in the Holy Scriptures, we are told distinctly that they were to be brought upon the land by Aaron. In allusion to this, our sages observe: "In the water of the river, Moses found shelter when a child, and the earth covered the Egyptian whom he had killed. It would have seemed ungrateful if, unmindful of their good offices, he had smitten the earth and the water with his staff." Such reflections of our sages must not be taken literally as explanations. In their intense admiration for the Holy Scriptures, they like to read all good and noble thoughts into them, or to give these thoughts to us as drawn from this favorite source. In the case under discussion, they want to impress upon us the excellence of gratitude, and they maintain that in the Holy Scriptures, they find it advocated by God, and practised by Moses to its utmost consequences. A man must not injure even the earth or the water that has been of service to him. The thought has, indeed, passed into a proverb, "*In einen Brunnen, aus dem man getrunken, soll man keinen Stein werfen.*" (Into a well, from which one has drawn water, one should not throw stones.)

Gratitude is a virtue that apparently reaps no reward, while its opposite, ingratitude, seems much more profitable. One may be ungrateful, and yet remain well,

prosper, grow rich, and attain a good old age. A man
may fail to return thanks for all that he is and possesses;
no earthly judge can arraign him on this charge.

Gratitude, indeed, may cost man dear, may lead him
through fire and water, and demand sacrifice after sacrifice on his part. No wonder, then, that we see this virtue
so frequently neglected.

The ungrateful man, like a dishonest debtor, repu-
diates his debt. The benefit is forgotten, or its value
minimized in the eyes of the debtor, and held unworthy
of any special thanks, or he looks upon it as an attention due him. If the beneficiary does remember the
favor, and acknowledges it as such, he seeks to attribute it
to selfish motives on the part of the benefactor. Finally,
as the benefit is underestimated, the return that he makes
for it is overestimated ; he holds that he has fully made
good his indebtedness.

What is the nature of gratitude? How must it first
manifest itself? When may it cease to be active? A
generous acknowledgment of favors received constitutes
the first element of gratitude. The Hebrew language has
no equivalent for our word "thank." Where we use
thanks, the Hebrew speaks of תודה, acknowledgment,
recognition. מודים אנחנו לך means not "we thank thee,"
but "we acknowledge thee," "we recognize thee." Upon
making the thank-offering of the first fruits, the farmer
did not say, "I return thanks," but "I acknowledge this
day before the Lord, that I am come into the land which
the Lord swore unto our fathers to give to us." When
Achan sinned, Joshua demanded a "confession" from
him, using for confession the same word תודה usually
translated by thanks.

And where may gratitude end? Only with the end
of the debtor himself. A man ought never to allow
himself to forget another's kindness towards him, nor
believe that the act of benevolence has been fully repaid
with a favor done the benefactor in return. Not alone
should a man be ever thankful to the benefactor himself, but towards the latter's children, who may survive
him, should he show his gratitude. He should say
to himself, " This man's parents treated me in a most
friendly manner; he shall reap the fruit of their kindness." A noble nature rather *over-* than *under*estimates
the value of benefactions received; if it underestimates
anything, it is its own return for kindnesses. The consciousness of an obligation is not a burden on the spirit
of the grateful man; he rather finds pleasure in it from
the assurance which his experience has given him that
there are good men on earth, that the world is not so
black as it is painted. The grateful man does not feel
his indebtedness limited to the benefactor, but looks
upon it as extending to all with whom he may come in
contact. It prompts him to reason thus: " I have
received benefits, I have been shown much kindness.
Let me be equally friendly, whenever the opportunity
presents itself. My fellow-man extended a helping-
hand to me, when I was in distress, and it was pleasant
to me. I now feel called upon not to hold back when I
see others in trouble."

And as in your relations to individuals, so let it be
with associations and congregations, with nations and
countries. Whoever has dwelt under the protection of
a community, and enjoyed its benefits, ought never to
forget it. Even if he experience unkindness at its

hands, the memory of the good that he has enjoyed ought, nevertheless, not to pass from his mind. In regard to such circumstances, the Holy Scriptures declare, most clearly and emphatically: "Thou shalt not abhor an Egyptian; because thou wast a stranger in his land." In spite of the injustice that Israel had suffered, it was still not to forget that it had learned many useful things from the Egyptians; that it had dwelt in the land of Egypt. Israel was never to return to Egypt, the land of its oppression, but whenever the people might come in contact with an Egyptian, they were to treat him with kindness.

With every kindness that is shown us, every sacrifice made for our sake, every gift that we receive, we thus take upon ourselves a life-long obligation; grateful natures, therefore, are reluctant to make use of the kindness of others, when not absolutely unavoidable. The ungrateful man is like the thoughtless borrower, who makes use of all his credit; the payment of his debts does not trouble him. The ungrateful man lightly says, "I thank you," and, thereupon, considers his obligation discharged. The grateful man, on the other hand, is like the honest merchant, who has an aversion to making debts if he has not money sufficient at his disposal to cover the debt.

Gratitude is scarcely a virtue; it is rather an endowment of nature. Even beasts know gratitude. Isaiah, in reproaching Israel with ingratitude towards his God, says: "The ox knoweth his owner, and the ass his master's crib."

Indeed, in uncivilized man, in savages, we find it most strongly developed. Civilization refines the coarseness

of nature. In this refining process, however, many valuable, natural qualities are lost, among them gratitude.
A cultured man, in the ordinary sense of the term, has
not, by reason of his culture, gained in the power of gratitude; he is rather deficient in the development of this
endowment. We find a deeper sense of gratitude in the ·
wigwam, in the home of the unassuming citizen or
farmer, than in the palaces of the great.

Nature has arranged that gratitude shall be the first
subject of man's instruction in the school of life. On
the very first day of our existence, we receive more benefits than we can repay in a whole lifetime. At best, a
child may discharge the interest of its debt by means
of life-long devotion, love, obedience and reverence to
its benefactors, namely, its parents. Upon the first day
of man's existence as a suckling, follow the days and
years of the helplessness of childhood, days and years of
boundless devotion on the part of his parents. This is the
school in which nature teaches man to know gratitude.
As the pupil, who learns to know his "Reader" well,
applies his knowledge outside of the school-room, and
reads other books, so he that has learnt to be grateful
in the school of parental care and devotion, will be impelled to practise gratitude in other spheres of life.

So, too, the good citizen of the United States will
never forget that France extended a helping hand to
his country in its struggle for existence, and Israel will
always retain a friendly feeling for Holland — the first
modern state to permit Israel to lead a human existence.

RIGHTEOUS INDIGNATION.

How bitter must have been the feelings of Moses, as he passed down from Mount Sinai into the camp of the Israelites! His people had been delivered from slavery, and deemed worthy of a divine revelation. The ten commandments had laid the foundation of a new social and religious order. Forty days and nights had Moses passed upon the mountain-top in spiritual activity, rearing, with the divine aid, upon this foundation, the structure of Israel's Law. Finally, the system stood before his mental vision, complete in every detail. Law and law-giver alike were prepared for their work. The chosen people of the future stood, at the foot of the mountain, awaiting his return.

The forty days and nights of the isolation of Moses had not been passed only in a literal sense upon a mountain-top; in imagination, Moses had reached the summit of his hopes. Suddenly the call came to him: "Descend from the height of idealism. Far, far below you lies hideous reality. Think no more of the proud structure which you fondly hoped to rear, for the very foundation is sunken. The sound of the first word of the commandment has died away among your people."

The descent of Moses from Mount Sinai and his return to the camp may most aptly be characterized by

the German phrase, "*vom Himmel gefallen;*"* truly he
had fallen from the heaven of his hopes and ideals.
Nevertheless, he took with him the tables of stone, and
surely not for the purpose of destroying them. He had
heard the evil news, and it pierced his very soul, but he
had not yet *seen* what had occurred; his heart was sad-
dened within him, but the dreadful tidings had not be-
numbed his reason. Thus Moses moved towards the
camp with troubled soul, but calm and deliberate of
mind. In his conversation with Joshua concerning the
meaning of the noise in the camp, he found it impossible
to tell his companion openly of that which he knew had
happened. When, however, he saw before his eyes the
evidence of the miserable backsliding of the people, the
full consciousness of the wreck of his life's work broke
in upon him. His wrath flared up in him, and the tables
of stone, testifying to his people's mission, lay shattered
at his feet. Without faithful believers, they were utterly
worthless.

He who, like Moses, has seen his life-work crumble
away before his eyes, or who, teaching in the fond belief
that he is training a community of wise and good men,
finds that his scholars are brutes and fools; whoever has
lived in the sweet dream of having established a new
order of truth and light, of love and justice, and awakes
to find the old misery, the old error, the same darkness
of the spirit as of old—he, indeed, will not censure the
faithful servant of the Lord for his loss of self-control,
nor chide him for acting like an ordinary mortal, and
breaking even the most precious possession of his house
in the moment of anger.

* An idiomatic expression for keen and sudden disappointment.—[Tr.]

His was holy wrath!

Nothing in this world is absolutely good or absolutely bad. Wheat, the bread-giver, is but a weed, if it grow in an inappropriate spot, while the deadly nightshade may, under certain circumstances, prove a precious plant. So, too, wise deliberation, and so, powerful wrath, dreadful to see and destructive in its effects; respectively, they are not absolutely good, not absolutely bad. The conduct of Aaron is a case in point. He beheld the stream of evil running ever higher. He saw that it threatened to break through all the dikes set up to resist its course. He carefully and prudently considered how useless it would be for him to attempt to stem this wild current of opposition. The flood-gates were broken down, and through them the rabble poured in an unchecked stream, leaving destruction in its wake. Aaron comforted himself, as any cool, deliberate man might do, with the reflection that the catastrophe was inevitable. When called to account by Moses, he said to him: "Thou knowest the people, that it is bent on mischief," meaning, "I could not prevent them from carrying out their wishes. Opposition, on my part, would have cost me my life." Thus is Aaron represented to us in this narrative, a reed bending before the storm, a sheep fleeing from wolves.

What a contrast to the behavior of Moses! In his righteous indignation, he stormed into the very midst of the intoxicated masses, dashing the tables of stone into pieces before their eyes, and seizing their god, he ground him into powder. The multitude gathered about the calf scattered in affright. Moses despatched the Levites to seize the ringleaders of rebellion, and the blood of three thousand of them was poured out on the desert

sands. Order was restored in the camp. Such was the
work of wrath, fanned into a flame by the spirit of holiness. In considering another Biblical section, we had
occasion to remark that cursing, a universal practice in
ancient times, was gradually vanishing with the spread
of culture; so, too, with anger. As civilization pro-
gresses, calm deliberation gradually takes the place of
passionate action, and especially does it supplant wrath
as a method of adjusting a difficulty. A cultured man
of our day is as ashamed of manifesting anger as of
swearing. Persons of intelligence discuss and argue
questions of state, of the congregation, of the family,
of business, etc., without passion. They fight with argu-
ments, but not with venom and blood. The uncultured,
on the other hand, in their intercourse with their fellow-
man, are ever on the verge of a crater. From its mouth,
the fire of wrath may burst forth at any moment.

It must, in justice, be said of the citizens of our country that outbursts of passionate wrath are less frequent
among them than in any other nation of the earth.
They act with prudence and deliberation in cases in
which others employ violent means to secure their ends.
The American may even commit murder, or wreak
bloody revenge without ceasing to be a gentleman in
outward bearing. But it must not be overlooked that
there is a dark side to this decline of violent passion. Crimes that arouse the righteous indignation
of all good people of other lands are here disposed of
with the utmost coolness by people and judge alike.
As evil courses lose the shame formerly attached to
them, indignation and stern justice also decline. Crimes
do not bring dishonor to the offender; they are simply

"settled," to use a common phrase. When brought before a judge they are adjusted, and pardon may be granted if sentence of condemnation be passed.

Our sages tell us the story that, in view of the havoc wrought by passion in the moral world, the evil genius was pursued, and finally driven into an iron cage, and the cage was carefully locked. Soon, however, it became evident that it was impossible for the world to exist without passion, and so passion was again set at liberty, but was first blinded so that it should no longer choose for itself a path of destruction, but would be constrained to act as a slave to the moral nature.

Pre-eminent goodness, truth and beauty are always the offspring of passion. Deliberation and careful thought do not fall into error easily, but, on the other hand, they lack the creative power which alone can raise actions above the level of the commonplace, nor can they boast the power of self-sacrifice, the inevitable price of greatness.

How excellent is a little righteous indignation in many of the affairs of life, the less important as well as those of greater moment! For example, if parents were always to take all possible, mitigating circumstances into consideration in their dealings with their children, they would in each case overlook the fault, ever excusing it and delaying punishment. Forbearance is a convenient virtue, and one appealing with force to a parent's feelings. Fortunately, however, fathers and mothers are now and again, to the great advantage of their children, filled with righteous indignation, and the children, in turn, under the inspiration

16

of wholesome respect, for once are made to feel the value of a serious education.

So, too, husband and wife, holding the sanctity of the marriage bond at its true worth, forbear to speak of each other's weaknesses; they go on their way without improving, and their mutual respect weakens in proportion to the strength of their failings. Suddenly, one or the other is filled with righteous indignation; involuntarily a word of censure is dropt, which, severely as it may smart, is salutary in effect.

A thunder-burst of righteous indignation might occasionally be of good service in clearing the air in the legislative halls of state and community, where excessive cleverness and hair-splitting debate so frequently hinder healthy progress.

Let us imagine Moses entering one of our synagogues. His eye would light upon the memorial tables, which usually occupy so prominent a place in our houses of worship, and he would ask one of the many Israelitish children present, probably a non-attendant or an irregular attendant at the religious school—if, indeed, a school exists—" Do you know the ten commandments? Can you read the words inscribed upon that tablet? Do you know the name of the first letter?" " No !" would be the answer to each question. I believe the spirit of his ancient, holy wrath would overcome him, and once more he would dash the tables of stone into fragments !

We no longer know righteous indignation in such matters. Civilization tames men and ennobles human nature. We see and hear much that is displeasing to us without giving way to ungovernable wrath. Blessed be this achievement of true culture ! It is well for us

Rabbi Meïr was the author of the infelicitous benediction, " Praised be thou, O Lord! who hast not made me a woman." If his spirit, sixteen hundred years after his demise, could look down from the heavenly heights, upon our time and circumstances, he would say, " Praised be thou, O Lord! who hast created women that they may arise to preserve the sanctuary of Israel in the hour of danger!"

MOSES AND HIS MISSION.

LEV. I : 1.

Shortly after the exodus from Egypt, Israel erected a common sanctuary, expending upon it energy and treasure in proportion to the means at its disposal. The people brought gold and silver and other costly material for the building and its ornamentation. The nobles contributed jewels of great price. Bezalel and his associates bent their strength and skill to the work. The women made perhaps the greatest sacrifice of all—they surrendered their mirrors of burnished bronze.

What did Moses contribute to the sacred cause?

In the Proverbs of Solomon, we read, " There is gold and a multitude of jewels; but a precious vessel are the lips of knowledge." This verse suggests the following to our sages: " Gold was brought by the people, and pearls the princes gave; but who brought the most precious vessel? Moses, we are told, gazed sadly upon the completed sanctuary, and said, 'Every one has contributed his share. I, alone, have come with empty hands.' God, therefore, comforted him, saying, ' Thy word is the gift most pleasing in my sight. Among all these men, thou alone wilt be called.' Therefore, the Bible says, ' The Lord *called* unto Moses, and spoke unto him.' "

The tabernacle was completed with its rich, golden ornaments. Upon the breast and shoulders of the high-priest flashed the jewelled wealth of kingdoms. The sacrificial service was in full progress; the incense ascended from the sanctuary in fragrant clouds. The people filled the space set aside for them, feasting their eyes upon the result of their labors, and giving generous praise to all whose material aid or artistic skill had assisted in the completion of the sanctuary. But no voice had as yet come from on high to set the seal of divine approval upon the work. Finally, the call came. "He called unto Moses." From among all the people, he alone was called. For without Moses' share in the work, the tabernacle and its service, with all its pomp and show, would have been without purpose. If the spirit of Moses dwell therein, even an humble house may be a glorious sanctuary, while an Israelitish temple, to which the Law and the spirit of Moses are strangers, even though it be decked with purple and set upon beams of gold, is naught but a monument to pride and vainglory. It matters not how solemn the chant of the service, nor how much apparent devotion and exaltation mark the progress of the prayers, it is all a mere form, if the call be not heard in the sanctuary, the call unto Moses.

The references to the construction of the tabernacle and the services held in it are of importance to us in our day. It is not the width of the street, nor the imposing size and magnificence of the structure, and the elegant decoration of the interior, nor yet the melodious choir, the majestic peal of the organ, and the dignified behavior of the worshippers that can make our synagogues what they ought to be. Neither can the size and thickness of the prayer-books compass this end.

The true spirit can be measured only by the reverence paid to Moses and his Law on the lips of the teachers, and in the hearts of the attendants. Through a newly completed sanctuary must resound the call determining its worth and purpose, the Lord calling " unto Moses."

In every Israelitish house of worship there is at least one copy of the written Law of Moses, and long or short portions are recited in the course of the service. But when God " calls " for Moses and his Law, he does not want the mere sound of the word, void of all life and intelligence, but the animating thought, the living soul of the Law. The soul receives no inspiration from the hasty recital of the Torah, and that in a language unintelligible to many in the audience. If the only source of Israel's knowledge of the Law be the weekly instruction—if such it can be called—received on the Sabbath day, then, indeed, may Moses ask, in sadness: " What has been my share in the erection of the sanctuary?"

It is the duty of every Israelite to familiarize himself with the Law of Moses in word and import while he is young, nor should he cease from its study in old age. And if he that occupies the pulpit likewise considers it his duty to aid in spreading " knowledge and understanding " of the Law, then we may hope to have sympathy and intelligence accompany the reading of the Torah. The call unto Moses, which is of so great a significance in our sanctuaries, does not merely mean an intimate acquaintance with his Law; it also requires a consideration of the qualities which fitted Moses for his life-work —to be a law-giver unto Israel, and in many respects, a standard for all civilized nations.

Moses was eighty years old, and as yet there was no

Torah, although, previous to this time, the call of God had come to him in Egypt. In that day, there was no trace of the mass of learning which a theological student of our time is expected to acquire. The Bible did not exist, still less was there any thought of a Talmud. Moses had absorbed the learning of the time, and, through thought and experience, had acquired much knowledge of the world and its ways. Such was Moses as God found him—not a theologian, but a *man*, qualified to proclaim his commandments, and worthy of the task, and the " Lord called unto him."

When God calls for Moses in the sanctuaries devoted to his service, he does not want the theologian Moses, expounding, both in his praise and in his censure, in his lamentation and in his rejoicing, a narrow Judaism ; he wants the Moses pictured to us in the Bible, the man of energy, rich in knowledge of man and the world, whose mind encompasses the whole of life and understands it; who does not forget God in his attention to worldly matters, nor does he ignore the earth while reflecting upon the greatness of his Maker.

Finally, the call for Moses does not enjoin upon us merely an intimate acquaintance with the Law and the wisdom therein contained. Of equal importance is the question, " What testimony do we bear to his Law and his example in our daily lives?"

While occupying an exalted position in Egypt, Moses risked his life for the sake of his helpless brethren. Even when a fugitive, an inner voice compelled him to aid those suffering grievous wrongs to obtain justice. Advanced in years, he took upon himself the liberation and the leadership of his unhappy people. The forty days and nights passed on the mountain-top were surely not spent in feasting. This is the lesson of this incident in the life of Moses, as narrated in the Bible; in the execution of his divine appointed task, the aged man denied himself many physical comforts, devoting himself wholly to the service of divine truth and the salvation of his people. Tireless energy was united in him with unparalleled modesty and inexhaustible patience, and therefore God called unto him.

And similarly the call resounds through our synagogues; the call for men willing and able to aid those to obtain justice that suffer wrongfully; the call for men to devote themselves to the service of the community, to advance the welfare of others in the narrow or wide spheres in which they may be called upon to labor.

OFFERING AND SACRIFICE.

"Speak unto the children of Israel, and say unto them, If any one of you wish to bring an offering unto the Lord ; of the cattle, either of the herds, or of the flocks, shall ye bring your offering"—LEV. I : 2.

אדם כי יקריב מכם קרבן ליי

This passage, if translated in the order in which the words occur in Hebrew, would read : "A man that offers *of you* a sacrifice unto the Lord." According to the *sense* of the verse, it ought to read, אדם מכם כי יקריב קרבן ליי "Any one of you that brings an offering unto the Lord."

Many interpretations have been put upon this text by the old Bible students, but not one of them is entirely satisfactory. In our morning's discourse, let us attempt to find a more pleasing interpretation of these verses.

In the passage, מכם, "of you," must be emphasized. If a man wishes to bring a true sacrifice to God, he must put a part of himself into the offering. A gift, whose bestowal does not demand any *self-denial* on the part of the giver, though it may be good in itself, by virtue of its application to a worthy cause, is, nevertheless, so far as the giver is concerned, not a sacrifice. Physical aid, rendered without effort, but at an opportune moment, may prove a most grateful help, a true service, but can lay no claim to the distinction of sacrifice ; it is not מכם, "of you," a part of your *ego*. So a man may bring an offering to the Temple, and think that he has brought a sacrifice. The sacrificial animal may bleed before the altar, or lie smoking upon it; it is, nevertheless, but a gift, not a sacrifice, and, in this instance, a useless one. You must bring a part of yourself with your offering, your heart and soul must be in it, if it is to be a true sacrifice. This, alone, constituted the worth of the sacrificial service at the altar, and upon this idea, the prophets ever laid great stress. A pious heart and noble intentions must accompany the sacrifice. The offering is not an end in itself. It is not food for the gods, as the heathen believe, but the expression of a pious, god-fearing frame of mind, beneficent in its moral effect upon the giver himself.

For us, the synagogue and its service must take the place of the Temple and the sacrifice of olden times; and we, too, must heed the injunction contained in the emphatic מכם, "of you," if the service in the synagogue is to partake of the efficacy of a sacrifice. Participation in the public service is always beneficial in its effect upon ourselves, and is, moreover, a worthy action. If, however, we attend service only when we have nothing else wherewith to occupy our time, only when the sun shines brightly and the air is clear, and the house of worship stands at but a short distance away from our homes; if, in brief, we are willing to sacrifice neither strength nor convenience, then, in truth, our מכם, *mickem* is wanting. We bring our prayer-books, but not ourselves to the synagogue.

The gift of the man of little means is usually a sacrifice. A gift, however small in value, demands strict self-denial on his part. The rich man can, naturally, not be expected to dispose of his riches for benevolent purposes to his own actual impoverishment. So long, however, as giving is a pleasure to him, requiring no self-conquest on his part, his gift, however deserving of gratitude, cannot be regarded as a sacrifice. It is not *mickem*. If, however, the man of wealth gives away more than he feels it his actual duty to give, bearing more than his share of the general burden of charity; if his heart is weary of giving and again giving; if he lacks sympathy for the applicant; if, indeed, antipathy prejudices him; if he is prompted not by his charitable impulses, but by his sense of duty, then giving is no longer a pleasure to him—even the rich man, under such circumstances, brings a sacrifice.

In actual, personal service, however, in the real *mickem*, rich and poor are alike. He that wishes to make a sacrifice pleasing in the sight of God, may not be sparing of his own efforts. Let us speak not of those that offer their fellow-man only censure and good advice instead of material aid and the helping hand, but of better men. Of these we may make two divisions. Those in the one class manifest their sympathy for suffering mankind in generous gifts, and by gladly sacrificing their money for the benefit of others; but no demand may be made upon them themselves, neither upon their time nor their energy; nor will they deprive themselves of any pleasure for the sake of their suffering fellow-men. In the other division are the real helpers in distress, the true workers in the field of humanity and religion. They grow neither tired nor impatient, but are ever ready to put their hands to the good cause, to deny themselves both rest and pleasure for the benefit of their family, of the community, of suffering mankind.

Many a father of a family is the very personification

17

of liberality towards his wife and children. Without a murmur, he pays his consort's bills. He employs the best teachers for his children, and considers no sum too large to be expended on procuring their happiness. But he himself must be left in peace. His wife receives no help from him; early and late, year in and year out, she must bear alone the cares of the household. There is no one with whom she may seek counsel or assistance, and the children, too, lack a guide and an educator. This is *giving* without *sacrifice*. It is not *mickem*. This same man may be a good member of congregations and societies. To their councils and meetings, he sends his delegate, the dollar, but he himself cannot be induced to come.

So there are many good and attentive children that do everything for parents and grandparents that can be done with money, but they are not self-sacrificing enough to take into consideration the wishes of their elders in the arrangement of their households, or in their mode of life; they find it impossible to leave desires ungratified for the sake of giving pleasure to others. Here, again, we have a lack of what the Bible calls *mickem*.

So with our relations to our kinsmen. We are not unwilling to render them material assistance, but we hesitate to associate with them, if they happen to occupy a lower position in the social scale. Such help is a gift, but not a sacrifice. We offer them our gold, but not ourselves.

Again: a man is a Jew, and wants to live as such, but his religion must not demand too much of him. He gladly celebrates the Holy Days if they happen to fall upon Sundays, thus not interfering with his business pursuits. Judaism must, likewise, not ask that a curb be put upon his appetite. His fellow-citizens of other beliefs need not discover that he is a Jew, for this knowledge might work him harm. Such Judaism has some virtue in it, it is true, but it is not the virtue of sacrifice. It is not *mickem*. Such religion does not penetrate the very heart and soul of man.

Again: a certain man is religious. But religion demands a continual abasement of reason. A truly religious person must acknowledge to himself that he believes in the highest truths, even though his reason does not grasp them as easily as the rule of three; they lie beyond the horizon of his reason. This means great self-conquest for man, proud as he is of his intellectual attainments. To him whose faith is bounded by reason religion is as a gift, not a sacrifice.

On the whole, the pleasant virtues do not allow man to become degraded, nor, on the other hand, do they raise him above the level of the commonplace. By pleasant virtues, I mean such as it is agreeable to exercise, whose practice makes our paths in life smooth and easy. The stern virtues, on the other hand, exalt a human being in the sight of God and his fellow-men. The stern virtues cause the heart of man to bleed. Against their practice, prudence enters its protest. A sharp struggle within the soul is the price of their triumph.

Revenge, for instance. How sweet! The long wished for hour of vengeance has come at length! Reason says to us: "Your opponent, your enemy is at your mercy. Take from him his power. Do unto him as he did unto

you, and let him feel all the bitterness that he has made
you suffer." Duty, however, calls to you: "You shall
not take revenge. You must not seek to wreak vengeance upon your fellow-man." Truly, forgiveness is
as difficult as revenge is pleasant; and great as is the
delight of laying hands upon your enemy, and punish-
ing him to your heart's content, so great is the self-
conquest required to allow him to go on his way un-
harmed, and, it may be, to render him assistance. He
that practises this stern virtue, doing his enemy no
harm, but rather acting as a benefactor towards him, he
indeed, brings a sacrifice—*mickem*, a portion of his own
heart. Thus, every struggle against a passion, every
self-imposed deprivation of comfort, ease, pleasure, dearest habits, favorite pursuits, or even renunciation of
well-founded opinion, for the sake of maintaining harmony and concord in the home circle and abroad, is a
true act of self-sacrifice, an offering of a portion of self-
love.

Everything great and noble in its nature demands
sacrifices. Virtue, religion, patriotism, friendship, conjugal affection, filial and parental love, affection among
brethers and sisters—all require sacrifices for their full
development. Their worth is great or small in proportion to the power of self-sacrifice manifested in their
exercise.

How large the price paid for truth! How difficult to
be faithful to its standard, and ever to acknowledge it
before mankind!

In the darkness of mediæval days, our ancestors sacrificed all that is most dear to man upon earth for the sake
of their faith, in defence of that which they held to be

the truth. Not individuals alone, but entire communities, from the child to the aged man, from the beggar to the man of wealth and position!

Those were times in which man sacrificed himself and all that was precious in his eyes to his God. How light a burden has Judaism grown to be in our day, and yet many murmur at its weight, and here and there it is thrown off as too oppressive to be longer borne. A heavy plank rests more securely on the shoulder than the light feather, which a breath of air may blow away. Thus it is with Judaism. The easier its profession and its practice, the more difficult appears to its bearers the task of balancing it in the strong winds of modern times.

The daily service in the Temple was begun with a prescribed sacrifice, and in the evening, it was closed with the same ceremony. At day-break, the priests were called to prepare the offering. We, too, are called upon every morning to bring our sacrifices in our homes and in our various pursuits. Man, gather up your forces for the work before you! Practise self-control, be peaceable, be benevolent! Strive to subdue indolence, desire, greed, envy, hatred, pride and arrogance, even though a piece of your heart—the corner in which these qualities reside—be sacrificed in the act. *Mickem!* Make an offering of this part of your *self* to your God.

PROVIDENCE OR CHANCE.

LEV. X.

Aaron, the honored high-priest, stood performing the duties of his exalted office on the most festive of the days celebrating the dedication of the newly-finished tabernacle. His heart was filled with emotions of solemn joy. Well might he praise that day as the proudest of his life. Probably not a few envious glances followed the hero of the day, the foremost among six hundred thousand men, moving about in his magnificent robes to perform the honored service in the sanctuary. But who can foresee the vicissitudes of a single day! The sun had risen brightly that morning for Aaron; at noon it shone above his head in majestic splendor, the evening saw it sink obscured by clouds and mist. Of his four sons, who had shared with him the honors, as the services of the day, the two older ones lay stretched before him in death, victims to their own wrong-doing.

"A fire went out from before the Lord." A similar incident, occurring in our own day, would not be reported in these words: "A fire went out from before the Lord," it would be spoken of as a *disaster*, an unfortunate *occurrence*, an *accident*.

Can we look upon the denial of the existence of a wise Providence as a mark of progress? Is it a proof of sound philosophy to say, under similar circumstances, " a fire broke out," and not to add "from God?" Nay, such omission rather bespeaks a relapse into a state of deplorable barbarism.

History can tell us but little of the earliest stages of human civilization; let us then close its vast tomes, and allow thought to carry us back to that dim past. A picture is there unrolled to us of men destroyed by fire and water, of men strangled and slain without looking up to any power higher than themselves. Chance and the wickedness of man alone are looked upon as responsible agents. In a later stage of development, petty, envious and malicious deities and spirits were regarded as the authors of the evil that afflicted mankind, till finally, in the Scriptures, the one, omnipotent God is revealed, who holds in his hand the destinies of all his creatures. Nothing is too great nor is aught too small to escape his all-seeing eye. It is he who has counted not only the suns, but every leaf upon each tree, every mote of dust upon the globe, who not only sees into the heart of man, and understands all his joys and sorrows, his thoughts, desires and ambitions, but who knows the very entrails of the minute creatures which, even when enlarged by the microscope to the ten-thousandth diameter, become visible to human eyes as a mere dot. Thus the idea of unity was introduced into creation.

Creation is a unity, the work of one mind, and the constant aim of science is naught but to show the relation of the individual to the universe.

Is it not an inspiring thought that we are all parts of one universe ruled by intelligence, in which the individual is neither lost nor forgotten? To take the reins of the rulership of the world from God, and place them

into the hands of blind chance, once more disintegrates
the whole into its component parts, and we have again
chance in the place in which the idea of God had erected
a structure, harmonious in all its details. This so-called
progress, which sets chance in the place of Providence,
restores the condition of those times in which the fratri-
cide asks, "Am I my brother's keeper?"

The incident under discussion, in which the hand
of Providence manifested itself visibly, is of a sort
familiar to our own every-day experience. The two
young men, Nadab and Abihu, heeded not the injunctions of their father and of their uncle, who was at the
same time their superior in position and their teacher;
regardless of authority and law, they played with the
forbidden fire. This heedlessness was their destruction,
and from the consequences of this very fault, we see
thousands and tens of thousands suffering day after day.
He that fails to obey his parents; that heeds not the
injunctions of teachers and superiors, is sure to bring
ruin upon himself, though consuming fire may not
always be the destroying agent.

Is there even one among us who, casting an honest
glance upon his past life, will not say, "I should be
better off to-day, had I always heeded the voice of my
father, my mother, my teacher?" In flaming letters
we see traced in every earthly career these words: "He
that uses fire like Nadab and Abihu will perish even
as did Nadab and Abihu." This is a law of God, as
natural and as unalterable as the change of the seasons.
Yet it must be admitted, that in the course of his life,
man is visited by sorrows which, in human estimation,
he has not brought upon himself, and he enjoys blessings

which he does not deserve. In these crises, it is hard for a believer to maintain his position. If this event is not the work of chance, but the conscious deed of your God, then he is a ruthless God, governed by caprice. But I say that he that believes in the existence of a Supreme Being, and at the same time believes that this Being could abandon his creatures to the mercy of blind chance, is guilty of grosser blasphemy, than if he ascribes to him caprice and ruthlessness. Neither of these descriptions applies to the true Israelitish conception of God. We believe that God is neither cruel beyond comprehension, nor beyond comprehension indifferent to the weal and woe of his creatures. He is wise and good beyond comprehension. It is true, the combination of kindness and justice in divine judgments is incomprehensible to us; neither can we understand the union of free-will and predestination. It is, however, rational to assert, "The God of my belief is an incomprehensible Being," for the concept deity presupposes inscrutability. A God whose purpose we could fathom, the significance of whose actions we could grasp with our mere spark of intelligence, would be no God.

The piety that traces everything to the will of the Almighty as its cause is, however, not always the source of comfort that it proved to Aaron. To one, the recognition of God's dispensations is the cause of much self-reproach and consequent unhappiness; to another, again, it offers an opportunity for uncharitable criticism of his neighbor. The one upbraids himself, thinking, that trouble and distress, death and destruction are God's decrees, and the other judges his fellow-man in bitterness; he says to himself, "God has afflicted that man for his misdeeds." With this thought in mind, Moses addressed to Aaron the words of consolation, "On those who are near unto me, will I be sanctified." The upright and the pious cannot be spared earthly woe and affliction; even the best among men must learn to know suffering. Not every stroke of misfortune is meant as a punishment, neither is every infliction a penalty for sin. Man honors God and sanctifies him in the measure in which he submits to God's will, holding firmly to the conviction, "God's will controls my destiny; what God does is for the best." Piety does not consist in loud wailing, much less in an open display of bitter grief, but rather in humble resignation to God's will.

"And before all the people will I be glorified." The mass of the people, incapable of independent thought, but ready to follow others in thought, speech and action, emulating your example, will honor God. And highly necessary it is that the people see before them a worthy example of willing submission.

Experience teaches that the illusion is common to all the nations of the earth, that the louder lamentation and mourning are among the people, and the more unrestrained the expression of grief, the greater their piety.

The contemporaries of Moses cut their flesh in sign of mourning, tore their hair and mutilated their bodies till the skin was dyed in blood. The expression of grief at funerals was heightened by the weeping and howling of women paid for their efforts. Moses now demanded of Aaron that by his good example he should discountenance these vicious customs. "Let not the hair of your head grow long, rend not your garments;" be not interrupted in the discharge of your duties.

Moses warned his brother against another vicious usage of the day. Just as on the one side, mistaken piety sought to aggravate the emotion of grief, so, on the other hand, the attempt was made at mourning feasts to deaden the natural feelings of sorrow by the use of intoxicating drinks. Man should, however, neither morbidly over-stimulate his natural feelings in a spirit of religious extravagance, nor frivolously seek to benumb them. Give unto nature its due, neither more nor less.

Such is the significance of the law for the sons of Aaron set down in this chapter—the law enjoining upon them abstinence from the use of intoxicating liquors.

INDIVIDUALITY.

LEV. X.

When men like Nadab and Abihu, who had already been given a share with their father in the service of the sanctuary, and had been appointed as teachers in Israel, seek to follow their own inclinations, turning aside from the course marked out for them by high authority, we must look for a more satisfactory reason for their action than the general observation that youth, by its very nature, is tempted to place itself in opposition to the views of the aged. Important principles must be at stake in this conflict between Moses and Aaron, on the one side, and Nadab and Abihu, on the other.

"Nadab and Abihu took each his censer, and they put therein fire, and put therein incense: and they brought near before the Lord a strange fire, which he had not commanded them."

It seems probable—and the view is advanced by our sages—that it was Israel's strong individuality, so pronounced as to be stigmatized by Moses as stubbornness, that rendered it fit for its mission as the bearer and the preserver of the pure conception of God together with all the ideas inseparable from that belief, so important in their influence upon other faiths. A nation of a more pliable nature, more ready to surrender its individuality for the sake of an easier existence among the

nations, could not have undergone the dreadful persecutions, the great oppressions, and the nameless sufferings
in the cause of truth endured by Israel.

The obstinate position taken in Israel on the question
of personal rights, and the intense repugnance ever manifested to a surrender of any of them, indicate clearly the
reason for Israel's failure to rear a permanent state.
With the exception of the reigns of David and Solomon,
and of a few years during the time of .the Maccabees,
Israel always lived in a state of dependency on other
nations, or else, as we read in the Book of Judges,
" Every one did what was pleasing in his own eyes," or
as the people exclaimed, after the death of Solomon, when
weary of the rigor of the central authority, " Let every
Israelite look to his own tent!"

Now we are ready to examine our text—a manifestation of this individuality in the earliest days of our history.

Moses and Aaron had arranged a program for the
dedication of the tabernacle, in which there was no mention of an offering of incense. When in accordance with
the arrangements, the various sacrifices had been offered,
and consumed by the fire, Nadab and Abihu seemed to
think the ceremonies still incomplete ; thereupon, each
took his censer, laid fire upon it, and made an offering
of incense—in opposition to the order of exercises planned
at the appointed place in the name of God.

If in our own time, at some public ceremony, at which
the exercises were proceeding with all due order and
decorum, some officious person were to interfere with the
order of ceremonies, surely the anger of the authorities
of the day would quickly be roused. It is true, with us

an action like that of Nadab and Abihu would not be
deemed worthy of the death penalty, since we have
learnt to discriminate between form and spirit; but in
the time of Moses, and especially in the sacrificial service, form was of great importance. In a lower stage
of civilization, a nation, as even now the mass of the
people, does not distinguish between the form and the
matter; to the people, they are the same, standing and
falling together.

One of the great ideas of Moses in regard to sacrifices
was the overthrow of all altars, so that but one should
remain to be devoted to the service of the Almighty;
upon it sacrifices were to be brought, under the super-
vision of the high-priest, according to a prescribed plan,
no option being allowed in the matter. Thus alone
could backsliding into idolatry be combated. The
myriads of Israel's followers were to serve God according to set ceremonies, and not as was pleasing in their
own sight. On the very first day on which this law was
to go into operation, opposition reared its head in the
camp. Nadab and Abihu wished to carry out their own
ideas; nor did the struggle end with their death; it was
prolonged throughout a thousand years. Again and
again do we find in the historical books of the Bible
the complaint, "The people continued to sacrifice upon
their private altars, and there to offer incense." And
if, after long years of idolatry, a pious king succeeded
in bringing about a revival of better things, still we
constantly hear the same refrain, "But the altars were
still without number; the people continued to sacrifice upon their high places." In short, the people
would not be deprived of their individuality; they

'were unwilling to submit to a common will and a common form.

This characteristic explains much in the history of Israel in ancient times, as at a later period and in our own days. At every page of its marvellous story, Judaism seems on the verge of disintegration. Not only the limbs of Israel's *body* lie scattered over the world; in spiritual matters, there is likewise no unity, no community of action, in truth, nothing but opposition and divergence. Again and again may it be said, "Each one takes his own censer, and puts thereon incense;" and worst of all, he also "lays a fire thereupon!" It has been said of the Bible that its words are capable of forty-nine interpretations. There is no other religious community on the face of the earth so entirely without central authority; the members think and act as they please, and yet follow a common path in spite of all divergence. The one community looks up to a Pope, a Delai Lama, or a Sheik ul Islam, as an authority; others again boast a consistory or a synod. But we have no institution corresponding to any of these. Each one takes his own censer. Rabbinical conventions in the old world, and Boards of Delegates in the new have sought to bring about unity of action, but their voices, too, die away ineffectual. The Union of American Hebrew Congregations has a like end in view, but as soon as it will require obedience of individuals and congregations, it is certain that the demand will meet with protest or silent disregard.

The Shulchan Arukh, it is true, was an acknowledged authority, to a certain degree extending its influence even to our own day; still its power was not so great as is generally believed. Strict as this code is, as a whole, it must still be said that many a one came with his censer, and laid fire upon it, " a strange fire which God had not commanded him." The cause of these phenomena in Jewish life must, indeed, be regarded as a fact; but the further cultivation of the national quality which they indicate, is not to be recommended. Many great afflictions are, in the end, recognized as beneficent in effect; even death is no exception to the rule; still it would not occur to us, on that account, to foster and nurse evil in the world. So this strongly marked individuality of Israel is an evil in its one-sided development. To it we must oppose, as a counterpoise, a strenuous effort to maintain a connection with the body of Israel, even if in pursuance of this aim, it becomes necessary to give up much that is dear to us; much that appears to us better than that which meets with the approval of the majority.

"After the doings of the land of Egypt, wherein ye have dwelt, shall ye not do; and after the doings of the land of Canaan whither I am bringing you, shall ye not do; and in their customs, shall ye not walk.

"My ordinances shall ye do, and my statutes shall ye keep, to walk therein : I am the Lord your God.

"And ye shall keep my statutes, and my ordinances, which if a man do he shall live in them : I am the Lord.

* * * * * * * * * *

"For all these abominations have the men of the land done, who were before you, and the land hath become defiled."—LEV. XVIII : 3-5, 27.

With these injunctions a heavy task was laid on our ancestors. They were ordered to forget what they had learnt in Egypt, and to learn nothing in that most efficient school in which many receive their entire education—the school of life, in which we are taught by association and example. They were to ignore completely the prevailing institutions and usages of the two most cultured states of the time, of Egypt and of Canaan, the neighbor of wealthy and cultured Phœnicia. They were to rear a new order of things in state and society, build according to a new law, making no use of old material or rules. The slow progress of the new idea in Israel, and the many backslidings of the people into their old faults are in nowise remarkable, for these faults were merely the difficulty of forgetting the past, and the inability to

resist the example of the nations among which the Israelites dwelt.

The law of Moses declared: "There is but one God!"
Egypt and Canaan contradicted this statement; every
hill and grove adorned with the image of a god; every
monument erected by pagan hands; every inscription,
wherever such existed, contradicted it. King and people,
the learned priest and the ignorant shepherd alike repu-
diated this truth. As with one voice, they exclaimed:
"There is but one God! That is not true! It is not
alone an untruth, but an heretical, dreadful thought, a
grievous offence against the gods, a profanity which the
gods will not fail to punish." Moses taught an ideal
faith; his doctrine was a voice from heaven, totally at
variance with the earth and its inhabitants.

"Love thy neighbor as thyself." Another strange
doctrine unheard of either in Egypt or in the land of
Canaan! "As one born in the land among you, shall be
unto you the stranger that sojourns with you." Here
we have a direct blow at an institution common to all
ancient communities, both great and small; among them
all, the stranger was mistrusted and hated, if, indeed,
death was not his portion.

"Ye shall be unto me a kingdom of priests and a
holy nation," that is the declaration of the equality of
the whole people before God and the Law. In order to
make this Law a part of its very life, Israel had to forget that in Egypt, slavery, inequality before the law, the
caste system, were equivalent to wisdom, and that from
time immemorial, they had been the pillars of the social
order. Above all these laws, however, stood the command enjoining strict morality, purity of life in the rela-

tions of the sexes, and a chastity unknown to Egypt and Canaan alike. As our text, we read only the introductory words of the chapter recited this morning. The whole chapter can be read at our public services only because we read it in the Hebrew language. Children and other weaklings cannot grasp the meaning of the section, and even to those that understand them, these things are less offensive when expressed in the Hebrew tongue than in the speech of our daily intercourse. That which in our day cannot, without outraging propriety and decency, be read aloud, even as a prohibition, was a common usage among the Egyptians and the Canaanites, and none thought of it as sinful. It was entirely in accord with the law and custom of the time. We may, then, imagine how difficult of execution was the behest to forget the sensual delights and the license of Egypt and Canaan, and to cultivate strict morality and chastity, in the midst of a population among whom debauchery formed a part even of divine worship.

Thirty-five hundred years ago, the Egyptians and the Phœnicians, ranking second only to the former, were the most cultured nations of the earth. Israel first lived in Egypt, and later in its career, was the neighbor of the Phœnicians. Suddenly Moses appears, standing alone in his ideas and convictions, and says to his people, Israel, "Forget Egypt, neither learn aught from the Phœnicians. Through me, God sends unto you a new Law; it does not teach you how to build houses, or dig canals, or guide vessels, or carry on your trades and occupations; neither will it teach you how to inscribe your thoughts upon wood and stone to preserve them for future generations, nor how to manipulate numbers, how to measure the surface of the earth, how to observe the movements of the sun and the stars. All these things it is well not to *forget*, these it is well to *learn*. No land could teach these arts better than Egypt and Phœnicia." Moses confined his teachings to religion and morality. His object it was to give to Israel a new doctrine of faith and humanity, by the application of which a new life was to begin for the nation. Had Moses brought his divine truths, his teachings, and his laws of universal love and benevolence from Egypt, as is boldly asserted by many a critic desirous of belittling mankind's debt to our religion, how could he have laid upon his contemporaries the prohibitory command, "Ye shall *not* do as the Egyptians do; ye shall *not* follow in their paths?"

Although it is highly displeasing to many a well-meaning but superficial critic that this chapter forms a part of the Bible, it is nevertheless one of the most valuable of its sections, for the prohibitions enjoined by Moses testify to the moral condition of the most cultured people of the time.

"Thou shalt love the Lord thy God with all thy heart, with all thy soul, and with all thy might." The gods, as pictured in the imaginations of the Egyptians and Canaanites, or as represented in visible form, or by them in the shapes of living beasts, were not beings to be loved; they rather inspired their adorers with terror and repulsion.

The highest ideal towards which our relation to our fellow-men should tend, is expressed in the maxim: "Love thy neighbor as thyself." The generic idea of *man*, a human being, the citizen of the world, was known neither to the Egyptians nor to the Canaanites.

When Pharaoh said to Moses, "I know not Adonai," he
might have added, "The idea of *man* is utterly strange
to me; I know only Egyptians and barbarians." And
finally, the most elevated conception of man's duty
toward himself is expressed in our text: וחי בהם—if a
man do my statutes and ordinances, "he shall live
by them," to which our sages add, in explanation,
ולא שימת בהם, "not die by them." The Israelite ought
to regard life, its preservation, maintenance and enjoyment as a duty, and not leave it entirely to nature's
control. This certainly required the Israelites to forget
Egypt, and to refrain from adopting the customs of
Canaan; for in those countries the underlying thought
of religion was worship of the gods, not the care bestowed by the gods upon man, while the religion of
Israel sought the happiness of mankind. "Not for my
sake do I demand obedience," says the Lord, "not for
mine own honor and glory, have I given laws and commandments unto you, that you should live according to
them, but for your sake, that you may live and be
happy."

וחי בהם, "he shall live by them." Heathenism does not
recognize that man has duties toward himself. What
matters it to the gods that man does violence to his person, or injures his health, that he scourges himself, and
denies himself the pleasures of life, if only the honor
and the offerings due to them from mortals receive
proper attention? The highest honor that could be
paid to the gods, the offering most pleasing in their
sight was a man's sacrifice of his own person upon the
altar. Most grateful to them was the incense of human
flesh arising from the earth.

In the Mosaic code, self-preservation is for the first time considered a religious duty.

On the one hand, to forget, and on the other, not to imitate have ever been, and still continue, Israel's duty. It is true, the land from which many of us came was no Egypt, neither do we dwell in Canaan. In both countries, we did and do learn much for which we ought to be truly grateful, not alone in trades, in science, in art, and in all other knowledge useful to us in our civic life, but in morality as well. The people among whom we dwell set us a good and worthy example. For, do they not use the same source from which we draw inspiration and knowledge—the Holy Scriptures? But in essential matters of faith and in all that touches closely our worship of God, we must follow the path especially marked out for us by the divine word, learning and adopting nothing from our former fellow-citizens, nor from those among whom our lot is now cast. In matters of morality as well, many an injunction has been handed down to us from the old, severe times which it would be well not to exchange for the usages and ideas of other nations; among such behests, may be included those contained in the chapter read to-day, offensive to the ear, but valuable to the heart. We have reference to the sanctity of marriage in the Israelitish community. The Bible knows no false modesty. In its pages are found in abundance words that we hesitate to pronounce, and on the other hand, the Holy Canon contains a song in honor of pure love; but no thought endangering the sanctity of the marriage relation, treating it in a frivolous light for the amusement of the public, no sentiment making fidelity ridiculous and glorifying breach of faith is to be found in its books. Holy family life! Foundation of the structure of morality! Remain with us in thy ancient strength. Israel! Exchange not the precious heir-loom of chastity in the marriage bond and purity in family relations for the glittering toys of frivolity common in the life about you!

We have still another precious inheritance from the olden days, the virtue of moderation in the use of intoxicating liquors. We rarely find an Israelite a member of a temperance society, for Israel's religion says to him וחי בהם, "You shall *live*, and enjoy yourself, ולא שימת בהם, but you shall not destroy in yourself the capacity for enjoyment." Nor is an Israelite often found among drunkards. Here again the warning advice of Moses is in place: "Do not act according to the usages of the land that you have left, nor of that in which you dwell!"

We have received many benefits at the hands of our fellow-citizens, both here and abroad; let us strive to make some return for these gifts by setting them a good example in our own lives.

EQUALITY.

"Ye shall be holy: for I the Lord your God am holy."—LEV. XIX : 2.

We have here no moral maxim, whose influence upon mind and heart can be but a variable quantity, but a law, a fundamental law upon which rises the very structure of the Mosaic state. The meaning of this law is more clearly indicated in the verse of the Bible which reads: "Ye shall be unto me a kingdom of priests and a holy nation"—I declare you all equal before God and the Law in dignity, in rights and in duties.

In Egypt, the home of Moses, the model state of antiquity, the doctrine of a holy *nation* and of a kingdom in which every subject possessed equal privileges with the priestly caste, would have been looked upon as revolutionary, a transgression against the divine and earthly order of the universe. The promulgator of such a doctrine, unless spared on the plea of insanity, would have met with a martyr's fate. Differences in rank, belief and race lay at the foundation of state and society in Egypt, as in all ancient, mediæval and even modern civilizations, the republics of the Middle Ages forming no exception to this rule. There had been holy men before this time, but no one had ever conceived the idea of a holy *nation*. The ancient world was familiar also with the idea of a *priest-nation*, *i. e.*, a nation controlled, in body and soul, by the priesthood. The Bible tells us

264

that the meanest Egyptian considered it beneath him to sit down to a meal with a shepherd. In India, the representative of a civilization even older than that of Egypt, one hundred Pariahs were not considered equal in worth to one Brahmin. A Brahmin would die of thirst rather than refresh himself at a well from which a Pariah had drawn water.

Such was the condition of the world through which resounded the proclamation of Moses: "Ye shall all form a holy nation; each one of you is of priestly worth!" A legend current among our sages audaciously says that God, too, binds phylacteries upon his brow, and that, as in the phylacteries of Israel lies the confession of the unity of God, so the Lord's phylacteries declare the unity of Israel as a single, harmonious community: "Where is there another people like thy people Israel, founded on unity?" For man's notions about divine rule exercise a determining influence upon the institutions of government made by man, and through them, upon the weal and woe of mankind. The heathen conception of heaven lacked the element of unity as well as of equality. Their gods and spirits were separated into grades and classes. How could the thought of human equality exist side by side with this conception of heavenly institutions? Not until the spread of the belief in *one* God, the promulgation of the doctrine of the creation of *one* human pair, and of man's creation in the image of God as narrated in the Bible, could the thought of the equality of all men inform law. The man that made all Israel kneel before one God could also call to it with the voice of authority, "Ye shall be a kingdom of priests and a holy nation!" or as set forth in our text, "Ye shall be holy: for I the Lord your God am holy."

When paganism clothed itself in the garb of Christianity, many gods were deposed from their high places in heaven, but this change did not bring with it the establishment of the idea of divine unity. In consequence, throughout seventeen hundred years, the Church tolerated and even approved the institution of rank in affairs of the state and of society; indeed, the Church herself had serfs and slaves in her possession. The division of believers into priesthood and laity exists even to-day; the ban of the Church would follow a contradiction of this dogma, and if temporal power were to lend its aid, the daring rebel would atone for his heresy upon the funeral pyre. In the highly cultured states of the old world, the pride and splendor of the nobility is not yet a thing of the past.

The desert was the scene of the promulgation of the new doctrine, the equality of all men in the sight of God. There, alone, could Moses find neutral ground, soil uncorrupted by the vicious husbandry of violence and injustice. The Puritans, too, were compelled to flee from the restraints of tradition, an antiquated doctrine of kingly authority, and the hopeless view of heaven and earth current in the old world; they, too, sought virgin soil, and came to these bleak shores, still covered with the primeval forest, that they might prepare the ground for the law of reason, and plan a life in accordance with the doctrine of the equality of all men.

The law and the doctrine of universal equality have become so thoroughly a part of our very flesh and blood that a word on the subject may appear super-

fluous, how much more making the idea the theme
of a discourse in a house of worship. Nevertheless, it
is well for us to be reminded occasionally that the
acquisition is, in truth, a very recent one. For more
than three thousand years, the law of equality was like
a grain of wheat lying in the hand of a mummy. The
law as it stood in the Bible was a beautiful flower in the
garden of morality. In the economy of human affairs,
in the fields of practical legislation and administration,
it was trampled upon, and violently uprooted, wherever
it ventured to sprout upon the surface of society.
Wonderful to relate! Three thousand years after the
promulgation of the doctrine, six thousand miles distant
from Mount Sinai, far over the sea known at that time
as the הגדול ים, and beyond a still greater הגדול ים, entirely
unknown to the ancients, in a quarter of the globe whose
existence was not suspected in that distant day—there the
Mosaic law, like the staff of Aaron, sprouted, blossomed
and bore fruit in one moment! The plant that had
been looked upon as poisonous in the old world, or at
the least, detested by the ruling powers as a rank weed,
now became a very tree of life for mankind. And
yet only a decade ago, how much blood was shed in
this very land, the traditional home of liberty, ere the
complete triumph of this glorious principle could be
achieved!

What is Israel's share in this achievement? There
was no Jew among the Puritans that came to this country
in the *Mayflower*, and planted the seed that was to bear
good fruit for the future Republic. None of our fellow-
believers participated in the struggles of the colonies
with the Parliament of the mother-country. The name

of an Israelite is not found among the signers of the Declaration of Independence, nor among the framers of the Constitution. Our share in the great work of the Republic is our Torah. The corner-stone of our national constitution—the equality of all men—was quarried at Mount Sinai. The Puritans, those men of irresistible strength and iron will, were the builders of the Republic. In them Saxon strength and Biblical spirit were united. They thought in the spirit of the Old Testament; they spoke in the language of the Bible; they preached in the style of the prophets; they sang in the words of our psalmists. As they also preferred to take their names from the Old Testament, only the sound of the Hebrew language was wanting in their camp for us to imagine ourselves in the midst of Davids, Joabs, Gideons and other Old Testament heroes.

Israelites! This is our part in the structure of a new world—our Torah! There is but one God in Heaven and one mankind on earth. Yet in our day, none know and study the Torah less than we Israelites. To the Spaniards belonged the gold and silver mines of the new world; but it was the Hollanders and the English-men that grew rich. The Spanish owners became im-poverished in their indolence. We possess the gold mine of religion, but in religious learning we grow ever poorer; our Christian brethren enrich themselves with our treasures.

Who can count the millions of dollars expended by Christian piety and liberality upon the translation of the Bible into one hundred and fifty languages, that it may be spread over the entire earth, and be placed in every lonely cabin? In the cars, in steamboats, in h itels, the Bible lies ready at hand, placed there by some pious hand ; and it is not merely read, it is *studied* by Christian scholars and by the common people, by priest and layman alike. And now behold the contrast —the Holy Scriptures and the Israelites! The picture is a sad one, even from a secular point of view, for any one that makes the slightest pretension to culture ought not to be a stranger to this book of the world's litera- ture. Will there soon be a change for the better? May God grant that Israel remain his holy nation and a kingdom of priests worthy of the name!

When we assemble in thy name, O God! to open the book of thy Law, we express our thanks to thee that thou hast selected us from among all nations to receive thy Law—to receive, but not to forget it; not, like sloth- ful servants, to lay the burden upon the shoulders of others, but to preserve it, to study it and to spread abroad its blessed truths. We thank thee in words, may we confirm our gratitude in deeds! May thy holy law be ever on our lips and in our hearts! May the words of the prophet find realization in us: "My spirit that is upon thee, and my words which I have put in thy mouth, shall not depart out of thy mouth, nor out of the mouth of thy children, nor out of the mouth of thy children's children, from henceforth and forever!"

THE MEANING OF THE WORD "HOLY."

"Speak unto all the congregation of the children of Israel, and say unto them, Ye shall be holy; for I the Lord your God am holy."—LEV. XIX : 2.

An action worthy of being called holy must be entirely free from selfish motives. If we shun sin because of our fear of earthly or eternal punishment; if we do good in the hope of reward, though this anticipated reward be but praise and gratitude and other acknowledgment, the action is, indeed, praiseworthy. Our sages say, "Whoever says, 'These alms I give that my child may live, or in order to secure for myself life eternal,' may be called truly pious." Yes, he is a pious man, for God is in his thoughts, and to him he looks for help. However, we cannot call him a *holy* man, for his motive is self-interest, even though of a most refined character. "Ye shall be holy." With no thought of selfish gain, sanctify your lives, devoting yourselves to good and avoiding evil.

A man may, however, do good and noble deeds with aims and spirit alike disinterested, and still not have the slightest claim to holiness, for in order to deserve the attribute holy, sentiment and act must be inspired by thoughts of God and his holy will. "For I the Lord your God am holy"—let this be the reason for your holiness. In this chapter, so rich in maxims concerning that which is good and just, every sentence is followed by the

270

warning, "I am the Lord your God." Be this the
motive of your actions. No one speaks of holy Socrates.
In our days, too, there are many good and noble men,
who have no claim to holiness, still less do they lay any
pretensions to such praise, for God is not in their thoughts,
probably they do not even believe in him, and hence the
divine idea can have no influence upon their feelings and
actions. Through Moses, God proclaims to Israel : " Ye
shall be holy ! It is God's will that, without a thought of
self, you devote yourselves to all that is pure and elevated, and let your inspiration be this thought, ' God is
holy !' "

Little justification as there is for calling that man holy
whose actions, though disinterested, good and noble, are
uninspired by any thought of God, still less is it proper
to ascribe this quality of holiness to one who acts
always in the name of God, and who lives and dies in a
firm belief in him, but whose sentiments and actions
cannot bear the searching light of reason and morality.
In the name of God, Torquemada and Arbues, Philip the
Second, Ferdinand and Isabella wrought deeds, the
very thought of which makes us shudder with horror.
Loyola, too, believed that he was truly serving God, and
all these the Head of the Church pronounced holy.
Granting that these men robbed, persecuted and tortured
their fellow-men to death in the firm belief that their
actions were pleasing in the sight of God ; granting that
avarice did not play a part in urging them on to action,
nevertheless, we cannot admit that they could lay claim
to holiness, since their doctrine, sentiments and deeds
were in direct opposition to the dictates of reason and
morality. Korach, too, laid claim to holiness. He said,

"The whole of the congregation are all of them holy, and the Lord is among them," but his *deeds* were base, prompted by vain ambition. Acting in the name of God and in a belief in God may make a man pious, but not holy. Holiness is greater than piety. Holiness includes piety, but piety may exist apart from holiness. There are, therefore, more pious men than saints in the world. A fanatic may be pious, and yet displeasing both to God and to man. Piety is of the heart, but holiness presses into service heart, hand and spirit. "Ye shall be holy, for I the Lord your God am holy." God is not called holy because of a pious belief in himself, but because he is goodness, justice and wisdom; because he dwells in our thoughts far removed from all that is earthly, all that is sensual. "Ye shall be holy" means, "I am not satisfied with piety that simply pays its addresses to me; I want not servants that think to gain my favor by praise and prayer."

Finally, holiness must be paramount and constant, suffering neither fluctuation nor change.

In every man's life there are moments of good inspiration, when noble impulses are stirred within him. So too, there are but few human beings, over whom there steals not, now and again, a presentiment or a consciousness of the existence of a divine, omnipotent Power, of an eternal life in which the soul will continue its existence. To some, such feelings, such moments may be familiar companions; to others, but fleeting and infrequent visitors, perhaps gaining entrance to their souls on the annually recurring Day of Atonement, or when affliction and death are visited upon them. Such moments and thoughts are like flashes of lightning, illuminating the heaven of night; but the light is unreliable. It does not always lighten, when one is sorely in need of light. So, too, the light of piety is often extinguished, even in the pious man, at the very moment when he most feels the want of it. But, "Ye shall be holy" means, "The fear of the Lord, a good heart and a willing hand must become second nature to you. In temptation and in the hour of weakness, they must not waver. Your fear of God and your moral instinct dare not be diseased, at times exciting your blood to fever heat; at others, chilling you to the heart."

After the principle of holiness has been laid down for us in the words of our text, the rest of the chapter, read to-day, gives the details for putting it into practice.

"Ye shall fear, every man, his mother and his father." Fear of one's father, *i. e.*, obedience to parents, lies at the foundation of education in holiness. Let no one speak of an education as good, in which childlike obedience is wanting. Opinions may differ as to the mode of compassing this end. Not the *method*, but the *result*, is important. "Ye shall be holy!" How beautiful are these words! Moses, however, was not a man of fine phrases, but of deep and sound sense. He says to Israel, "You are destined to become a holy nation, to devote yourself entirely to all that is divine, good and noble. Towards this end must tend the education given you by your father and mother. Holy men are not *born*. In obedience to one's father and mother one learns obedience to duty.

"Ye shall fear, every man, his mother and his father, and my Sabbaths shall ye keep." If your children are to obey you, fathers and mothers, *you* must keep my Sabbaths. Yet important as the observance of the Sabbath

19

is, it is but one duty, selected as an example out of many duties, and saying to us, "If the education of your children is to be successful, you must guide them by your good example; if your children are to obey you, *you* must be obedient to God." It is true that, in the work of education, the observance of the Sabbath is a most important factor, and hence especially fitted to be chosen as an example. "My sanctuary shall ye reverence" is a further means to holiness. In using these words, Moses had in mind the sanctuary of his time, though the structure was but a simple tent and not a magnificent temple. The tabernacle and later the two Temples were replaced by synagogues and schools as seats of education in holiness. Reverence the holy purposes that the house serves, be the structure but one of boards! Divine service, the school, education in the home with the observance of the Sabbath as an aid, are the means of sanctifying Israel. When we enter the house of the Lord let us heed the call, " Reverence for my sanctuaries!" Assemble here in an elevated, an earnest mood ; leave frivolous thoughts and ungodly meditations without these walls. Let devotion hold your souls in thrall! Upon joining our family circles, let us attend to the inward voice saying, "Render obedience to your parents!" When we pursue our callings, in our business intercourse, let us heed the warning, "Be upright in your dealings with your neighbor." And in all conditions and vicissitudes of life, may sympathy with our fellow-man be our constant companion ! Love your neighbor in a spirit of disinterestedness, of unselfishness, of holiness.

"Ye shall be holy !" Be not only synagogue and prayer-book saints, but be holy in thought and action, holding aloof from everything base and impure.

SELF-RESPECT.

Lev. XIX : 18.

"Love thy neighbor as thyself!" "This law," says
Christianity, "I gave unto the world," and thereupon
proceeds to call itself, to the exclusion of all others, the
religion of love. The Jewish religion is said by it to be
narrow in its sympathies, and the God of Israel is called
a God of wrath. It is impossible to understand how the
authorship of the doctrine of humanity can be denied
to Judaism, for the tenet is taught here in the Pentateuch with all possible clearness and force. "That may
be true," they say to us, "but you use the word רֵעֲךָ 'thy
neighbor,' which means belonging to your own people.
Non-Israelites are excluded from this circle, while our
religion teaches an unrestricted and universal love of
mankind." This objection, too, is entirely without foundation. In the verses that follow, Moses says: "If a
stranger sojourn with you in your land, ye shall not vex
him. As one born in the land among you, shall be unto
you the stranger that sojourneth with you, and thou
shalt love him as thyself."

The moving force in this dispute between the two sets
of adherents is the vain ambition of each to make the
greater *boast* of the faith professed by each. In theory,
this law is highly prized, both in churches and in synagogues; it is found in all catechisms. But in practice,

it is equally neglected by both bodies of men. This contest between the religions for the honor of being the true mother of the idea of humanity reminds us of the dispute of the two mothers before the judgment seat of Solomon, concerning the ownership of the living child and the dead one. In that altercation the living child nearly lost its life. At times, both religions have acted like unnatural mothers towards this offspring of heaven. It is but a poor consolation for us that rivers of blood, mountains of human bodies, seas of tears testify against the younger mother, while the older one, the Synagogue, for seventeen hundred years, like the lamb in the fable, did not muddy the stream for the wolves, and stands before the world clean of hand. The theory is good, even of heavenly excellence. It is, indeed, but too good for this world. Earth would turn into a heaven for its inhabitants, if the doctrine of humanity were in practice applied with the zeal with which it is advocated as a theory. There is probably no one among us so little versed in knowledge of himself as to boast, " I, for my part, love my neighbor as myself." There has been no human being on the face of the earth, from Adam's day down to our own, who has not loved himself more than his fellow-man. Taken in its strict sense, the law is against human nature. It was set up by Moses as an ideal to be approached more and more nearly, but without any prospect of its complete realization. In the development of the religion of Israel, as shown in the religious writings that followed the books of Moses, there is no reference to the law of humanity promulgated in the Torah. Not until twelve hundred years after the time of Moses do we hear the famous Golden

Rule of Hillel. This law, however, is not "Love* thy neighbor as thyself," but "Do not unto others what you would not have others do unto you." In idea, this is very far removed from love, but as a duty, it lies within the range of man's powers. Synagogues and churches are not wanting in men and women obeying this Golden Rule in their lives, and even going far beyond it in their *works* of love.

The law of love of our fellow-man is to be our ideal; its meaning, therefore, deserves a somewhat closer investigation. We translate the word ואהבת in our text as "thou shalt love." Love, however, is stubborn, and will not be made a matter of duty. Sympathy comes and goes, and gives no reason for its erratic course. As we noticed earlier in the discussion, the demand for love for our fellow-man is against human nature, and is not man's nature also the work of God? But ואהבת may also mean, be charitable, be benignant. This demand is not unreasonable. Man can comply with it, if such be his will. Rejoice in your neighbor's prosperity; judge him in the best possible light; give him all due honor, and in your intercourse with him, make all allowances for his deficiencies. Sympathize with him in his sorrow, pity him in his distress, even if you are unable or unwilling to aid him in deed. Such is the construction that our sages put upon the verse, "Be humane," they say, "even in the manner of executing sentence of death upon a criminal, for 'thou shalt love thy neighbor as thyself.'" To ask love for a criminal would be demand-

---

* ואהבת "Thou shalt love" is here followed by the dative case. The verse may, therefore, be translated, "Love *for* thy neighbor," etc. Hillel evidently thus translated the verse, for his Golden Rule is merely the negative of this injunction.—[Tr.]

ing too much, but one may be kindly disposed even towards those going to the scaffold.

The words " as thyself" demand a somewhat more thorough discussion. These words seem to make the doctrine still unsafer as a guide in life. In too many instances, our neighbor would be but hardly used, were we to love him as ourselves, act towards him as towards ourselves. Let us examine our lives with strictly impartial scrutiny, with vision unobscured by fatuous self-love. Who has wrought us more harm, has made life harder for us to bear, has done more to embitter our joys, than we ourselves? And we consider ourselves as belonging to the better classes! How is it, then, with the thousands lying in prison; with those wandering aimlessly about the streets; with the uncounted hosts of thieves and cheats, who bring upon themselves want and distress, amid which they perish, ending their lives in poor-houses, or it may be by their own hands? All these men loved themselves, but we should scarcely feel grateful were they to show us in our intercourse with them such love as they have shown towards themselves.

Therefore, *let man first learn to love himself wisely;* that is the higher duty. A man must be of worth to himself, before he can be of worth to his neighbor. Beneficent and enduring love is founded upon respect. If we advance " Love thyself," as the higher principle, it is in the sense, " Man respect thyself." Far be it from the spirit of religion to demand love for yourself, in your wild, brutish inclinations, your boundless selfishness. To love one's self wisely and in a god-pleasing manner, means to keep far from one's self all manner of impurity, for every sin is an act of unkindness toward one's self. To

love one's self means to do good to others, for your reward
is great in your own heart and in the hearts of those
about you. Your friends will be double the number of
those befriended by you. To love one's self means to
enjoy God's gifts, but only in such a way as not to lose
one's self respect. Be pure, be honest, be upright, be
true, kind and useful, be grateful to God and man, be
courteous and sociable ; thus, your love for yourself will
rest upon respect ; you will be a friend to yourself, and
your friendship and your love may then possess some
value for your neighbor !

The principle of love of self is thus developed before
the idea of love of one's fellow-man, and it likewise
takes precedence in its mention in the Bible. Man, we
are told, is created in the image of God, which means,
" Man, do not hold too mean an opinion of yourself, as if
created for no other purpose than to eat, drink and sleep ;
to be born and to die like the beast. You are destined for
higher things ; you have free-will ; you can do good and
evil to others. You have an immortal soul extending
beyond this earthly life ; you have intelligence. Like
God, the soul is invisible, but its being is felt, just as the
being of the Almighty and his omnipotence and his wisdom are perceptible in his works. Upon your countenance, the Lord has breathed the living soul."* Both
mind and heart speak in the face of man. The face is
the mirror of our thoughts and emotions. In it, we may
read acumen and stupidity, benevolence and malice, deep
earnestness and unbounded covetousness, fidelity and

---

* Luther, in his "Table Talk," translates this passage in the Bible thus·
" He blew *upon* his countenance a living spirit." This rendition was
approved by Herder.

deceit, wrath and equanimity, love and hate, despair and
resignation, cunning and simplicity, pride and humility,
and even more than all this may a watchful observer
note in the face of man! Therefore, man, hold not too
low an opinion of yourself! Pay honor and respect to
your own soul. Even your fellow-man may read your
nature in your face, and he will regard you with respect
or contempt, according to his decision; how much better must your soul be known to your Creator! If, when
you look into your mirror, you see unamiability stamped
on your countenance, you ought to feel ashamed even in
your own eyes. You will thus learn to love yourself
wisely, to grant yourself every pleasure that does not
make you lose the respect of good men and of yourself.
And thus, seeing it to be rooted in yourself, a part of
your very being, remember the law of humanity, the
subject of contention between Christianity and Judaism.
In the strife, let us not allow this heavenly child to perish; let both rather cherish it with tender care.

SUCCESS AND FAILURE.

LEV. XXII : 27.

Success is the all powerful argument, deciding beyond appeal the question of merit. Reason, morality, the warning voice of history, are all mute before the spectacle of obvious triumph.

The world does not inquire whence came the gold. It matters not whether it be of low and sordid origin, or the reward of honorable service; whether it shine on the breast of the hero, a token of self-sacrificing courage, or gleam in the hand of the spy, a reward for treason. Gold is gold. So with success. Success is proof of right-thinking, of cleverness, of wisdom and of justice. Success is success. The path on which the goal of victory was attained is of no moment. As soon, however, as fortune deserts a man, he loses, in a moment, not only the results of his labor, but the good opinion formerly held by his fellow-men of his endowments of heart and mind. Such is the fate of human beings, and of ideas, currents of thought, and fashions as well. They rule, their triumph is manifest, and hence they are considered beautiful, good, true and right, until their kingdom is taken from them; but when that time comes, they are no longer conceded the slightest merit.

Our attention is directed to this subject to-day by a commentary of the Midrash on the morning's portion.

We read in Ecclesiastes, האלהים יבקש את־נרדף, "God is on the side of the persecuted;" whereupon the Midrash remarks, "God espouses the cause of the downtrodden against the oppressor. Cain was the oppressor of his brother Abel, and the Lord turned away from the former. So with Noah and his contemporaries. God chose Noah from all the men of his time. Abraham and Nimrod, Jacob and Esau, Joseph and his brothers, Moses and Pharaoh, David and Saul, Israel among the nations of the earth—in each instance, God is found on the side of the oppressed. So with the sacrificial animals; the ox is hunted down by the lion, the goat by the leopard, the wolf chases the lamb. None of these pursuers is deemed worthy of being sacrificed; only the pursued and long-suffering animals may be led to the altar. Therefore, we read, 'When a *bullock*, or a *sheep*, or a *goat*, is brought forth.'" (Lev. XXII : 27.)

In his faith and in his practice, Noah stood alone, in opposition to all the men of his time. Such was the relation of Abraham and of Moses to their respective contemporaries, and such was the position of Israel and its faith in all lands and times. Every epoch furnishes examples of men of intellectual strength and of moral power, holding an isolated position in thought, feeling and tastes.

The masses do not regard with indifference the voluntary spiritual separation and independent position of such individuals; no, they harass and persecute the men and women that dare hold different opinions and beliefs from those current with their contemporaries. The non-conformists are jeered and vexed in a thousand ways, and abused until their discomfiture seems complete.

"God sides with the oppressed." Many a man, occupying a solitary position in his generation, and many an idea struggling against the current of the time, are on the side of right and truth, while aberrations of feeling, taste and thought may make up the sum of the spiritual life of entire epochs. Noah, holding himself aloof from the rudeness about him, suffering violence but doing none, avoiding wickedness in the midst of a sinful world, must have seemed a fool in the eyes of his contemporaries. From a human point of view, success was not on his side. Abraham's new faith, as the legend tells us, brought him mortal danger. His hours of leisure were filled with meditations, not conducive to material welfare. He remained true to a God, who led him from one temptation into another. His new moral code set certain bounds to his earthly pleasures. All this must have made his life appear a failure to the men of his time; nor could they think his idea the correct one, nor regard Abraham himself as a wise and far-seeing man. Joseph's peculiar way of thinking made him appear an idle dreamer to his brothers. For eighty years it was Moses' fate to be regarded as a foolish man, who had interfered in a quarrel that did not concern him in the least, and, in consequence of which, he had to live as a stranger in a strange land.

And how low was the opinion held of Israel and its faith in the times and on the scenes of its oppression! Verily, throughout centuries, Israel and its faith seemed anything but triumphant. But God is with the oppressed. God looks not upon success, but upon the spiritual attitude. If the *principle* be good, though it lack the support of the multitude, God will be with it and its upholders.

The poet says: "Right is with the living," or as Ecclesiastes expresses it, "A living dog fareth better than a dead lion." Hence, every period of time is looked upon as the best, by those living in it; ours is no exception to the rule. "The nineteenth century!" With this exclamation, all possible praise and approval are heaped upon its institutions and the opinions of the multitude; for the century is alive, life is success, and success means everything that is good and right. The ancient times are dead and gone, and, therefore, they are dismal failures. Others, again, hold that the olden times achieved more than the new in faith and morality, in domestic and social life. They think that a dead lion is *better* than a living dog. But the important point is that whether the oppressor takes a stand on the side of the old or of the new, God is not with the oppressor. Success is of no avail as an argument in the sight of God. If justice and right be on their side, God takes part with the minority against the majority, with the weak against the strong, with the living against the dead.

Let us, too, not allow our judgment to be biased by success or failure. When we form our opinion of a man, let us look not upon the fruits of his life, but upon the seed sown by him. Many a one sows thistles, and reaps rich and luscious fruits; do not decide, on that account, to sow the seed of thistles. Another, again, plants rarest grains, and rank weeds spring up, and choke them. Do not, therefore, cease to sow good seeds in your path in life. Man does his share, be it good or bad. Success—

the earthly harvest of our deeds—is influenced by the winds and storms of fate, which lie beyond human control. Let no one, then, believe too firmly in his own moral and mental strength, because fortune smiles upon him, nor hold too mean an opinion of himself, and despair of his powers, because success does not crown his efforts. Look with impartial eye upon the condition of your *soul*. See whether your intentions are good, whether you have done the best in your power. Let success not make you arrogant, nor defeat dishearten you. And let us all make it a rule of life ever to be the partisans of the oppressed and the weak.

But why are the weak ones weak, if God be on their side? Why are the oppressed persecuted, and the down-trodden abused? . We may as well ask, "Why is the bullock strangled by the lion? Why does the leopard rend the goat? Why is the lamb torn by the wolf? What is the reason for the sorrows of the helpless?" This is one of the great problems of the universe.

Hence, hold not too high an opinion of the lions, the leopards and the wolves of your acquaintance, because their efforts meet with success. Neither think meanly of the sheep, the weak, those that are hunted down, because failure is their lot in life.

"LET THY BROTHER LIVE WITH THEE!"

LEV. XXV : 25–44.

The Hebrew language is especially rich in expressions for poor. We have רש, הילך, כסכן, אביון, עני, דל. On the other hand, it is very poor in words for the idea of wealth. We have the word עשיר, and possibly also שוע. This peculiarity in the language proves how much attention was paid to the poor by the people that spoke it. In our text a certain term is used to describe the change from wealth to poverty (מכך or מוך). We read, "And if thy brother become poor, and fall in decay with thee: then shalt thou assist him, yea, though he be a stranger, or a sojourner, that he may live with thee. Thou shalt not take of him any usury or increase; but thou shalt be afraid of thy God: that thy brother may live with thee." And again we read, "*If thy brother become poor, and sell away some of his possession: then may his nearest of kin come and redeem what his brother hath sold.*" The time set for the redemption of a house within the city was one year; country property could be redeemed within any length of time. If the property was not redeemed, land and village property alike had to revert to the original owner in the jubilee year. And, finally, we read a third time, "*And if thy brother become poor near thee, and (he sell himself unto thee, or) be sold unto thee: thou shalt not compel him to work as a bond-servant.*

"But as a hired laborer, as a sojourner shall he be with thee; until the year of the jubilee shall he serve with thee.

"And then shall he depart from thee, he and his children with him; and he shall return unto his own family, and unto the possession of his fathers shall he return."

If a man sells a part of his estate, he cannot properly be called poor. According to the Mosaic laws, a man's sale of his own person, or his sale by warrant of the court, to satisfy an unpaid debt, signifies only that he pledges himself to the service of another man for a length of time not exceeding six years. But he is not poor who is able to pay his debts with the fruit of his labor, and to support himself by service rendered to others. To this class of unfortunates, our morning's text refers, men declining in fortune, but not yet fallen, struggling with adverse fate, but yet holding out against its attacks.

The phrase, "Thou shalt love thy neighbor as thyself," is extolled by all, and refuted by none; many a one, however, feels that he has discharged the duty here laid upon him by the gift to the poor of a few cents or a few dollars. The man so reduced in means that he is undeniably poor has passed the time of sorest distress. Not only will the benevolence of others not allow him to want, but the inner struggle, the anguish of sinking ever lower, no longer makes his heart heavy within him. Poverty itself is not so hard to bear as the journey leading to it from a position of affluence. How difficult to part with the first acre, the second, the third! "I was a well-to-do farmer and am still considered such by my neighbors, but I shall soon be compelled to become a simple day-laborer." Judge of the feelings of the man, once the possessor of

a broad estate, with none to dictate to him, but many in
his service to do his bidding, when forced by necessity
to enter with wife and child, into another's employ, he
and his wife as well compelled to act as the servants of
strangers! This sorrowful journey from wealth to
poverty is frequently made even more difficult by the
painful efforts to maintain the appearance of prosperity
before the eyes of the world. Though the heart aches,
a smile of contentment must play upon the lips! Sore
distress under the thread-bare cloak of affluence!

To render assistance to struggling and sinking fellow-
creatures, to extend to them a helping hand, and aid
them that they may not fall—this is the active love of
our fellow-man enjoined on us by the Holy Scriptures.
Moses wrote this chapter only to impress the importance
of this duty upon his people. It is by no means an
exhaustive treatment of the subject, but merely a cita-
tion of examples. In it, our sympathy and help are
not invoked for naked poverty, crying aloud for bread,
extending the begging hand, and ever ready with a
word of gratitude in return for the gift; but for him
" who falls in decay with thee," or literally, whose hand
sinks helpless at his side. He does not stretch forth his
hand to receive help, but you cannot fail to notice that
it drops nerveless. He may be. endowed with excellent
qualities of mind and heart, but to amass and maintain
a fortune requires skill of hand as well. To you, not to
the world at large, it is plain that his hand hangs useless at his side.

For the care of the destitute, for orphans and widows,
for the helpless and aged, charity provides. Their distress is alleviated by public institutions and the united

efforts of benevolent men and women. But public institutions are powerless to aid those succumbing in their struggles against fate, for the publication of their distress would be an even greater trial than want itself. They shrink from confessing to themselves how sad is the future that awaits them. A tender heart, a heart filled with love for humanity, must here seek to bring help in word and deed, unseen of all but God alone. "Thou shalt be afraid of thy God!" And the text adds, "I am the Lord." The thought, "God, the Holy One, sees me, I shall find grace in the sight of the all-merciful Father," is most precious to him who acts as an unknown benefactor to his fellow-creatures in distress. More precious than tears of gratitude; than expressions of praise and approval in countless newspapers; than monuments of marble and of bronze, is the reflection, "I am acting in God's spirit, for God, too, unseen of any one, heals the heart wounded by sorrow, and from his invisible hand, the whole world is fed."

"That man is not poor," some may say, "he has still resources upon which he may depend for his sustenance. 'He has sold away *some* of his possession.'" Thou, who art a friend to mankind, do not wait until all the resources of thy fellow-man are exhausted. As soon as he is compelled by necessity to *begin* parting with his possessions, "then shalt thou assist him," lend him a helping hand. "But we cannot all be rich! Let him sink into poverty. There is still time to help him when he has become quite needy." "Let thy brother live *with* thee." Let it be a pleasure to thee, to have him live *next* to thee, in undisturbed prosperity, not oppressed by care and sunken far *below* thee in worldly station.

We read further, "Thy money shalt thou not give him upon usury." In another place נשך כל־דבר אשר ישך is added (Deut. XXIII : 20); that is, nothing that bites, that makes him suffer shalt thou impose upon him. Do not accompany thy charitable deed with *biting* words. Thy benevolence does not give thee the right to assume the character of a lordly patron.

What Moses calls *selling*, would in our days be considered entering into the service of others. How many young and old men, women and girls nowadays consider themselves fortunate, if the opportunity be afforded them of earning their living in the employ of strangers! Many of them have seen better days, when they themselves were masters and had servants of their own at their beck and call. "Thou shalt not rule over them with rigor." If now thou art become a master over them, be not only their superior, lording it over them at will, but be also a helpful friend, of whom they may seek advice; do not treat them as slaves.

In the Æneid, Virgil makes his hero prophesy as to the future of Rome, and he says: "Others will surpass thee in fluency of speech, in arts, in science; thou wilt show thy pre-eminence in exercising rulership over the whole world." Israel can apply this description to its own career, but in a different and nobler sense. Israel is surpassed by others in the number of artists, of men of wisdom, of discoverers and inventors. As men the achievements of Israelites in all human arts may compare favorably or unfavorably with those of others; their *Judaism* plays no part in their worldly success or failure. But in faith and in theoretical and practical humanity, Israel ought to become the ruling power of the world.

Thirty-five hundred years ago these doctrines of humanity stood alone in the world; to-day they are no longer
good enough for those that consider themselves representative of the best thought of our day.   The belief in one
God, and in his pure, moral Law, with its great chapter
on humanity, stands upon a royal road of the world's
history, and is destined to ride in triumph over the whole
earth.   A language reveals the spirit of those that
speak it. The Germans say *dein Nächster* or *Nebenmensch;*
the Englishman speaks of his *neighbor* and *fellow-man;*
the Hebrew language uses the word *friend*, as in
ואהבת לרעך כמוך, or, as in our morning's text, the still
more loving term, *brother*.   Not the Israelite alone is
spoken of as a friend or a brother; the term is also
applied, as our text again illustrates, to the strangers
that sojourn in the land.

We live among a nation not inferior to Israel in charity and humanity.   Let us strive not to fall short of its
standard in acts of benevolence; let us rather exert ourselves to keep in advance of it, so that, when our Law
has won for itself the rulership of the world, Israel's may
be the undisputed right to bear aloft the banner bearing
the inscription, " Let thy brother live with thee !"

KNOW THYSELF.

"And the Lord spoke unto Moses, saying, Speak unto Aaron, and say
unto him, When thou lightest the lamps, then shall the seven lamps
give light toward the body of the candlestick."—NUMBERS VIII : 1-2.

According to our text, the six lamps upon the six branches of the candlestick were to be so turned as to shed light upon the body of the candelabrum. The lamp was to be a light unto itself, its beams were to serve primarily for illumination of itself.

These instructions form a fitting introduction to the whole chapter, which treats of the conduct of the Levites in their sacred calling. The tribe of Levi was to be a light unto the people, shining before them in precept and example. It was, therefore, necessary for the Levites to be a light unto themselves, examining their own souls by the searching rays of scrutiny and trial, before they could be able and worthy to guide others by the light of their example.

All of us may well take to heart the instruction here given to the Levites. Let us allow our light to penetrate our own souls, before we concentrate its rays upon the thoughts and feelings, the words and actions of others.

To know himself is man's most difficult task as well as his most imperative duty. As we find suitable Biblical verses or pious sentiments inscribed upon the doors of our houses of worship, so over the portal of a Greek temple might have been read the legend, "Know thyself."

The twofold evil—lack of self-knowledge and excessive illumination of the actions and sins of others—grows worse with the progress of civilization. Among civilized nations, appreciation of right and wrong is almost universal, but not every one possesses the moral strength to be virtuous and live according to law. Hypocrisy lends its aid in concealing deficiencies, and in the place of true morality of conduct we have the *appearance* of morality. When the Empress Catherine of Russia was journeying through the Crimea, her all-powerful favorite had the country lying along the road on which she was travelling decorated, to some distance on each side, with representations of pleasant villages, neat farms, smiling fields and grazing herds of cattle in order to deceive the ruler as to the true, desolate condition of the country.

These painted villages correspond to the gestures, forms of speech and action current in civilized society; they are really painted virtues. Were the civilized world in reality as it appears to the superficial observer, earth would be a glorious, nay, a heavenly abode. The few human beings in the houses of correction are as nothing compared with the vast numbers of men on earth. The men that are at large, if taken to be what they pretend to be, are the very impersonations of virtue.

Yet we know in our hearts that such is not the case. We know that in the forms of speech and intercourse of the most cultivated circles, mere show is offered in place of reality. At the very zenith of Roman culture, Augustus reigned for forty-four years, the most powerful

man in the most powerful realm on earth. In his dying
hour, he said to his friend and adviser, Mæcenas,
"Have I played my part well?" If a man with the
power of Augustus, before whom a world lay prostrate,
felt compelled to throw the cloak of hypocrisy over his
purple robes; if, in the solemn hour of death, seeing
himself as he really was, he made the confession that
he had been acting a part in life—surely we can feel no
surprise at Kant's assertion that men, in general, in
becoming more civilized, develop more and more into
actors.

These observations are not recorded as an accusation
or a reproach against society. If such were our idea,
we should necessarily have to regard civilization as an
evil. In reality, no greater honor could be shown to
virtue, nor could her divine origin be more clearly
manifested, than in the phenomenon that those possessing neither the strength nor the inclination to lead a life
of virtue, feel it incumbent upon them to honor it by
simulating its appearance. Virtue is like the sun; the
reflection cast upon the earth at dawn is followed by the
sun himself. So he that practises the appearance of
virtue accustoms himself to virtue itself: he grows to
love it as we love everything that is habitual, and
finally becomes truly virtuous.

Simplicity alone is deceived by appearances. Every
thinking civilized being knows that marks of affection,
of respect, of decorum, of unselfishness in word or
action, may be either a mere pretence or a proof of real
feeling. If a person says to me, "Consider my house
your home," he is not using an hypocritical phrase
for I know that the offer is made with the assumption

that it will not be taken seriously. A savage, on the other hand, would look upon the invitation as a genuine offer.

Imagine a world entirely wanting in decorum, in manners, in a sense of ·shame, in courtesy, in refinement, a world in which all the poison seething in the heart of men, were poured out in society, in which the number of good actions would be limited by inclination, in which kind words and pleasant smiles would be exchanged only when prompted by true kindliness of feeling—how miserable were human existence in this world! Such a condition would mean the end of all sociability, of all tranquillity, of all contentment. Were no word to be spoken, no act performed, however good in itself, unless called forth by correspondingly good feeling, true virtue, which gradually develops under cover of the assumption of virtue, would be but a rare phenomenon.

Decorum, a regard for appearance, politeness, the friendly exchange of sentiments of regard, make up the small coin of virtue. Small change is always alloyed with baser metal, and therefore does not possess the intrinsic value of gold, but nevertheless, it is indispensable as a medium of exchange.

If a fellow-being manifests a kindly disposition towards you, if he is polite and attentive, give him credit for his kindness, even though you think that his heart is not in the act. If a friend fails to meet with your expectations of him, be not too bitter in your denunciations; you should have remembered that you are dealing with a civilized being, who drops many a phrase that he does not mean seriously, because he takes it for granted that he will not be held to his word. Aristotle commences an address with these words, "My friends! There are no friends!"

On the other hand, let the light of criticism penetrate deeply into your own heart, into the recesses of your thoughts and feeling. Turn the seven lamps of your reason inward upon yourself. Examine, by their light, how your sentiments and actions harmonize with each other. Be not content with the simulation which you excuse in others. You must not pry too deeply into the motives of your fellow-men, but bring the searching light of scrutiny sharply to bear upon the grounds of your own action. Strive *to be* that which you find it well to *appear*. When you light the lamp of reason, let its light be cast principally upon yourself. Be like Augustus, the mighty emperor; like Kant, the strict moralist, the great thinker, and let us add, on the authority of our text, like Aaron, the first high-priest!

CHARACTER SKETCHES FROM THE BIBLE.

MOSES, KORACH, DATHAN AND ABIRAM.

NUMBERS XVI.

Korach speaks of the "people of the Lord" and its holiness. He accuses Moses and Aaron of tyranny and presumption in the administration of the sacred office. We, however, understand the purpose of his accusation; we can clearly see the secret design of his speech to the people. He adopts the tone of all demagogues and office-seekers, flattering the masses, misrepresenting the conditions of the time, and slandering the party in power. "The people! The people's rights!" is their cry. The meaning of their harangue is ever, "Place the power into our hands! Let us guard your rights!" We know well the design of Korach's agitation. His eye is on the high-priest's office. *He* wishes to rule the "people of the Lord." Ambition was the mainspring of his action.

Among all the passions, ambition is the most dangerous. The darkest pages in history have been painted in its lurid colors. When ruled by any other passion, man is fully conscious that he is doing wrong. The gambler, the drunkard, the rake, the thief, the swindler, the voluptuary, all well know that they are pursuing

the path of evil; but they are, or think themselves, too
weak to forsake their wicked ways, and follow their inward promptings to a better life. , The man of ambition,
on the other hand, believes himself worthy of the honor
to which he aspires. He thinks that he is laying claim
merely to that which is his due; he holds that the world
is defrauding him of his rights. The stronger his confidence in the justice of his claim, the bolder and the
more decided will be the stand taken by him.

Ambition, unlike the other passions which generally
rule petty souls, is usually most active in men of genius,
of extraordinary ability. To this peculiarity, it is due,
that, as far as the public welfare is concerned, it is the
most dangerous of all the passions. The power stirring
within the man of ambition seeks an outlet for its exercise, a field wherein it may turn its energies to account.
The endowments of the man of ambition are not always
imaginary; they may be of undeniable excellence.
Recognition of his abilities alone is wanting, nor does
the opportunity offer itself for procuring this recognition by proper means. In his impatience he shakes the
very foundation of society, calling to his aid the powers
of deceit and violence.

Such was the case with Korach. His unsatisfied ambition wrought havoc in Israel, and brought misery to
thousands upon thousands implicated in the rebellion.
Before Korach's appearance upon the scene, the material for insurrection lay ready in the community, need-
ing but the necessary touch to set it aflame; ignoble
purposes stirred in the hearts of many in Israel. But
the order of the community would not have been dis-
turbed thereby. The disaffection of petty minds would

not have burst forth into the flames of rebellion. Courage and decision were lacking. The ambition of one man, however, served to set the whole mass ablaze. All the passions, seething in the hearts of petty men; all the malice which had been ashamed to show itself in the light of day, now burst forth in united strength. The master-passion, ambition, broke the dam of public order, and the full flood of cowardly sinners poured into the camp.

As ambition is the most dangerous of the passions, it is also the noblest of them all. To devote thought and scheming, toil and energy to low, sensual delights, to material gain in gold or goods, to drink, to gambling, is the mark of a base and vulgar nature. For, when our objects in life are so unworthy of our dignity as human beings, as are these, then the nobly-born soul must degrade itself to the position of slave to the body. But honor is one of the finest of the pleasures of life; honor is a true delight to the soul. The body must deny itself much, must sacrifice much, must do its utmost, so that the soul may enjoy the fulness of honor. Korach, as the most dangerous of the mutineers, merited the most severe punishment. His name, therefore, is identified with the rebellion; heavy was the penalty paid for his guilt. He was the guiltiest among the rebels, but not the worst. Therefore, despite his guilt, we find that, in other sections of the Bible, the descendants of Korach are men highly honored in the community. We find poets among them and famous singers, by their efforts contributing much to the beauty of the Temple service.

Therefore, the Bible says, " But the sons of Korach did not die." The error of the father was not visited

upon the children. His noble qualities, his ability to
work his way out of the common mass, and, from the
height attained, influence the life of the community—
this was the inheritance of his children and his children's children.

The children of Korach, who, according to the Holy
Scriptures, did not die with their father, include not only
the heirs of his body, but his *spiritual* descendants as
well. Whoever feels within himself the ability to be of
use in the community; whoever seeks to be the right
man in the right place, will also feel the desire to occupy
this place, and stepping forth from the seclusion of
private life, to take upon himself the burdens, the cares,
the dangers, and in the end also the ingratitude of
public service.

Korach's spirit thus lived again in Alexander, in
Julius Cæsar, in Napoleon—all of them great men,
fitted for the high position which they won for themselves by virtue of their superior powers, but censurable
for the means employed in attainment of this end; for
their violence, intrigues, breach of faith, and bloodshed.
Like Korach's, theirs, too, was an end of horror.

Let us turn to the picture presented by the life of
Dathan and Abiram.

Quite unlike Korach, these men seem neither dangerous nor worthy of the least respect. Their characters
were low, and their motives mean, nor did they possess
the necessary strength to do harm. They met the ad-
vances of Moses and his offer of a peaceable adjustment
of difficulties in a malicious spirit, with foolish and irrational words. Like all low-minded men, they looked
with hatred upon any one of noble aims, and, therefore,

they were instinctively the personal enemies of Moses, the idealist, the man of lofty thought. They reproach Moses with having led the children of Israel out of Egypt, the land of slavery, it is true, but of slavery sweetened with milk and honey. They failed to appreciate the work of Moses as the savior of the people, their teacher and leader; even the promise of fertile lands for their children was without value for them. They wished to have fields and vineyards for themselves. They belonged to that class of people, to whom nothing is worth the effort expended on obtaining it, except money and worldly goods, fields and meadows; to the class that would joyfully surrender Mount Sinai for a vineyard, a world of ideals for a tangible possession.

Dathan and Abiram, too, have passed away, but their vulgarity of soul still lives on in the world.

In every undertaking, the question is raised, " Will it bring us to the land flowing with milk and honey? What is the use of diligent study of the Law, of scientific investigation, of poetry and art, if they cannot help us to obtain fields and vineyards, if they will not fill our coffers with gold?"

Material blessings are by no means to be despised. Who does not strive to possess them? But side by side with our efforts for earthly possessions, we must still find time for higher things. When our interest or our participation in a good cause is asked, we should not always inquire as to the worldly advantage that we may gain from our efforts. In his anxiety for his acres and vineyards, his milk and honey, man must not lose sight of the demands of the heart and the soul, the welfare of mankind, the good of posterity, immortality and the life hereafter; otherwise he will perish in the desert of worldly interests as Dathan and Abiram sank into the earth, and were lost forever.

The third character sketch is that of Moses.

Dathan and Abiram seek indemnity in fields and vineyards for the losses which, they maintain, they have suffered in leaving the land of Egypt. To them, Moses says, "'I have not taken away an ass of any one of them.' Have I asked for one beast of burden in return for my services? I have sacrificed my life, all my strength in this cause; where are *my* fields and *my* vineyards? 'Nor have I done wrong to any one of them.' Where is even *one* man, whose rights I have injured in the fulness of my authority?"

Here we have the picture of a man sacrificing himself for the world, for its improvement and elevation. He took upon himself the leadership of the people, and wielded his power like a great man, and that, at a time, when there was little prospect of honor or success, when he could see only labor and care in store for him. When he made his first petition to Pharaoh, there surely was none to envy him : no Korach, no Dathan, no Abiram showed his face then. Later, however, when seeming impossibilities had been achieved, when the daring undertaking had been crowned with success, and Moses stood before them in the fulness of his power, then the envious sought to injure him, and to wrest from the leader, tried and true, the reins of authority. From his height, however, he could call to them : " For whose sake do I stand here upon the watch-tower? Not for my own sake, and not for the sake of those near unto me. I climbed this height, and now hold it in *your* interest. My office has brought me no field and no vineyard, neither milk nor honey has been my reward. Mine was the very beast of burden that carried me on the journey, from Midian into Egypt, undertaken in behalf of your liberation."

"PEOPLE OF THE LORD."

NUMBERS XI : 27-29 and XVI.

In the "Sayings of the Fathers," we find the sage advice to scholars to choose their words carefully in their discourses, so that their pupils may not misunderstand them, and thus be led to spread erroneous doctrines.

The quarrel between Moses and Korach furnishes a striking example of the harm that may be wrought by the misconstruing of even the sublimest truths. Sin is rarely shameless enough to show itself in all its nakedness, and say, "I am sin ; I know what I am, and you, too, may know it. It matters not to me that you recognize me in my true character." No ; sin speaks not thus, but rather loves to clothe itself in the garb of virtue. Many a misdemeanor is not committed, solely because it is impossible for the offence to maintain the appearance of respectability. Rudeness seeks to excuse itself, saying, "There is no deceit in me. I am perfectly frank and open." Hard-heartedness explains its position thus: "We must not spoil the poor by heaping benefits upon them," and the Israelite that seeks to make his religion as convenient to himself as possible says, "This is philosophy !"

In the last Sabbath's portion, we were told how two highly-esteemed laymen in Israel had prophesied to the people, because "the spirit rested upon them." Eager informers lost no time in telling Moses of the occurrence. To them, Moses said, "O, that we might render all the people of the Lord prophets; that the Lord would pour out his spirit upon them!"

Moses had spoken of Israel as a "people of the Lord." Shortly afterward, Korach appeared at the head of a misguided party in rebellion against the existing order, with an argument taken from Moses' own speech—"people of the Lord!"

No doubt, the greedy office-seekers were ashamed to oppose their petty malice and their utter worthlessness to the sterling character of Moses. Therefore, they acted in the capacity of advocates of the "people of the Lord." The majesty of the whole people could, despite his greatness, be boldly set up in opposition to Moses. Had not Moses himself called them "people of the Lord?" If it was true, as Moses had said, that every one in Israel might be a prophet, then surely every Israelite was worthy of the high-priestly office. Thus sin reared its head in the camp, under the mask of an advocate defending a people defrauded of its rights. The Israelites, dupes as they were, marked the words of their leaders, and though they failed to grasp their meaning, they hurled at Moses and Aaron the reproach, "It is you who have caused the people of the Lord to die!"

In using the phrase, "people of the Lord," Moses did not mean to imply that every Israelite, from the fact of his Israelitish birth, was a better, a more gifted man than others; that he was, on that account, fitted for highest honors. Moses adds the stipulation, "That the Lord would put his spirit upon them." God, however, does not lay his spirit upon one unworthy of it,

21

even though he be of Israelitish birth. Upon Eldad
and Medad, who worked earnestly in the camp as
teachers and preachers, without any thought of reward
in gold or land or honor, upon them rested the spirit of
the Lord. Their *ability* to teach, their *willingness* to
teach, and the *modesty* which led them to choose to work
for the common welfare without honorary titles and
badges of office, such must be the characteristics of the
men that can form a veritable "people of the Lord!"

Not so Korach. To work quietly and unostenta-
tiously for the common good was not to his mind.
Strange to relate, in Israel's entire camp, there were but
two men who, as "people of the Lord," offered themselves as teachers in the camp, while more than two
hundred and fifty, as "people of the Lord," offered
themselves as candidates for the office of high-priest!

Would it ever have occurred to a common Egyptian
to stir up a revolt for the purpose of obtaining a priestly
office? Our knowledge of the history of Egypt is constantly having fresh light cast upon it, but as yet we
have had no account of a rebellion against the priestly
order, or of any uprising of the lower against the upper
castes. In Egypt, the idea of a holy nation, of an
entire people forming a kingdom of priests, was utterly
unknown. On the contrary, the people, in general, were
filled with the consciousness of their ungodliness, and of
their unworthiness to approach their gods as priests.

Moses corrected this error. He maintained that the
whole of the Israelitish nation is holy with reference to
rights and privileges; but he asserted as well that not
every Israelite is therefore a saint. "The Lord will make
known who is his, and who is holy, that he may cause

them to come near unto him; and him whom he shall choose will he cause to come near unto him." Accident of birth cannot sanctify an Israelite. A holy life alone can bring a man near to God, and only the " chosen " one, not he that thrusts himself forward, may approach the Lord.

How frequently in life do we see teachers and preachers, statesmen and philosophers misunderstood, their words and speeches misinterpreted! The unfortunate division of the Israelites into Pharisees and Sadducees, for instance, is said to have owed its origin to the misunderstanding of a doctrine concerning retribution. Who can measure the rivers of blood, whose source may be traced to the misuse or the misconception of the terms, liberty, religion, enlightenment, and the like? Is it not to the misinterpretation of certain passages in the Holy Scriptures that the origin of the Christian religion has been traced—of that mighty religion, whose adherents are scattered far and wide; whose influence has changed the very current of life in hut and palace, in village and town; whose numerous sects control completely great sections of our globe? There are, in our nineteenth century, millions of men that adhere to political parties, knowing naught but the watchword, and swearing by it, though they comprehend the underlying principle as little as Korach's followers knew the meaning of their cry, "people of the Lord." Phenomena, similar in character to these of world-wide import, may be observed, on a smaller scale, in our daily lives. How much trouble and strife might be avoided in the home, in business, in social and congregational affairs, were but this wise saying constantly borne in mind:

"Ye sages, be careful in your speech, that ye be not misunderstood, nor your meaning misconceived." Words are like fire: useful if carefully guarded, but dangerous when employed, as children use fire, without thought or caution. A single word of doubtful meaning in compacts between nations and kingdoms not infrequently has been the cause of long years of bloody warfare, and, in private affairs, of weary law suits and great losses.

The wise lesson which we may clearly read in our text ought to impress two things on our minds: it is well to accustom *one's self* to a mode of speech that cannot be misunderstood. Again, the words of *others* must not be weighed upon too exact a scale, nor should the worst possible construction be put on them. It may be that your brother expressed himself infelicitously; but as well may it be that you have been infelicitous in your interpretation.

QUALITY AND QUANTITY.

"And Balaam said unto Balak, Build me here seven altars, and prepare me here seven bullocks and seven rams."—NUMBERS XXIII : 1.

Upon this verse our sages comment thus: "Why *seven* altars? Because up to that time seven pious men had erected altars, pleasing in the sight of God, namely, Adam, Abel, Noah, Abraham, Isaac, Jacob and Moses. 'Their sacrifices were certainly pleasing in thy eyes; but is it not more fitting for thee to receive offerings from seventy nations than from seven individuals?' Balak asks of Deity. He was answered, we are told, by a saying of Solomon's, 'Better is a piece of dry bread and quiet therewith, than a house full of the sacrifices of contention.'"

In the physical world, quantity often supplies the place of quality, bulk is substituted for strength. Two weak men may succeed in vanquishing one strong opponent, a thick board may bear more than a thin bar of iron.

The experience that quantity may compensate for lack of quality leads to the application of this principle in the intellectual and moral world. The bungling artist seeks to hide his lack of skill by laying on his colors in thick patches; the poor musician covers the bareness of his composition with the noise of instruments; the liar seeks to give strength to his statements,

of whose incredibility he is well aware, by repeated pro-
testations of his veracity. The hypocrite employs countless words and kisses, pressures of the hand, and all
other possible outward signs of good-will as proofs of his
friendship and good faith, which in reality, are almost
minus quantities. So, too, in religion, it is believed that
lack of quality may be made good by added quantity.
For instance, the followers of a belief or the members
of a sect are counted, and the great number of believers
is looked upon as the religion's chief glory. God is
supposed to be honored by a great number of meaningless religious practices. The strength of a religion is
judged by the outward glory and magnificence of the
temple, the service and the machinery of divine worship.
It is the chief pride of the vast majority in religious
communities to see their spacious temples well filled.
The truth and excellence of one's belief are attested by
the crowd of its professors, by the power and wealth of
those that bow beneath its yoke, by the worldly prosperity enjoyed by believers, and denied to unbelievers,
or at best grudgingly bestowed upon them.

Were we to allow such witnesses to the truth as numbers, power and social success to have weight with us in
judging religious truths, then we Israelites would hold
but a poor opinion of our faith. We are not numerous nor powerful, neither does Judaism pave the way
to social success for its followers. But truth does not
always dwell with the majority. How frequently have
the champions, the teachers of truth yielded up their
tortured souls on the funeral pyre, while tens of thousands of the people in their wild delusion looked upon
the horrible scene as a sacrificial service pleasing in the

sight of God. So, too, thought Balak, in the song of Balaam. "Why," says he, "wilt thou find pleasure only in the altars of this little nation? Why wilt thou recognize the homage of only seven men in the long period of time between Adam and Moses? Behold seventy nations are at thy service. Comply with their wishes. Be God as they conceive him, the God of the majority!"

Let it, then, be a matter of indifference to us how many millions we count among our followers. Our confidence in the truth of our belief is not shaken, because some statisticians estimate the number of Israelites at only five millions, nor are we strengthened in our faith, when others, exaggerating, assume eleven millions to be the correct number. We, likewise, refuse to swell our ranks with proselytes. Yes, even though thousands fall away, and are lost to us through seduction or frivolity, not the least harm is thereby done in our eyes to the truth that we profess. "The righteous is an everlasting foundation." Were a supporter of the truth to stand alone in his belief, _he_ would be the pillar, the upholder of his world.

The split in Israel, in religious matters, is so open that it cannot be ignored by silence on the subject. Israelites of the old way of thinking are still in an overwhelming majority. That, however, does not prove that they are in the right, nor can this fact alone make their future secure. Quantity cannot compensate for lack of quality. On the other hand, the defection of so many highly cultured men, of men of wealth from orthodoxy, proves nothing against its tenets, for, "Better is a piece of dry bread, and quiet therewith, than a house full of the sacrifices of contention."

Young Israel, the Israel of reform, is still in the
minority. It cannot be reproached with this paucity of
numbers, as a weakness, for the question is one of quality
not quantity. It is striving earnestly to increase its
forces, but even should it succeed, should tens of thousands join its ranks, it would be intrinsically no better.
In order to prove true superiority, young Israel must
show its advantage over the old in benevolence, in a
stern sense of justice, in cultivation of heart and mind,
in moderation, in modesty, in peace and chastity of
family life, in the domestic virtues in general.

When a Balak of the future ascends the seat of judgment to pass sentence on the party contests in Israel,
and cries out in his animosity, "Behold, how this people
is divided against itself. Here thou seest a portion, and
there a portion. Surely, then, thou mayest curse them
and denounce them"—let us hope that this will be the
answer: "I see neither wrong on the one side, nor per-
verseness on the other. The Lord his God is with each
of them." Balak said, "Behold, I have built seven
altars, and offered seven bullocks and seven rams thereupon, and," as our sages continue his speech for him,
"Abraham brought only one small ram as an offering.
I, however, have brought seven rams, and even seven
bullocks besides." This is the climax of heathen piety.
Every grove had its own altar, every height its idol.
Festivals, assemblies of the people, innumerable religious
practices, meaningless and irrational, filled up the measure of a heathen's days; countless sacrifices, culminating
in the sacrifice of the best-beloved children, constantly
bled on the altar. Moses, in forbidding private sacrifices, destroyed thousands of altars at a blow. Only one

altar was allowed by the Law—the altar in the one Temple in the land.

He that keeps within due bounds in his religious life, he that lays more stress upon quality than upon quantity, he is pious after the manner of Abel, of Noah, of the patriarchs, of Moses, who, in the outward expression of their adoration of God, limited themselves to building *one* altar, to sacrificing *one* lamb. Whoever, on the contrary, holds that piety demands many religious observances—he is a follower of Balak, who built seven altars, and let seven bullocks and seven rams smoke upon them.

In the Biblical section, from which our text is taken, we read that at the sacrifice, the king " was standing by his burnt-offering, he, and all the princes of Moab." The heathen idea that eye and ear must be attracted by the pomp and show of the public service has been banished neither from the church nor from the synagogue. Excessive importance is still placed upon appearances, upon costly show, upon the presence of individuals prominent in the community by virtue of wealth or position. Abraham sacrificed a ram without peal of organ and chant of choir; he stood alone with his son and his God. Mount Moriah was made sacred for all time by his sacrifice; even to-day it is ascended with emotions of reverence, while the site of Balak's pompous sacrificial service is forgotten ; neither does any one care to seek it.

Every feature that contributes to the dignity of the services and to its attractiveness for the visitor is of value in our eyes, but it would be highly un-Jewish to overestimate the importance of these outward things, and to look upon them as essential, and err to so great an extent that we should not consider a service worthy of the name, one that we could really attend with propriety, unless the rich dresses of the ladies rustle; unless organ and choir pour out a flood of music; unless a preacher appeals in grandiloquent language to the congregation from the pulpit.

"Better a piece of dry bread, and quiet therewith," better a house of God filled with devotion, which is after all the satisfying bread of the pious heart, "than a house full of the sacrifices of contention," *i. e.*, a house of worship, beautifully finished and decorated, but wanting in the true devotion that brings peace to the heart.

THE TESTIMONY OF OUR LAW AMONG THE NATIONS.

"See, I have taught you statutes and ordinances just as the Lord my God commanded me; that ye may do so in the midst of the land whither you go to take possession of it.

"Keep therefore and do them ; for this is your wisdom and your understanding before the eyes of the nations, that shall hear all these statutes, and they shall say, Nothing but a wise and understanding people is this great nation.

"For what great nation is there that hath gods so nigh unto it, as is the Lord our God at all times that we call upon him?

"And what great nation is there that hath statutes and ordinances so righteous as is all this law, which I lay before you this day?

"Only take heed to thyself, and guard thy soul diligently, that thou do not forget the things which thy eyes have seen, and that they depart not from thy heart all the days of thy life ; but thou shalt make them known unto thy sons and unto thy sons' sons."—DEUT. IV : 5-9.

No age or clime has failed to produce individuals of pre-eminent wisdom and justice, within the ranks of Judaism as well as beyond its pale. But in this morning's text, Moses exhorts the Israelites, saying, " It is not sufficient for Israel to produce individuals of ripened judgment and ability. Israel must show the world how an entire people may be elevated above the level of the surrounding nations, through the influence of the divine Law, which I gave unto it." The actions of the child of worthy parents or of the pupil of a school of good repute are observed more closely, and his faults of omission and commission are censured more severely than the deficiencies of him whose training has been neglected,

315

both at home and at school. We proudly extol the
merits of the Law of Moses, vaunting its antiquity, its
existence as a light in Israel, at a time when all the peoples round about were sunk in the darkness of heathenism. Since, then, we acknowledge that we have had so
greatly the advantage of other nations in enlightenment
and truth, it will naturally be inferred that we ought
equally to excel other and less favored classes of mankind in piety and nobility. If we, scattered members of
Israel, were content to rank merely among the average
members of the communities in the midst of which we
reside, severe censure would be our rightful portion.
Abraham was our father; Moses, our teacher; the Torah,
our text-book in religion; the prophets, our guides; from
our midst, the Psalms rang out into the world. Surely,
then, we ought to raise ourselves above the level of me-
diocrity. We have no right to complain then, if an
Israelite is more severely condemned for violations of the
truth, or of right and morality in general, than the many
sinners of other religious beliefs. Neither must we consider ourselves victims of injustice, if the errors of individuals among us are laid to the account of the entire
community. Do we not ourselves say, "Every Israelite
is responsible for his brother?"

Not the Law of Israel, but the life of Israel in accordance with the Law can win honor and respect for us
among the nations. Then, too, the talent or the genius
of one of our fellow-believers should not be expected to
elicit from the surrounding nations the exclamation,
"Nothing but a wise and understanding people is this
great nation!"

The honor which Israel shall enjoy among the nations,

according to Moses' prophecy, and which he exhorts the people to strive to deserve, is not in the least affected by our relative position to the followers of other beliefs in commerce, in art or in science. Enlightenment and nobility of soul, piety and morality, manifested by the mass of the people—these alone are the conditions under which Israel will win the respect of the nations of the earth. Let the wisdom and piety of Israel, which Moses promised should be rewarded with the regard of mankind, be practically applied, in the conduct of Israel in the ordinary relations of men—in the intercourse of husbands and wives, of parents and children; in a moderate enjoyment of the good things of life; in the erection of benevolent institutions; in humanity; in unswerving fidelity to religious convictions.

But is not this promise of reward, as a spur to the fulfilment of duty, in opposition to the requirements of strict morality? Is it right for the Bible, that divine volume, to find room in its pages for the demand that man allow human approbation to influence his conduct? Would it not have been better to say, "Do what is right, regardless of the opinion of the peoples round about you?" There is, however, no nation on earth that does not pride itself on the possession of some real or fancied pre-eminence, and it is by the thought of these excellencies that the bond of nationality is strengthened, and popular pride in nationality stimulated. Moses wished to inspire such pride in his people. Could he, then, have set a loftier aim to their ambition than the hope of wresting from the lips of the nations the praise, "This nation has the most rational conception of God. Its laws are laws of justice and mercy. The people serve their

God, and live a life of righteousness, manifesting justice, truth and love in their relations to each other and to strangers!"

Let us not boast of our written Law, looking upon it as a crown for our heads, if the Law resides not within our heads as well; nor is it proper for us to array ourselves in the cloak of humanity and justice, of truth and the knowledge of God, as taught by our religion, if the being, enveloped in the cloak, is a stranger to these virtues. The Law is not meant as an honor to *us;* *we* must rather honor it in our daily lives by living in accordance with it; that is to say, we must "sanctify the name of the Lord."

There remains for our consideration only that part of our text which reads, "For what great nation is there that hath gods so nigh unto it as is the Lord, our God, *at all times that we call upon him?*"

This verse emphasizes, in the first place, the omnipresence of God in contradistinction to the heathen deities who were local in jurisdiction. "Our God," says Moses, "is everywhere the same, upon the land and on the sea, upon mountain-tops as in the valleys, on earth and in heaven. He hears us, and is nigh unto us whenever we call upon him. He is near to us also in the sense that we have no mediator between God and ourselves." Another lesson is here taught us as well. God is nigh unto us only if we call upon him. If we wish to keep alive within us the consciousness of the existence of God, we must turn to him from time to time, thus reminding ourselves that a God reigns over us, a God of mercy and justice. The blessed result of prayer is not always a direct response to our petitions;

but few prayers are answered in the sense that we have changed the will of God according to our own will. Surely, it is best that God's will and not ours is done. Prayer is, however, never without its reward, for through it, we refresh in ourselves the feeling that God is near to his creatures. A voice within us seems to say, "Son of man, there is a God, the director of the fates of men, who is ever nigh unto you. Trust in his wisdom, fear his justice and his tribunal! Let the thought of his holiness fill you with a solemn dread!" This is the echo, the answer, in a pious heart, of the earnest prayer ascending from its depths.

If God is not to be forgotten in Israel, we must direct our attention more earnestly to our Law; we must be more zealous in our attendance at public worship; there to join the assembled congregation in praising God, and in listening to the exposition of divine truths, so that God may, indeed, be near unto us in heart and spirit.

NEITHER ADD THERETO, NOR DIMINISH THEREFROM.

"What thing soever I command you, even that shall ye observe to do: thou shalt not add thereto, and thou shalt not diminish therefrom." —Deut. XIII : 1.

This prohibition is contradictory to the development of religious law and life among us; truly, there has been much "added thereto" as well as "diminished therefrom."

Nor could it be otherwise. The Law was not made for angels. Man is ever subject to the vicissitudes of time, place and circumstances, and these influences are responsible for the continual flux and flow in his spiritual life.

This, however, is the meaning of our text: "Leave the Law of Moses as it is. Add nothing to it, claiming for your interpolation a divine origin, and thereby giving added value to the *Law* and more authority to *your* views and ordinances. Neither take anything from it, nor force any meaning out of it, if there happens to be something in my Law displeasing to you, or inconvenient, because out of season. Your lawful religious authorities may regulate your life according to the demands of time and place, as the Holy Scriptures say, 'Thou shalt not depart from the sentence which they may tell thee;' but these decrees must be promulgated on their own responsibility."

320

The old teachers remained faithful to this injunction. It was not a matter of idle play, when they ascertained the exact number of letters, words and verses in the Mosaic Law, or estimated the number of Mosaic ordinances, fixing the positive commands at two hundred and forty-eight, and the prohibitions at three hundred and sixty-five. However religious law and life might be modified and altered by additions and eliminations of the rabbis and by popular custom, the Law of Moses, as such, the basis for all these changes, was never to be affected. A sharp, dividing line was carefully maintained between divine and human additions—between "Mosaic" and "rabbinical." Hillel established seven rules, and Rabbi Ishmael increased their number to thirteen, as guides in the interpretation of the Law of Moses. The results of these interpretations—the true explanations as well as the distorted complications—were always looked upon as rabbinical. The six hundred and thirteen Mosaic commands and prohibitions were neither increased nor diminished in number by the labor of scholars. The Talmud—the repository of the mental activity of the rabbis—never became a New Testament. It served, and to some extent still serves, as a religious guide, but it was never regarded as other than a human, a rabbinical product.

We, in our days, ought to be especially mindful of the words of our text, neither "to add thereto nor to diminish therefrom," to honor the book in the form in which it has been handed down to us. In forcing its way out of the narrow bed of the Holy Scriptures, life has torn away much of their banks; it has spread itself over many fields, now a source of blessing, and again

22

leaving destruction and devastation in its path. Let us take heed that we may not lend a hand in the destruction of the dikes still remaining. ,

Holy Writ must patiently permit many of its decisions to be disregarded by impetuous life. It must allow science to examine its pages with a critical eye. But we ought not to put upon it the indignity of so wresting its sense as to find sanction and approval in its pages for the very havoc wrought in it by the force of circumstances. Israel has often returned to the Law after long intervals of neglect. As a good mother keeps the modest rooms of their early home ever ready against the possible return of her haughty children, so the Holy Scriptures are always prepared for returning Israel. Whenever Israel *does* return, let it find everything just as it left it.

Neither should we "add thereto." We should not attempt to make the Holy Scriptures more beautiful than they are. Nor should we seek to read into them great ideas, great truths and principles of humanity, which have come to us "with the process of the suns," and which we fail to find in the Holy Book. We should be grossly unjust towards the world, towards the many generations with their men of great endowments of mind and heart that have come and gone, were we to ascribe to our Holy Book every possible development in doctrine and legislation, in enlightenment and nobility. Many of our most honored, our most highly valued spiritual possessions, many ideas contributing greatly to man's welfare on earth and in the hereafter, were produced, taught and put into practice simultaneously with the teachings of Moses, as well as after the time of that great law-giver. In comparison with the moral order of our day, the Law of Moses may be likened to the acorn by the side of the mighty oak, whose wide, many-leaved branches throw dense and far-reaching shade upon the ground. The acorn went through various processes, became warmed in the earth, sprouted and developed, and when it had penetrated to the surface, and stepped forth into the sunlight, it had to pass through many seasons, drinking in their changes of light, heat, rain, air and gases; it had to be blown about in all directions by storm and tempest, and add ring by ring to its circumference, ere it grew to be the heaven-aspiring oak. In like manner with the Holy Scriptures as the nucleus, the germ, the root of all development, our system of morality has grown ; our views have become clearer, our feelings have become ennobled, our ideas of justice have become purer and more elevated, and especially has science advanced with giant strides. Excessive praise provokes criticism. He that insists upon finding all our modern conceptions of nobility and virtue in the Bible, is responsible for the consequences, if the sharp critic, seeking such ideas, and failing in his attempt, pronounces harsh judgment upon the sacred documents.

Time and all nations have been working at the structure of religion for four thousand years. We Israelites occupy a position in the very midst of this work of culture. Upon us there lies a twofold obligation : to co-operate heart and soul in the structure of a religion for all mankind, and not to imagine that the Israelite whose conduct seems unexceptionable when judged by Biblical or rabbinical standards, appears perfect before God and the world. Religion is never complete, nor is man ever perfect in his relation to himself, to God and to his fellow-man. Not Mount Sinai alone bears the heaven of our laws and doctrines; the Alleghanies and the Rockies ought also to be supporters of these sublime ideas. Not only by the seventy elders in the desert and seventy-one revered heads of the Sanhedrin, which sat in *Lishkhath haggazith*, but also in the legislatures, in Congress, even in every common council, is the cause of religion advanced or injured—in Boston as in Rome, in each place according to its character. Religion makes up our whole life. We either sin against it, or live a worthy existence according to its dictates. In reading a book, we read religion either as ennobled or degraded, as adulterated with frivolity or deepened with thought. He that writes a book writes religion even though religion be far from his thoughts while he is at work. Thus Humboldt, Dickens, Schiller, Longfellow involuntarily have added more to the circle that our century, too, is making about the trunk of religion's tree, than many a rabbi who devotes his whole life to the *conscious* study of religion.

Religious communities should, therefore, always maintain friendly relations with one another. All can learn from one another. All are filled with the desire to advance the cause of religion. Side by side with this aim, we Israelites have yet another task. We must guard strictly our ancient religious documents, that nothing be "added thereto nor diminished therefrom." Let him, who may seek them in hundreds or thousands of years, find them as they were when handed to us: neither better nor worse, neither increased nor diminished in contents. Mountains may be moved, and hills be levelled; the heavens may grow old even as a garment, but the word of the Lord will stand forever!

COMPETITION.

"Thou shalt not remove the landmarks of thy neighbor, which they of old time have set, in thy inheritance which thou shalt inherit, in the land that the Lord thy God giveth thee to possess it."—DEUT. XIX : 14.

Although the removal of a landmark is neither more nor less than theft, and though robbery and depredation of all kinds are distinctly prohibited by the Bible, this kind of stealing receives especial mention, as peculiarly deserving of punishment. In all ancient codes, the removal of a landmark is condemned in the severest terms. The art of surveying was not known in those days, nor had the ancients registers in which landed possessions were recorded according to their size and boundary. The landmark was, therefore, the only absolute proof of the possession of real estate. In view of the great importance of fixed boundaries, the Romans had a special tutelary diety for them—Terminus; in our text, also, God is mentioned particularly in connection with the prohibition against removing a neighbor's landmark—"in the land which the Lord thy *God* giveth thee to possess it."

In the course of time, this commandment lost its significance ; even after the removal of a landmark we can find the correct boundary. But it is only in its application to fields and meadows that this law has lost its importance ; respect for the boundary marking off our right from that of our neighbors still forms a great chapter in the book of morality.

Upon careful examination, respect for existing boundaries will be found to constitute a great part of our
idea of morality. In the home, boundary lines are
rigidly drawn between husband and wife, between
parents and children; in business houses, between buyer
and seller, between lender and borrower, between
laborer and employer, and between civil functionary
and citizen. Each one has his own peculiar rights
and privileges, and to the rights of each, certain boundaries are set. Of him that steps beyond the limit
of his authority, it may be said, " he removes the landmark of his neighbor." In our morning's discourse, we
shall consider only one phase of this far-reaching prohibition—the interpretation put upon it by our sages,
which, under the designation גבול מסיג (unfair competition), was held in high regard in truly pious Jewish
circles. According to this conception, an Israelite is
not allowed to cripple a fellow-man's means of gaining a
livelihood through competition. In the Bible, the height
of popular felicity is thus described : " They shall sit
every man under his vine and under his fig tree with
none to make them afraid." This indicates peace at
home and abroad. But, in our days, no one could,
even under such favorable conditions, dwell in security
" under his vine and his fig tree," not even in the most
powerful state, guarded by millions of soldiers; not even
under the watch of the most vigilant police force. The
name of the destroyer of a quiet, comfortable existence; of the thief of the spiritual peace of the merchant;
of the noiseless war between man and man, is competition, or as our sages express it גבול מסיג. The official cannot find unalloyed pleasure in his office, nor the business

man in his daily pursuit, nor the workman in his hire.
A man says to himself: "My field is bearing fruit.
After much honest and arduous toil, I may at length
hope to reap a rich harvest." Suddenly competition
stretches its hand beyond the boundary line, and his
hopes are dashed, his harvest blighted.

Alas! this unlimited liberty to bring ruin upon one's
fellow-man is the very pride and boast of our time! It
is true, the results of this competition in increasing
means of intercourse and in developing industry can
scarcely be estimated; they have indeed attained a
dazzling height. In progress, one year at present is equal
to one hundred of former times. But how great the
price that we have paid for this advance! How has morality suffered! If a man feels uncertain of his future,
he hastily seizes upon every means in any way justifiable
before the law in order to reap the richest possible harvest in the field of the present. And how many true,
honest, industrious men does competition daily drag into
financial ruin! How many worthy families fall into
misery and decay, how many struggle for existence, wag-
ing a daily fight with the current of competition—a fight
that makes all rest, all enjoyment of life impossible!

We do not speak of inevitable competition. When two
are constrained to seek bread in the same field, and must
snatch from each other one-half the means of subsistence,
it is dire want that oversteps the boundary. We speak
only of the thousands with whom competition is not a
matter of necessity, of those that can reap a rich harvest within their own limits, and nevertheless cross into
the boundaries of others, that they may glean there as
well.

Even here, the individual is scarcely to blame. The
spirit of the age looks up to competition as its good genius,
calling upon it for aid, and burning incense before it as
before a deity. What can the individual do but yield
himself up to the current of the time, and extend his ter-
ritory as far as possible beyond his own boundaries?
Every one must be prepared to have his boundaries
invaded on the morrow, even as he oversteps the boundaries of others to-day—to have the waters drawn away
from the source of his existence, even as he guides the
stream of another's livelihood into his own channel.
The warning of Moses is unheeded to-day. "Thou shalt
not remove the landmarks of thy neighbor," sounds like
folly in the ears of the present generation. But little
remains of the old Jewish respect for the "landmark"
of one's neighbor.

If the command to love one's neighbor, in its application in deeds of benevolence, could heal the wounds of
society, the problem before us would be a comparatively
easy one. The many institutions for the relief of human
misery speak well for the active charity of our days.
Neither can we complain of lack of justice. Good sense
and good-will are ever present to give us the best possible
laws, although the law, it is true, has not always the best
servants to see that its bidding is done. What we do
lack, however, is *equity*. Equity lies midway between
justice and benevolence; it is unwritten justice and
charity towards all, rich and poor alike.

It is vain to hope to dispel the serious and dangerous
questions of the time that lie like threatening clouds
over all countries, by multiplying charities, or by means
of legislation. "Thou shalt not remove the landmark

of thy neighbor is sound *morality*, and belongs under the head of equity, not of justice or law. This is the great work for future generations: to procure universal acknowledgment for the Mosaic doctrine of respect for the landmark of one's neighbor; so to limit the jurisdiction of competition that it may prove, not a curse, but a blessing to society. The conscience of the people must be awakened, must be made as alive to the force of the unwritten law of equity as of the written law of justice. A disregard of the demands of equity ought to seem, to the public sense of justice, as dishonorable as a violation of the written law of the country; it ought to seem as dishonorable to remove an invisible landmark, as to climb into a window for the purpose of committing a theft.

"Let thy brother live with thee." As far as it lies in thy power, let him enjoy his life and be secure in his happiness "under his vine and his fig tree." This is not the land that thou hast seized for thyself, but the land that the Lord has given to thee.

CHIVALRY.

"Remember what Amalek did unto thee, by the way, at your coming
forth out of Egypt.

"How he met thee by the way, and smote the hindmost of thee, all that
were feeble behind thee, when thou was faint and weary ; and he
feared not God."—DEUT. XXV : 17-19.

I believe that I can guess the thoughts of many during the reading of this text. The sound of this cry of
revenge from barbarous times, you think, ought not to be
heard in these days of enlightenment and humanity.

And even granted that we, peace-loving Israelites,
were eager to give heed to this cry; were eager once more
to seize the sword of revenge, to wash out with blood old
scores against this hereditary enemy, where could we
find Amalek to-day, inasmuch as the command to extir-
pate the Amalekites was carried out to the letter in the
days of Hezekiah ?

Let us consider the significance of this command in
the days of Moses and its importance to us.

According to one principle of division, the history of
civilization falls into three great periods.

The first includes the time in which man led a life of
complete lawlessness ; then followed the period of the
rule of unwritten law, which, in turn, led to the sway
of the written code.

It would be impossible to determine the length of the
first period—the time in which men led a life of license,

fighting and destroying one another in the struggle for existence—the time pictured to us in the Bible in the story of the first brothers. This subject constitutes a boundless field for investigation, a field in which Darwin, his predecessors and his followers have garnered rich harvests. So much, however, we can state with absolute certainty: the moment of man's first impulse towards culture must have coincided with his earliest suspicion of the existence of higher spiritual powers, powers of superhuman strength, surrounding him in invisible form. Or briefly stated, civilization took its rise in the fear of gods. We say fear of *gods*—for this fear must have assailed the savage on all sides to restrain him on the path of wild desire, to make him voluntarily do or leave undone what he would have preferred to neglect or to perform. The idea of one God does not carry with it sufficient terrors for primitive man to curb his wild nature. This vague fear of the gods, which fills the savage with sudden dread, without giving a decided bent to his thoughts and actions, develops into the religion of the second period of human civilization —a fixed system of doctrines and statutes directing thought and action with binding force.

Upon the field thus picketed by religion, custom flourishes, developing into the law of habit, which in turn becomes the unwritten law of society.

Whatever may be said of the worth or worthlessness of early religions, they must be allowed one merit—they taught man obedience to binding laws.

The law of chivalry was the most important of these unwritten laws. An exhaustive definition of this idea, a consideration of its development in the course of time,

especially during the Middle Ages, would fill a volume.
It suffices for our purpose to bring before the mind, the
seed and kernel of the virtue—honor in arms, the only
honor recognized by half-civilized peoples, the honor of
strong bones, of muscles of iron, and nerves of steel;
of a hand unswerving in directing the club or other
weapon of attack and defence. Such honor could be
gained only in the contest of the strong with the
strong, of the armed warrior with him who was chal-
lenged to fight and hence prepared for defence. In
a further stage of development, not only did it bring
no honor to a man to attack another from behind,
to fall upon the unarmed man with weapons, to overthrow the weak, but, on the contrary, it brought
him only shame and disgrace. In a still higher stage
of development, it became a matter of duty for the
man of honor, not only to *spare* the weak, but, indeed,
to grant them protection, to constitute himself the cham-
pion of women, children, the aged and—the priests.

As the fear of the gods may be considered the a-b-c of
culture, the first impress of the shovel on the path of
civilization, so the virtue of chivalry may be called the
first reading lesson, the first outpost of civilization.

Amalek had taken none of these first steps in civilization.

"He met you by the way"—you, who were travelling
onward, not suspecting harm, unprepared for battle.

"He smote the hindermost of you; the aged, the
women, the children, the sick, the lame, when your
warriors were faint and weary," not in a condition
to invite the attack of men of chivalrous honor and
feeling.

" He feared not " the gods. The very first impulse, the earliest germ of civilization was wanting in him.

A community so uttery devoid of law, of honor, of fear of God, bore in itself the seed of destruction. It would surely have met its fate—extirpation—without the command of Moses. The Mosaic decree merely shows us, by means of an illustration, the phenomenon that we have observed as the result of a law of nature, in the history of many other equally barbarous hordes. There is no decree in the United States ordering the extermination of the Indian, and yet the remnants of his people are melting away like snow in the sunshine of spring; for, in the Indian of our day, there lives, also, no spark of chivalry. He fights from ambush, attacks peaceful travellers, murders in cold blood women and children, the aged and the sick, and puts his defenceless prisoners to death by horrible means, untroubled by any thoughts of his gods. So Moses summoned the children of Israel to the task performed, in their time, by the Regulators of the South, or the Vigilance Committee of California, who though criminals before the law, were yet benefactors of society. He wished them to free the nation from this public scourge, to remove this stumbling block from the path of civilization.

Such was the significance, in the ancient Biblical days, of the commandment of revenge in our text. But what lesson can it teach us? What can we, in its annual repetition, gain from it?

The answer to this question brings us to the third epoch in civilization—the period of written law.

Written law has limited the activity of the virtue of chivalry, but it has not completely discarded it. Written law is gross matter, unwritten law fine spirit. He that makes the written law the sole guide of his life, leaving undone only those things that it forbids, and performing none but its injunctions, may be a good, tax-paying citizen, an important man on exchange, a man whose honesty, according to the letter of the law, cannot be impugned. He may live without shame, and be buried with pomp and glory—nevertheless, he is but a poor creature; he is not of the knights; in spite of his liberty, he is a slave.

We have defined chivalry as meaning, honor in arms. Such it was at one time, and still remains in those states, in which great, standing armies are necessary as a protection against foes from within and without. In those countries, the bearer of arms is highly respected, and in point of honor, he is more sensitive than other men. In the United States, the bearing of arms in time of peace is not accounted an especially honorable profession; if a man were habitually to walk our streets girt with a sword, he would be laughed at and jeered. But our definition speaks of "*honor* in arms." Even if we omit "arms," the best part—honor, the unwritten law of chivalrous manhood—still remains; it cannot be couched in writing, nor formulated into a law. It is the *bouquet* of character, the delicate perfume of the soul, which, despite its delicacy, makes its presence manifest in the whole man, in his every act and thought.

The written law says, "Thou shalt not lie." But how much falsehood there is in the world which the law cannot touch—falsehood under the protection of equivocation in speech and action, under all possible evasion and excuses made to appease conscience! Not so the man of chivalrous honor. He is filled with that noble pride

which will stand before no man with eyes downcast, he
wants to look every man openly and honestly in the eye.
But he cannot do so, upon whose tongue there is a lie,
who finds it necessary to conceal speech and countenance
behind the screen of equivocation. Therefore, the man
of chivalrous honor is true, where hundreds are false.

The man of chivalrous honor is faithful. Falsehood is
the weakness of a heart that dares not show itself in its
true colors. A man of chivalrous honor scorns such
weakness and timidity.

For the same reason the man of chivalrous honor is
better equipped to resist sin than others. Open sin
brings shame, and to sin in secret betokens fear of man
and his criticism. Both these emotions are foreign to
the nature of chivalry.

The man of chivalrous honor stands erect before the
great ones of the earth. He bows no lower than they
before him. He is no flatterer, but he shows kindness
and lenity towards the weak and the lowly; he is never
brutal.

The man of chivalrous honor does his duty without
boasting; he is too proud to covet the applause of men.

In view of the great competition in business life, and
the poor equipment, with which so many are compelled
to enter the struggle for existence, it would be unjust to
condemn those that lie in wait to pounce upon any
opportunity of gaining an advantage; that feel driven
to employ any artifice within the boundary line of
threatening law. Such action, however, is not chivalrous. The man of honor does not lie in wait in the
path of life. He marches straight forward in his daily
occupation, as the lion goes forth for his food.

The chivalry of man manifests itself most strongly in his attitude towards the weak.

He whose capital is large and whose soul is noble and chivalrous, suffers his weak competitor to live side by side with him. He crushes him not with the great power at his disposal. The mighty stream allows the brooklet to ripple on at its side; it does not swallow it up in its own greatness.

If a man is hard-pressed by business troubles, power-less in his relations to a man of chivalrous soul, unable to impose conditions, but compelled to submit to any that may be offered—the high-minded man will spare the weak man, nor will he take all possible advantage of the misfortune of his neighbor which the written law may allow him to take with impunity.

Any one attacked from behind is weak. To speak evil of a man behind his back is sinful, but it is especially offensive to the spirit of chivalrous honor, which requires a man to take the part of his unjustly slandered fellow, to defend the absent, who is unable to defend himself.

Woman is weak, not only by virtue of her frailer, physical constitution, but also by reason of her tempera-ment and the restraint put upon her by nature, custom and propriety. The man of chivalrous honor is, there-fore, especially distinguished by his delicate considera-tion for the weaker sex.

The minority is ever the weaker element in a com-munity. It is unchivalrous for the majority, because of its written right to do so, to tyrannize over the minority; especially is this true in cases in which the questions are of a religious nature.

There is, however, an obverse side to the virtue of

chivalry. Even in the olden times, when chivalry constituted the very basis of society, the knights were wont
rather to arrogate to themselves more rights than were
their due, than to help others to rights of which they
had been defrauded. So, in our days, we find men of
chivalrous nature, who go far beyond the requirements
of the written law in their performances, but who also
frequently fail to come up to the requirements of the
law, when it becomes inconvenient for them to do so. In
this way, they lose a proper standard of judgment for
themselves and for others.

The confusion of the chivalrous honor of manhood
with outward marks of honor presents a still darker
picture. Undue anxiety and effort for distinction in
public life show aught but a knightly spirit. The more
a man or woman struggles for honor among men, the
further does he or she travel from the path of true
honor. So great are the means required for obtaining
the gauds of public honor, the path to this goal is often
so degrading, if indeed, it be not impure and filthy,
that a few years of *honors* frequently pave the way to a
lifetime of shame. And even should this dearly-bought
outward distinction of a worthless soul last through life,
what boots it? Nothing is gained thereby except that
thousands of eyes are fixed upon the man, and thousands
of lips pronounce his name, but truly not to honor him.
For the more a man steps into the foreground, the better
target does he become for the critical shots of envy;
retributive justice feels called upon to do its duty.
Character, not social position, makes the knight. The
lord may be a slave, and his serf a nobleman.

Our text thus teaches us that the virtue of chivalry,

23

the bud of civilization, which, in our day, has opened
into the full blown flower—the unwritten law of honor
—is an ornament to man. It further tells us that,
though the days of coat of mail, of shield and battle-
axe be past; though the times of Charlemagne; of the
Cids, the Bayards, the Richard Cœur de Lions; of Sala-
din, of Götz and von Hutten lie far behind us, there is
still plenty of opportunity for the simple citizen to perform deeds of chivalry. "Thou shalt blot out the
remembrance of Amalek."

Strive to keep all vulgarizing influences far from you.
Avoid everything that may dishonor you in your own
eyes, and strive further to root out every remnant of the
deceitful, cowardly Amalekite spirit that may still lurk
in your heart. In the temple of God, "everything
speaketh glory" and honor.